WIN AT
ANY COST

WIN AT ANY COST

The Sell Out
of
College Athletics

by FRANCIS X. DEALY, JR.

A Birch Lane Press Book
Published by Carol Publishing Group

Copyright © 1990 by Francis X. Dealy, Jr.

A Birch Lane Press Book
Published by Carol Publishing Group

Editorial Offices   Sales & Distribution Offices
600 Madison Avenue   120 Enterprise Avenue
New York, NY 10022   Secaucus, NJ 07094

In Canada: Musson Book Company
A division of General Publishing Co. Limited
Don Mills, Ontario

Manufactured in the United States of America

10   9   8   7   6   5   4   3   2   1

Dealy, Francis X.
    Win at any cost : the sell out of college athletics / by Francis
X. Dealy, Jr.
        p.   cm.
    "A Birch Lane Press book."
    Includes index.
    ISBN 1-55972-052-2 : $18.95
        1. College sports—United States—Moral and ethical aspects.
    2. College sports—Economic aspects—United States.   3. Doping in
    sports—United States.   4. National Collegiate Athletic Association.
    I. Title.
    GV351.D43   1990
    363.4'5'0887960973—dc20   90-47203
                                                                     CIP

To Ellen

ACKNOWLEDGMENT

In the course of writing this book, I interviewed more than 200 people. Not all of these sessions were pleasant, but every subject received me courteously. I am grateful for their time and opinions.

I am indebted to Steve Byers who helped me immensely in no small task: compiling the pictures for *Win at Any Cost*.

I am also thankful to Nancy Wright, Director of Legislative Services for the NCAA, who never failed to answer a question willingly and thoughtfully.

Finally, I'm grateful to Hillel Black, editor of *Win at Any Cost*, and Henry Dunow of Curtis-Brown, Ltd., my agent.

Contents

1. Hank Gathers   13
2. Drugs   32
3. 100 Years Ago   56
4. Academic Fraud   78
5. The Black Gladiator   96
6. Proposition 48   111
7. Beer   125
8. Greed   144
9. Recruiting   168
10. Reform   197
    Epilogue   208
    Notes   216
    Bibliography   231
    Index   235

WIN AT
ANY COST

Panem et circenses.
JUVENAL

Hank Gathers

At 5:13 P.M., on Sunday, March 4, 1990, Loyola Marymount's Hank Gathers timed his jump perfectly, caught the pass high above the rim and slammed the ball through the net like Zeus hurling a thunderbolt. The dunk put Loyola Marymount ahead of Portland, 23-12, in the opening minutes of a tournament game that would decide which school would represent the West Coast Athletic Conference in the NCAA's 1990 Men's Basketball Championship.

The ability to make plays like that was why Hank Gathers, six-foot-seven, 210 pounds, made the 3,000 mile jump from the Philadelphia projects to sunny southern California five years before. His coach, Paul Westhead, had dubbed Gathers "The Bank Man," acknowledging his role as the heart and soul of the team, and the nation's leading scorer and rebounder.

At 5:14 P.M., after slapping a high five, Gathers's expression went from triumph to bewilderment as he staggered sideways and crumpled to the floor. For a moment, he sat with a stunned expression, as if to say, "How could this be happening to me, the strongest man in America?" When he tried to get up, his body convulsed and he fell back to the floor, his left leg twitching violently as his mother, aunt and two brothers rushed from the stands to help him.

The Loyola Marymount team physicians, Drs. Benjamin Schaffer and Daniel Hyslop, plus the team trainer, Chip Schaefer, and a third doctor, quickly joined the family. Gathers's boyhood friend and teammate, Bo Kimble, stood over him, helpless, while Paul West-head, Loyola Marymount's coach, hovered off to the side. Every-one looked indecisive and awkward, as if they were trying to determine if Gathers really needed help. Finally, Carol Livingston, Gathers's aunt, prodded the group into action by shrieking, "Some-body do something, please! Somebody do something!" Chip Schae-fer, the trainer, crouched down and took Gathers's pulse.

Several confused minutes passed while the doctors conferred before moving Gathers by stretcher out of view of the 3,500 fans to an outside alley. Once there, Schaefer connected two giant defi-brillator paddles to Gathers's chest and then sent 220 volts through his body to jump-start his heart. But it didn't work and Schaefer could not get a pulse. All that remained were Gathers's stone silence and the smell of his burnt flesh from the electric shock.

At 5:34 P.M., an emergency rescue team took Gathers to the Daniel Freeman Marina Hospital in Marina del Ray, California, two miles away.

At 6:55 P.M., on Sunday, March 4, 1990, one month before starring in The Final Four and three months before being a first round pick in the NBA draft, Eric Wilson "Hank" Gathers was pronounced dead.

An autopsy later revealed Gathers died from idiopathic cardio-myopathy with residual interstitial myocarditis. The autopsy also showed that Gathers had not taken his prescribed drug Inderal for at least eight hours before he died.

Hank Gathers was taking Inderal because on December 9, 1989, in a game against University of California, Santa Barbara, he collapsed at the foul line. He was down for only an instant before jumping back up, but the team physician took him to Centinela Medical Center anyway.

"I walked off the court with my arms up to show everyone I was strong," Gathers said later.[1]

After two days in the hospital, Dr. Michael Mellman determined that Gathers had an irregular heartbeat. He referred Gathers to Dr. Vernon Hattori, a cardiologist, and Dr. Charles Swerdlow, an electrophysiologist, for extensive cardiology tests.

A week later, Dr. Hattori delivered the bad news. Gathers suffered from cardiomyopathy, a thickening of the heart muscles that causes the heart to beat quickly and irregularly when stressed. Sometimes it can be fatal, especially for athletes. But Hattori added that Hank could be treated with Inderal, a drug that would slow Hank's entire body down, including his heart beats.

Five days later, Hattori permitted Gathers to resume practice provided Hank take 240 milligrams of Inderal a day, and provided he submit to weekly tests to determine the drug's on-going effectiveness.

Gathers suited up for the Loyola Marymount home game against Oklahoma on Saturday, December 23, but did not play.

The Tuesday after Christmas Gathers took a stress test which measured his heart beat at over 200 beats per minute, a dangerous level. The average twenty-three-year-old athlete, going all out, never exceeds 120 beats per minute.

That Friday, Paul Westhead met with Dr. Mellman, Dr. Hattori, Chip Schaefer and Gathers and confirmed their previous decision to allow Gathers to play. Again, the doctors emphasized to Gathers the importance of taking Inderal as prescribed and submitting to weekly tests.

The next day, Gathers returned to Loyola Marymount's starting lineup for twenty-four minutes. He scored twenty-two points and grabbed eleven rebounds.

On Tuesday, January 2, Loyola Marymount began an important road trip to Philadelphia where Gathers and Kimble were returning like prodigal sons. The team stopped off in Cincinnati to play Xavier. Gathers scored twenty points and grabbed eight rebounds while playing only thirty minutes.

Two days later, Loyola Marymount beat St. Joseph's of Philadelphia at the buzzer on Bo Kimble's three-point shot. In front of friends and family, Kimble was the hero, Gathers was the goat. Hank played like he was drugged and scored only eleven points.

On Saturday, Loyola Marymount beat another Philadelphia

school, LaSalle, 121-116. It was LaSalle's only loss of the regular season. Gathers played like the Gathers of old, scoring twenty-seven points and dominating both backboards.

Later, Gathers admitted to his high school coach, Rick Yan-kowitz, "Don't tell anybody but against LaSalle, I took only half my dose."[2]

In the next five games, Gathers's performance on the court improved as he decreased his dosage. His best game was against LSU where he scored-forty eight points. Gathers said,"I was out to prove something to the NBA scouts who were all there. Whatever team gets me will be lucky. They are going to get a quality, sound player who comes to play every night."[3]

At that time, it appeared as if Hank Gathers had beaten his heart ailment like he had conquered other obstacles in his life.

Hank's father, Eric Wilson Gathers, was an alcoholic who aban-doned the family when Hank was five years old. Shortly thereafter, his mother, the high-strung and determined Lucille Gathers, moved Hank and his two brothers, Derrick and Charles, and half-brother Chris Marable into the Raymond Rosen Projects of North Phila-delphia. The Rosen projects are eight blocks of government-issue bleakness where 11,000 people live amidst drugs, violence, litter and hopelessness. Perfunctory, battered chain link fences separate nothing from nothing.

"It looks like Germany must have looked after the war," said Mary Toy, a Philadelphia high school administrator.

By the dint of her ambition and fiery temperament, Lucille Gathers made sure her boys got the most out of life, even if it was in the slums of North Philadelphia. Although a Baptist, Lucille Gath-ers knew the value of a private education and she entered her sons Hank and Derrick in St. Elizabeth's, the neighborhood Catholic elementary school. There Hank and his brother met Father Dave Hagan, the parish priest who was one of the neighborhood's few sources of support and hope. Father Hagan also coached St. Eliz-abeth's seventh and eighth grade basketball team. "You could tell even when he was in the eighth grade that Hank Gathers was going to be a great basketball player and a great leader. A lot of people, especially his family, counted on Hank," Father Hagan said.

From St. Elizabeth's, Hank and Derrick went to the Murrell Dobbins Vocational High School. As if they needed to be reminded,

Dobbins categorized the Gathers brothers as severely disadvantaged.

Later, Gathers would say to his southern California college classmates. "I have lived in a project all my life. There is trash everywhere. I came to Los Angeles to get as far away from Philadelphia as possible. Ever since I was nine, I have wanted to get out. I know there is more to life than that."

Gathers played basketball for Dobbins where he teamed up with Bo Kimble, his brother Derrick, and Doug Overton, now starting guard for LaSalle, and won the Pennsylvania state championship in 1985.

Lucille Gathers was extremely active in Dobbins's Home and School Parents Association, always ready to defend the interest of her sons. Gathers's high school coach, Rich Yankowitz, said, "She was in anyone's face who messed with her boys." One time, after a game against Dobbins's arch-rival, Franklin, Lucille Gathers accosted Kenny Hamilton, Franklin's coach, and berated him for taunting Hank during the game. Lucille Gathers became so angry she spat on Hamilton's shoes.

Hank was as intense and as volatile as his mother.

When Dobbins Tech played Dunbar High School, the number one high school team in the country, Dobbins was up by sixteen points in the third quarter, and the game had all the earmarks of a rout. But one time down the floor on offense, Gathers did not get the ball as was planned. He went haywire, screaming abuse at the errant teammate. The teammate and the other players became so rattled they let down their guard and Dunbar came back to win by one point in double overtime.

When Hank was not on the basketball court, he was either with Father Hagan or Marva Crump, a girl from the projects with whom he had been going since they were both thirteen. Marva gave birth to their son, Aaron, in Hank's junior year at Dobbins.

Although not a great student, Hank Gathers graduated from Dobbins in June 1985 with a college prep degree and a trade certificate for refrigeration and air conditioning. After graduation, both Gathers and Kimble, known as "The Hank and Bo Show," were recruited by Dave Spencer for the University of Southern California. Spencer liked Gathers and Kimble because "they were

Philly ball players, tough and hungry. They'd dive for a loose ball, whereas the California players would all kind of stand around.''

About this time, Hank's older half-brother, Chris Marable, was arrested for stealing $80,000 worth of jewelry. He was sentenced to thirty to fifty years in jail for grand larceny. When this happened, Hank's determination to rescue the Gathers family became even more pronounced.

"I remember when he went to Los Angeles," said Derrick Gathers, "he didn't know anyone. But he went to get an education and to be a star and play in the NBA. There was a lot riding on him.''

Gathers and Kimble both started as freshman at USC, and they had a pretty good year. But Stan Morrison, USC's head coach, was fired after the season ended. In what would turn out to be an ill-considered move, Kimble and Gathers and another freshman star, Tommy Lewis, demanded to have a say in hiring Morrison's replacement.

Their request was ignored, but Morrison's replacement, George Raveling, later learning of their demands, became incensed. In an effort to establish his authority, Raveling delivered an ultimatum to the freshmen. Rather than comply, Gathers and Bo Kimble, at Kimble's urging, quit the team.

Father Dave Hagan advised the two to look up his boyhood Philadelphia friend, Paul Westhead, who was the coach of Loyola Marymount. Impressed with Westhead's promise to install a "run-and-gun" offense which would center around the two of them, Gathers and Kimble enrolled at Loyola Marymount. They sat out the 1986-87 season according to the NCAA rules.

Gathers, a communications major at Loyola Marymount's College of Fine and Communications Arts, aspired to a career in sports broadcasting after his basketball days were over. Like everything else, Gathers worked hard at broadcasting. During his summer break, he attended Roy Englebrecht's Sportscasters Camp where he broadcast some California Angels games.

Gathers loved an audience and he would entertain virtual strangers with his imitations of Eddie Murphy and Richard Pryor. One year, he hosted Loyola Marymount's team banquet, roasting Coach Westhead and his teammates. He was so funny that people urged him to try his routines at some of the Los Angeles comedy clubs.

But there was a serious side to Hank Gathers, too. He never relaxed when it came to his appearance, even if it were just to go to the corner store. He was not ostentatious, just always classically well-dressed. Hank Gathers stood in ironic contrast to his affluent classmates, products of California casualness with their Grateful Dead T-shirts and droopy cut-offs.

Gathers held to a fastidious diet, always certain to eat the right foods, including plenty of salads and fruit. He would cut out caffeine three days before a game. On game day, Hank would consume four bowls of oat bran at one sitting.

When it came to drugs and alcohol, no doubt because of his father, Gather was a militant abstainer. In fact, when he saw teammates drinking too much, he would say, "Don't you love yourself? If you did, you wouldn't be doing that to your mind and body."

But basketball was Hank's life, and he played it with a vengeance. Before every game he would say, "Let's go to war." Teammates who grew up surfing never knew if he was kidding or not.

After sitting out the 1986-87 season, the "Hank and Bo Show" led Loyola Marymount to a 28-4 record in 1987-88. The team averaged an incredible 110.3 points a game, proving that Westhead was a man of his word by installing the promised run-and-gun offense.

The next season, 1988-89, Gathers became only the second man in NCAA history to lead the nation in scoring—32.7 points per game—and in rebounds—13.7 per game.

Hank Gathers was well on his way to fulfilling the 10,000 to one dream, playing in the NBA and earning millions. In fact, an Italian team, Il Messagero Roma, offered Gathers over $1 million after his junior year at Loyola Marymount.

There was some speculation that Gathers would declare hardship and forgo his senior year for the pros. Gathers called a press conference in May 1989 to announce he was withdrawing from Loyola Marymount to fight Mike Tyson. Several moments passed before the press realized it was the butt of another Hank Gathers joke. He went on to say he was remaining in school another year to obtain his degree, to help Loyola Marymount win its third conference title in a row, and to do "real good in The Final Four."

Gathers borrowed $6,600 from a bank to pay for a $1 million disability insurance policy from Lloyd's of London to protect him against injury in his last year at Loyola Marymount. The policy did not cover his death which it could have for an extra premium of $735.

Hank's coach at Loyola Marymount, Paul Westhead, is an enigmatic, razor-thin man who, like Gathers, used basketball to flee from Philadelphia. Usually there is a pinched, furtive look about him as if the struggle between Paul Westhead, the coach, and Paul Westhead, the creative writing teacher, takes its toll.

In the late fifties, Westhead attended St. Joseph's College in Philadelphia where he played basketball for the future NBA coach, Jack Ramsey. After graduation, he coached basketball at Cheltenham High School in a Philadelphia suburb. Westhead then coached at LaSalle College, also of Philadelphia, where he was considered "an educator, very deliberate and controlled. He played an established, almost slow type of offense. No one made many mistakes or many points."[4]

After nine years at LaSalle, Westhead followed another Philadelphian, Jack McKinney, to the Los Angeles Lakers as the latter's assistant. In November 1979, thirteen games into the season, McKinney sustained a serious head injury while riding a bicycle to meet Westhead for a tennis match. Westhead was named the Lakers' interim coach.

For the remainder of the 1979-80 season, Westhead followed McKinney's game plans exactly and the Lakers won the NBA championship with help from Kareem Abdul Jabbar and rookie Magic Johnson. People felt Westhead and Johnson were on their way to brilliant NBA careers. Jabbar, of course, was already a superstar.

The next season, 1980-81, with McKinney still disabled, the Lakers appointed Westhead the team's permanent coach whereupon he installed his own style of play which was much more deliberate than McKinney's. Because of difficulty adjusting to Westhead's slow game, the Lakers had a bad regular season, and lost to Houston in the opening round of the NBA playoffs. In November 1982, the year-long feud between Magic Johnson and Westhead became public. Westhead insisted on running set plays, while Magic wanted to improvise more. After losing four of their first eleven games, Magic went to Dr. Jerry Buss, the Lakers owner, and gave him a choice—either him or Westhead. Magic won.

Westhead sat out the rest of that year and then coached the Chicago Bulls for the 1983-84 season. It was before Michael Jordan, and the Bulls finished with a disappointing 28-54 record, which got Westhead fired again.

Westhead went from being NBA world championship coach to being twice-fired in less than three years. He remained out of basketball for another year and then, through the intercession of Jesuit friends, he landed the Loyola management job in September 1985.

The Jesuits established Loyola Marymount University in 1917 in the Westchester section of Los Angeles. Before Hank Gathers made the school famous, Loyola Marymount was a compromise selection for those students who could not attend Georgetown. Today, it has 3,922 undergraduates, mostly affluent Los Angeles suburbanites, who pursue liberal arts, business administration, science, engineering, and fine arts. There are only 185 (4.7 percent) blacks in the student population, yet eight out of the fifteen basketball players are black. The average Loyola Marymount SAT score is 1,100, versus an average of 834 for the team. Gathers scored the minimum, 700, to get a scholarship.

Paul Westhead, the introvert, had an unusual relationship with Hank Gathers, the extrovert. At Gathers's funeral, Westhead said, "Hank the Bank. He was our guy, the fibre of our team. We called him Bank Man because we went to him for everything, for rebounds, for points and for life."[5]

Westhead was known to have a soothing effect on the explosive Gathers. After Loyola Marymount had beaten his alma mater, St. Joseph's, Westhead did not meet the media to enjoy the limelight. Instead, he was back in the lockerroom, comforting the disconsolate Hank Gathers who, so he thought, had been humiliated before his family and friends.

The 1989-90 season, right from the start, was laden with pressure for Westhead. Loyola Marymount was heavily favored to win its conference again, and to do well in the NCAA Men's Basketball Championship.

"It's always hard when you're the favorite," said Rich Yankowitz, Gathers's high school coach. "Paul was feeling the pressure. He became more unavailable than ever. I tried to talk to him when he came east in January but you could tell he was preoccupied."

Until December 9, Westhead was on track to reclaim his former fame. And then, the Bank Man went down.

But Gathers came back and played well in late December, even if he was a step slower.

Against stiffer competition, however, Hank Gathers's slower step cost him and the team. But when Gathers reduced his Inderal, he and the team surged again. And since the middle of January, after he scored forty-eight points against LSU, Gathers had reduced his daily dosage of Inderal to one-fourth what Dr. Hattori originally prescribed. From the LSU game to the day he died, Gathers and the team played brilliantly.

No one knows for sure who was responsible for allowing Gathers to reduce his lifesaving drug and still play. But the coroner concluded Gathers had not taken Inderal for at least eight hours before his death.

On April 20, 1990, Dr. Bruce Fagel, a physician and an attorney representing Lucille Gathers and her remaining sons, filed a $32.5 million negligence suit against Paul Westhead, Loyola Marymount, and twelve other university officials and doctors charging them with the responsibility for Hank Gathers's death. Fagel, who drives a 1989 Lincoln with vanity license plates JUGLR, excerpted a letter written by Dr. Vernon Hattori to Dr. Michael Mellman in which Hattori claimed that Westhead, once in early January and then again two days before Gathers died, called him and said, "Hank's athletic performance was substantially subpar and that he [Westhead] felt strongly that the medication should be changed." The suit also alleges that Hattori systematically reduced Gathers's dosage from 240 milligrams of Inderal to less than eighty milligrams per day and that none of the many doctors involved in the case ever told Hank he had a condition that was potentially fatal.

Fagel claims the doctors should not have allowed Gathers to play. He cited the December 1985 issue of the *Journal of the American College of Cardiologists* which stated that athletes suffering from cardiomyopathy who have fainted or who have heart rates that exceed 150 beats per minute should not participate in athletics. The suit also alleges that while Gathers lay helpless for two minutes and forty-five seconds after his collapse on March 4, the team doctors failed to use the defibrillator the school had bought expressly for Hank Gathers after his first fainting episode.

Both Loyola Marymount and Westhead issued separate statements denying any responsibility for Gathers's death.

Earlier, Westhead conceded to the *Los Angeles Times* that he had been present at a meeting with Gathers and his doctors a few days before New Year's Day, 1990, where the doctors gave their approval for Gathers to play again provided he continue to take his medicine and be tested. Westhead further admitted he did not follow up to see if Gathers took Inderal as prescribed. "Nobody ever asked me to watch if he took pills or anything like that," Westhead said.

Westhead also confirmed he knew Gathers had missed a test a week before his death, and that Hattori was frantically trying to get to Gathers before he played the March 4 game. In fact, Westhead relayed one of the messages from Hattori to Gathers. But, again, Westhead never followed up to see if Gathers went to be tested before the fateful game. "I assumed Hank called him," Westhead said.[6]

Barry Zepel, Loyola Marymount's assistant athletic director, when asked about the suit, said, "We did not think he was that seriously ill. There is a big distinction between collapsing and fainting, you know, and Hank Gathers did not faint in December. He got right back up."[7]

Asked why the school bought a defibrillator for $5,200 after Gathers's December collapse if Loyola Marymount viewed his condition as not that serious, Zepel replied, "We bought [it] for the old people who come to the games. We have a lot of old Jesuits. We did not buy the equipment necessarily for Hank."[8]

Perhaps sensing the school's indifference, Father Hagan, in his address at Hank's memorial service several days after he died, said, "He broke his body for this university. I hope the university will break its body for Hank."[9]

The team, led by his friend, Bo Kimble, and inspired by Hank's tragic death, made it to the final eight of the NCAA's 1990 Men's Basketball Championship before losing to the eventual champion, UNLV, 131-101. Loyola Marymount earned $1 million for their performance.

Why did Hank Gathers die?

Gathers's diagnosis was perfectly clear, cardiomyopathy.

The consequence of cardiomyopathy —possible death—was also equally clear.

Hank Gathers died because he played. And he died because he reduced the dosage of the one drug that could have saved him. And he died because his support system—his mother, friends and coach—were blinded by the stakes of his basketball career. They stood by and watched Hank Gathers kill himself.

Hank Gathers had little choice but to cheat himself and try to beat the odds. Basketball was his life. It wasn't a game like it is for most suburban kids. From the time he was nine, Hank Gathers was "the Bank Man," the person people turned to when they needed help. He was a twenty-three-year-old kid who was within months of erasing a lifetime of desperation for his mother with the millions he was sure to make in the NBA.

A team led by Hank Gathers playing in the NCAA Men's Basketball Championship would have done better than the team that played without him, an achievement that would have vindicated Paul Westhead.

With Hank Gathers, Loyola Marymount would have earned more money and recognition. A team led by Gathers would have made the reputations of his teammates more glowing. Finally, a team led by Gathers would have made "March Madness," the NCAA Men's Basketball Championship, that much more exciting for CBS, the NCAA, and their advertisers.

But in situations like these, where judgment might be impaired by money and glory, who makes sure the welfare of the athlete is protected?

When asked why the National Collegiate Athletic Association did not play such a role in the Hank Gathers case, Frank Uryasz, the association's Director of Sports Medicine, said, "There was no call for it, really. We never get involved in something like that. We leave that up to the individual situations."[10]

Yet, the party most responsible for making the stakes of college sports so tempting, and the pressure so intense, is the NCAA, itself.

CBS, for example, will pay the NCAA $1 billion over the next seven years to telecast The Final Four basketball tournament. In turn, the NCAA will distribute over eighty percent of this money to the top sixty-four schools that participate in the tournament. With this kind of money at stake, and the attendant glory, no wonder the major college basketball coaches are at once incited and intimidated by the chance to be invited to The Final Four tournament.

The NCAA has become the agent provocateur it was founded to apprehend.

In the fall of 1905, after a Union College football player died of a cerebral hemorrhage in a game against New York University, President Theordore Roosevelt summoned leaders of college football to Washington. True to form, Roosevelt delivered a trenchant message. Reform or abolish football.

Two months later, the National Collegiate Athletic Association was founded, but not before an additional seventeen young men died on the gridiron that season.

Today, the NCAA is comprised of nearly 800 universities and colleges that compete in over twenty-seven different sports for men and women, ranging from swimming to volleyball. The membership is divided into categories or divisions roughly corresponding to size and competitiveness. In the case of basketball, for example, there are 292 schools in Division I, 188 schools in Division II, and 287 schools in Division III, where athletic scholarships are not awarded. All told, the NCAA has over 1,100 schools, conferences and affiliated members, which is up from 600 in 1950.

But the problems of college sports are restricted to the top sixty-five schools with the best football and basketball programs, the so-called big-time schools where big-time revenues provide the temptation to cheat. In the next decade, for example, the top sixty-five college football and basketball programs will generate over $1.5 billion in revenue.

Yet, the NCAA is forever stating that only a small percentage of its member-schools cheat. If the NCAA were to be more forthcoming, it would admit that at least seventy percent of the big-time college football and basketball programs are either proven or suspected offenders. The lacrosse program at Wooster College is not the problem.

At least the founders of the NCAA tried to do the right thing when they adopted this purpose, ''the regulation and supervision of college athletics throughout the United States so they may be maintained on an ethical plane in keeping with the dignity and high purpose of education, and a high standard of personal honor, eligibility and fair play.''

Unfortunately, eighty-five years later, too many people, including many of its own members, believe the NCAA has never fulfilled its mission.

From 1905 until the 1950s, the NCAA functioned as a part-time federation squabbling with rival organizations for supremacy in amateur athletics. Although it did manage to stop the violence-related football deaths, the NCAA accomplished little else.

But in 1951, the NCAA hired its first full-time executive director, Walter Byers, who ruled the organization for thirty-seven years, one of the longest and most autocratic reigns in all of sports. Using his considerable negotiating and promotional skills, Byers forever changed the nature of intercollegiate athletics when he put college football and basketball on television. The day this happened was the day the rewards of mass entertainment became a permanent concern of the NCAA big-time institutions.

As good a promoter as Walter Byers was, he handicapped the NCAA enforcement responsibilities by creating the very promotional events that would prove to be the cause of scandal. Once schools tasted television's money, it was virtually impossible to wean them from it.

With television money, and its resulting power, came athletic departments incorporating themselves to enhance their independence and power. These separate legal entities are run by boards of directors completely independent from the university whose name they now only nominally bear.

As an example of how independent a separate athletic corporation can be, Louisiana State University's athletic corporation compiled such a profit in recent years that it donated over $2.7 million to LSU, itself. Other university athletic corporations are not nearly as generous, preferring instead to build more athletic facilities, pay higher wages, and keep surpluses in the hands of the people who earned it, namely, athletic directors and coaches.

Today's NCAA objectives, when compared to the association's original purpose, read more like the aims of a small town's Rotary Club. Paraphrasing from the NCAA General Information 1989-90 pamphlet, the association exists:

• To promote intercollegiate athletics.

- To uphold the principles of institutional control of all inter-collegiate athletics events, the "home rule" regulation.
- To encourage NCAA members to adopt recruiting and eligi-bility standards that will ensure satisfactory scholarship, sportsmanship and amateurism.
- To formulate and publish playing rules governing inter-collegiate athletics.
- To keep intercollegiate athletics statistics.
- To conduct national championships in intercollegiate ath-letics.
- To legislate any national issue pertaining to intercollegiate athletics.
- To maintain intercollegiate athletics on a high level.

If it were not for home rule, which is the regulation that permits an individual NCAA member-school to determine its own athletic fate, the NCAA would have had clear license to step in and control the Loyola Marymount-Hank Gathers situation better. But the in-herent conflict between protecting the interests of an individual school versus protecting the interests of a group of schools explains the NCAA's overall ineffectiveness. As it now stands, the NCAA openly encourages individual institutional autonomy and discour-ages a strong central authority. The association re-raises the age-old question of federalism versus states' rights, with the conservative Republican answer prevailing.

The authority of the NCAA resides in its annual conventions, held each January. These are the only occasions where rules may be either created or modified. They are dominated by the politically sophisticated NCAA old-guard defined as athletic directors, faculty athletic representatives and college presidents, sympathetic to ath-letics.

The NCAA Council, a forty-six-member body comprised of proportionate numbers from all three divisions, runs the NCAA on a day-to-day basis between annual conventions.

The NCAA Executive Committee oversees the association's multi-million annual budget which, because of the increased popu-larity of The Final Four basketball tournament and CBS's passion to broadcast it, has outpaced even the most explosive economic indices in the last ten years. In 1982, for example, before CBS was involved, the NCAA annual budget was only $28 million. In 1991, nine years after CBS took over the tournament, the NCAA annual budget is expected to exceed $165 million.

Reporting to the NCAA Council are eighty-nine NCAA committees consisting of 870 people who deal with everything from negotiating The Final Four television contract to establishing future convention sites.

Since there is great safety in numbers, the NCAA committee system offers the perfect opportunity to evade responsibility. When pressed about its role in the Hank Gathers situation, Frank Uryasz, the NCAA head of sports medicine, said, "The Committee on Competitive Safeguards and Medical Aspects of Sports might look into it when it meets in July."[11]

Another pressing question involving athletes received an equally evasive answer from an NCAA official. Athletes account for less than one percent of the nation's undergraduate population, yet studies show they represent thirty-three percent of those accused of campus rape and sexual assault.

When asked to comment on the problem, which is increasing yearly, David Cawood, assistant executive director of the NCAA, said, "It's a major problem for higher education. But it's a concern the NCAA has no jurisdiction over. It's unfortunate that athletics bring focus to the problem that doesn't get noticed otherwise."[13] If the NCAA does not have jurisdiction over a disproportionate number of intercollegiate athletes raping co-eds, then who does?

The NCAA executive director, Richard B. Schultz, who replaced Byers in 1987, supervises a staff of 300 full-time employees who are located in a brand new building of Overland Park, Kansas, a suburb of Kansas City. The NCAA staff assists the various committees in formulating and implementing policy approved at the annual conventions.

For the most part, the NCAA staff still feels Walter Byers's presence because Dick Schultz is absent so often. Three out of five working days, Schultz is not in his corner office. Instead, he is personally flying the private plane the NCAA bought expressly for him, visiting NCAA member-schools around the country. By doing so, Schultz exhibits his administrative strengths and weaknesses.

Because he likes to visit them frequently, members invariably refer to Schultz as "accessible," "open" and "collegial." They used to describe Walter Byers as more dictatorial and iron-fisted. The members respected Byers, but few liked him.

Walter Byers was not nearly as peripatetic or as accessible as Schultz is. Byers preferred to stay in Kansas City, overseeing his obedient staff.

Al Witte, current president of the NCAA, cited Schultz's wanderlust as his biggest weakness. Witte said, "He [Schultz] likes to travel too much. The staff is still pretty much Walter's people and they continue to run the place the same way Walter did. Dick has failed to move on one or two key staff people when he should have long ago."[14]

Walter Byers was a firm and precise boss, leaving very little to chance. In 1956, Byers wrote the following passages in the NCAA Office Manual which are still scrupulously adhered to:

Rule 6.1.1. Office Conduct
Male administrators are to wear suits or sports coats and slacks, shirts and ties. Women administrators and nonadministrative employees are to wear dresses, suits, skirts and blouses. All blouses must cover the waistline and below at all times.

Rule 9.3.1 The NCAA Building
All office drapes, including thermal drapes, are to be drawn at the time the occupant leaves his or her office for the day. Beverages (coffee, milk, soda and juice) are not permitted at desks.

Byers worked hard at creating and projecting the image of a plain, honest man from Kansas who stood in sharp contrast to, say, the slick New York executives with whom he negotiated the NCAA television packages. But *The Washington Post* contradicted this self-portrait when it revealed in 1985 that Byers had secured a $500,000 interest-free mortgage for himself from the United Missouri Bank of Kansas City, the bank that had the NCAA multi-million dollar business account. It appeared that Byers made the interest-free loan a provision for the bank to retain the association's business. Neither the NCAA then-president, John R. Davis, nor its secretary-treasurer, Wilford S. Bailey, knew or approved of the loan.[15]

Most of the senior staff members are Byers appointees who have been with the NCAA for over twenty years. When judged by the education and experience required by NCAA member-schools for comparable positions, many headquarters staffers lack the proper credentials for their jobs. Louis Spry, the NCAA controller, a graduate of Pacific Lutheran College, is not a CPA. Frank Uryasz, who heads up the sports medicine department, lacks a medical degree.

Membership in the NCAA is similar to any other sports federation. Volunteers start at the bottom, and progress through the various committee chairs. The speed with which they rise in the organization depends entirely on how well they cooperate with the NCAA conservative culture. Patience, not brilliance, determines who succeeds.

"I've been in the NCAA for twenty-five years," said Al Witte, who is not only the association's president but also faculty athletics representative of the University of Arkansas. "I started coming to the conventions as a means of getting out of the house and I just got hooked on it."[16]

The NCAA amply rewards forbearance and compliance. Witte travels throughout the country, first-class or in Schultz's private jet, staying in the best hotels and receiving unlimited media attention. He even is provided with a brand new Oldsmobile.

In theory, the president or chancellor of each NCAA member-school heads the delegation to the annual NCAA convention. But the member-school's athletic director or faculty athletics representative actually wields the power. Over the years there have been many power struggles between athletic directors and college presidents that violate traditional notions of what a boss-subordinate relationship should be. Bo Schembechler, when he was the athletic director of Michigan, said, "College presidents ought to stay out of the NCAA. They know nothing about college athletics, and always screw them up."[17]

In the early Eighties, college presidents, led by Harvard's Derek Bok, attempted to reform the NCAA. Their efforts resulted in the formation of the Presidents Commission. But the old-guard NCAA members — athletic directors, faculty athletic representatives —

refused to entrust the commission with any real authority. In 1989, Peter Likens, president of Lehigh University and a founding member of the Presidents Commission, quit the commission because it "has no power worth mentioning."[18]

Along the way, the Presidents Commission has been led by several would-be reformers who turned out to be in need of reform themselves. John Slaughter, chancellor of Maryland University, chaired the NCAA Presidents Commission while the Len Bias scandal rocked the nation.

When asked why he recruited athletes who were inferior students, Lefty Driesell, Maryland's basketball coach at the time, said, "I'm only the coach, and I never admitted anyone. Ask Slaughter how all those boys got into school. Ask him about Terry Long!"[19]

Later, when the question was raised with John Slaughter, he admitted, "Yes, from time to time I interceded on behalf of basketball players with the admissions office. And I did try to help Terry Long. That did not work out."[20]

Terry Long, who snorted cocaine all night long with Len Bias and then hid from the police for sixteen hours after Bias died, had been rejected by Maryland's Admissions Office when he first applied through normal channels. Driesell then prevailed upon Slaughter to help, and Slaughter admitted Long to Maryland via a remedial program over the program director's objections. Long then flunked out of Maryland, twice.

The report of the grand jury investigating Bias's death said, "Maryland University's decision to have a major athletic program based, to a large extent, on the talents of students who had less than a reasonable chance of graduating, was not only appalling, but abominable."

When asked if the Bias incident embarrassed his reign over The Presidents Commission, Slaughter said, "No, I wasn't embarrassed. Saddened, but not embarrassed."[21]

CHAPTER 2

Drugs

At noon, on Tuesday, June 17, 1986, eleven college basketball stars—all black, excessively tall and beautifully dressed—sat in the Felt Forum of Madison Square Garden waiting for the NBA draft to begin. Kenny Walker of Kentucky, Chuck Person of Auburn, Johnny Dawkins of Duke, Brad Daugherty of North Carolina, Chris Wasburn of North Carolina State, Len Bias of Maryland and others affected a joshing nonchalance. But their eyes appreciated the miracle of having made it to the pros.

Of the twenty-four NBA teams participating in the draft, Cleveland had first pick, and the Cavaliers selected the six-foot-eleven Brad Daugherty because they needed a center desperately. Red Auerbach of the Boston Celtics was second and he chose Len Bias, Maryland's consensus All-American. It was a toss-up as to who looked happier, Auerbach or Bias. Voted that year's best player in the Atlantic Coast Conference, Len Bias, six-foot-seven, had broken virtually every scoring record at the University of Maryland, a major spawning ground for the NBA. People who knew ACC basketball thought Len Bias was more explosive and exciting than Michael Jordan. On and off the basketball court, Bias was like Icarus, always soaring towards the sun.

The moment his name was announced, Bias bounded to the stage for the obligatory photo with NBA commissioner David Stern.

Since it was a New York crowd, The Forum cheered warily, knowing that Len Bias and the Celtics made too good a match.

Bias and Stern made an incongruous pair. The roly-poly commissioner, dressed in a dark pin-stripe suit that accentuated his squatness, could hardly tilt his neck back far enough to look up to the player wearing an elegant Armani suit that accentuated his litheness.

James Bias, the only father present, sat in the last row, smiling shyly as his son waved to him. Sitting next to the elder Bias was his son's newly retained agent, Bill Shelton of Advantage International, a sports management firm that also represented Moses Malone, John McEnroe, Sam Perkins and Steffi Graf.

Len Bias endured the endless questions, saying over and over again how happy he was to finally make it to the pros. One reporter asked Bias if he were going to be a million-dollar rookie, a question that made Bias grin and Auerbach frown.

At 2:00 P.M., Len, his father and Bill Shelton made their way to LaGuardia and took the 3:00 P.M. shuttle to Boston in time for Len to appear on the 6:00 news. Again, more questions requiring the same answer: "It's going to be great playing for Boston, understudying Larry Bird. I've always dreamed of it."

On Wednesday, June 18, 1986, Lee Fentress, the senior partner of Advantage International, and Phil deCicciotto, another executive with the firm, flew from Washington, D.C., to join the Biases and Shelton at the headquarters of Reebok International to negotiate an endorsement contract for Len. Representing Reebok was Paul Fireman, its youthful president, and Betsey Richardson, its blonde and pretty vice president of marketing.

"The thing I remember most about Len Bias," Richardson said, "was that he shared this moment with his father. I've negotiated a lot of these deals, and I had never seen another player bring his father with him before."[1]

Various Reebok personnel presented the company's product line to the Biases and took them on a plant tour while Fentress, Fireman and Richardson talked in another conference room. At about 5:00 P.M., Fentress emerged to report that Reebok had agreed to a five-year, $1.625 million deal. Both Biases were stunned. Between the Reebok endorsement contract and what he could expect from the Celtics, Len Bias would earn in one year what his father, a medical equipment repairman, and his mother, Lonise, a bank teller, earned in twenty-five.

After everyone shook hands, Paul Fireman invited the Biases and their agents to a party he was giving at the Royal Sonesta Hotel in Cambridge for key customers. Other Reebok endorsees Danny Ainge and Dennis Johnson of the Celtics were also going to be there. Len accepted, provided he could make an 8:30 P.M. flight back to Washington, D.C. He was anxious to see his mother.

Firemen introduced Bias to the party guests as Reebok's newest star. The dealers and the two Celtics were curious to meet the man who, together with Larry Bird, would make the Celtics World Champions again. Len left the party triumphantly, carrying an enormous bag full of Reebok shoes, clothes and Celtics mementos.

All five men made New York Air's flight #67 that left Logan Airport at 8:35 P.M., bound for Washington, D.C. Lee Fentress, the senior man from Advantage International, sat next to Len and reviewed what had happened in the last several days.

"The first thing I told him is to be patient. It would take several weeks for the Reebok contract to be drawn up and signed," Fentress said. "Then I told him that the Celtics had a salary-cap problem and that all they could afford was $500,000 but that I had persuaded Red Auerbach to get an additional $300,00 from somewhere." Fentress did not explain where the extra money would come from.

He continued, "Len was excited about the Celtics and the Reebok deal. But because he also was a little irresponsible. . .he wasn't going to school. . . I told him in no uncertain terms that he had to go to class."[2]

In mid-March of 1986, after starring in The Final Four basketball tournament—fifty-seven points and thirty rebounds through two rounds—Len Bias stopped going to classes, twenty-one credits shy of a degree.

"Yeah, that's true about Leonard," Lefty Driesell, Maryland's basketball coach, said later. "But what was he worried about? He was going to be a damn millionaire! Hell, I wouldn't have gone to class either."[3] Despite his comment, Driesell himself graduated from Duke University, Dean's List, and earned a Master's, with honors, from William and Mary.

Three other members of Maryland's basketball team—Terry Long, Jeff Baxter and Tom Jones—flunked out that semester, as well. Two months later, in the summer semester, freshman center Tony Massenburg was expelled for cheating.

But out of deference to his parents, Len Bias had returned to Maryland in early June to attend summer school. His parents were aspiring, determined people who brooked no interference from their children, when it came to born-again Christianity and education.

"Len Bias was no inner-city nigger," said Colonel Tom Fields, president of The Terrapins, Maryland's booster club. "He was an artistic young man, not a dumb kid, from a good family."[4] A few Maryland citizens, including members of its university's athletic department, still exhibit a red-clay ignorance.

The plane landed at Washington National at 9:53 P.M., and shortly thereafter, Len and his father said good night to Fentress, deCicciotto and Shelton.

In his newly-leased Datsun 300ZX sports car, Len drove his father to their Landover, Maryland, home, a small bungalow with a meticulous lawn, located four doors down from The Wayside Holiness Assembly of God Church. They arrived at 10:30 P.M. Len greeted his younger brothers, Jay, sixteen, and Eric, thirteen, and sister, Michelle, twenty-one, who were waiting for him on the front stoop, ecstatic over their brother "Frosty's " good fortune. Lonise Bias, a born-again Christian, had yet to return from one of her church activities.

About a half hour later, at 11:00 P.M., Len said good-bye to his family, and drove off to his dormitory suite at Maryland University. He promised to call his mother in the morning.

Bias drove up Route 1 past College Park and into the Maryland campus, arriving at the parking lot outside his dorm, Washington Hall, at 11:15 P.M. He proceeded to the four-bedroom apartment, Room 1103, which he shared with basketball teammates Terry Long, David Gregg, Keith Gatlin, and Jeff Baxter (Bias's roommate) and two members of the Maryland's football team, all-Atlantic Coast Conference player Keeta Covington and Ben Jefferson. All were there, plus a young woman, Marilyn Woods, waiting for Len to return. They laughed as Bias threw the Reebok bag into the living room and cried out, "Santa Claus is home."[5] Bias quickly changed into jeans, Reebok high-tops and a T-shirt. A gold neck chain, obscured by the tie his father made him wear, became visible.

After Len amused his friends for an hour or so with what it was like to meet the NBA commissioner David Stern and the Celtics' Red Auerbach, everyone retired. But Len, too excited to sleep, telephoned another friend, Brian Tribble, and said he was coming over with a pair of highly prized Reebok athletic shoes.

Tribble, twenty-three, a rug and upholstery cleaner, lived out his rich but unfulfilled basketball fantasies through Len Bias. Bias, in turn, lived out his social fantasies through the startlingly handsome Tribble who was often compared to Rudolph Valentino. Together, the six-foot-seven Bias and the Latin-lover Tribble were an "awesome combo with chicks." It was also suspected that Tribble augmented his income, and his social appeal, by selling cocaine.

Bias arrived at Tribble's apartment in nearby Beltsville at about 12:45 A.M. A pair of English bench-made shoes could not have provoked more appreciation than the high-tech Reebok "pumps" did. In fact, Tribble was so excited, he insisted on putting the shoes on and taking Bias out to celebrate.

Bias and Tribble left the apartment, thrilled with the Reeboks, Bias's future and the prospects of the night ahead.

The pair drove back over to a liquor store near the Maryland campus. On the way, while the two were stopped at a red light, Corporal William Conaway of the University of Maryland Police Department pulled alongside Bias's Datsun and recognized the driver. "I congratulated him," Conway later said, "on signing with the Celtics."[6]

Several minutes later, Bias and Tribble arrived at Town Hall Liquors, near the Maryland campus. Bias entered the store alone and bought two six-packs of Private Stock beer and a fifth of Hennessey Cognac from Michael Cogburn. After the transaction was completed, Cogburn sheepishly asked Len to autograph a Bias photo that was pinned to the wall. "We're all gonna turn Yankee and be Celtics fans now," Cogburn chuckled.

Bias and Tribble then drove to southeast Washington, D.C., and visited an older woman for about an hour.

Bias and Tribble returned to Bias's dormitory around 3:30 A.M. Upon entering the suite, Bias yelled out to his sleeping roommates, "Wake the fuck up, we are going to celebrate."[7]

Terry Long, a tall, powerfully built man from Richmond, Virginia, and David Gregg from nearby Hyattsville were the only two to respond. Long suggested they use his bedroom so as not to disturb the others. After closing the door, a large quantity of cocaine appeared on Long's desk.

As they speculated whether Bias would change once he became a millionaire, the four became increasingly inebriated drinking beer and the cognac and snorting the cocaine.

At 6:15 A.M., the party took a dangerous turn.

"Bias became all fucked up and laid his head back on my bed and closed his eyes," Terry Long testified later.

Moments later, with only the whites of his eyes now eerily evident, tremors passed through Bias's body while his head, legs and arms trembled furiously.

Long grabbed a pair of scissors and inserted the handles in Bias's mouth to keep him from swallowing or biting his tongue. Long also checked Bias's pulse and heartbeat.

Near panic now, the three men removed Bias from the bed and put him on the bedroom floor. Long began to administer CPR while Gregg held Bias's legs to prevent them from flying about. Bile seeped down his chin because after each seizure, Bias would vomit on himself.

Tribble finally had the presence of mind to call the Prince George's County Emergency 911 number.

Within minutes, eleven Prince George's County Fire Department paramedics arrived. They immediately took Bias out of Long's bedroom and laid him on the living room floor and administered additional lifesaving techniques.

While the paramedics frantically attended to Bias, Gregg Long and Tribble filled a plastic garbage bag with beer cans, the Hennessey bottle and various drug paraphernalia. At no time did the threesome volunteer to the paramedics that Bias had snorted a large quantity of cocaine.

After working on Bias for nearly forty minutes, the paramedics transported him to Leland Memorial Hospital in Hyattsville. Word spread quickly that "Len Bias was down." By 8:00 A.M., Bias's parents, Maryland basketball coach Lefty Driesell and fifteen team members and friends, including Tribble, Long and Gregg, had gathered outside the operating room where Len Bias lay.

The group was somber but hopeful, believing that nothing too serious could ever happen to this powerful athlete.

Tipped off by the paramedics, Homicide Detective Michael G. Ferriter of the Prince George's County Police Department arrived.

Terry Long told Ferriter: "Lennie was drafted by the Celtics, you know, and we were partying. He [Bias] had a couple of beers and maybe a shot of Hennessey. All of a sudden, he just went into convulsions."[8]

At 8:51 A.M., the slight, dark-skinned Dr. Amjad Rasul came came out of the operating room and announced to no one in particular that Len Bias was dead. James Bias escorted his wife Lonise, who was near hysteria, out into the parking lot. An ashen Driesell was using the wall pay-phone, whispering to Lee Fentress, Bias's agent. Jeff Baxter, Bias's roommate, approached Brian Tribble, David Gregg and Terry Long, who stood huddled together, and asked: "What went down last night, man? What went down?" The three shrugged and made no reply.

Just twelve hours before, Len Bias had fulfilled two ambitions most men only dream about. Now he lay on a hospital gurney, without his life and his dignity.

Len Bias's jeans were down around his ankles, his T-shirt pulled up around his neck. His head was tilted carelessly to one side, his eyes staring blankly beyond the ceiling. An airway tube, inserted in Bias's mouth and right nostril, obscured sections of his gold neck chain. Curdled vomit and foam clung to Bias's mouth. Six puncture marks below Bias's left breast, three puncture marks in the middle of his chest, and one puncture mark on each of Bias's inner thighs indicated where Dr. Rasul had applied the pulmonary resuscitation techniques.

After the hospital staff made Bias's corpse presentable, James Bias left his wife for a moment and came back to the operating room and identified the body of his son.

Before leaving the hospital, David Gregg and Terry Long took Coach Driesell aside and told him exactly what had transpired the previous night, drugs and all.

Coincidentally, while Long and Gregg were confessing to Driesell, Detective Michael Ferriter asked for a drug test of Bias's body which turned out positive. "So right from the start," Ferriter said, "we knew cocaine was involved."

His opinion was confirmed later that morning by Maryland's Chief Medical Examiner, Dr. John E. Smialek, and the Assistant

Medical Examiner, Dr. Dennis E. Smyth. The two concluded that Len Bias died of cocaine intoxication which interrupted the normal electrical control of his heartbeat, resulting in the sudden onset of seizures, vomiting, bile release and cardiac arrest. Len Bias's blood cocaine level was 6.5 milligrams per liter, twenty-five percent over the lethal concentration level.

After Bias died, Driesell went back to his office on the Maryland campus and called Lee Fentress again. This time Driesell told Fentress, "There's a rumor drugs are involved."[10]

On the advice of Fentress, Driesell asked Oliver Purnell, an assistant coach, to remove or destroy any evidence of drug use in Len Bias's room.[11]

At about noon, Driesell convened a meeting of the basketball team at his home in Wheaton, Maryland. "Before the police could meet with anyone," State Attorney Arthur Marshall said, "Coach Driesell met with the team, and then he met privately with David Gregg and Terry Long. He instructed the players, and these two men in particular, not to say anything to the police, not to cooperate."[12]

Shortly after the meeting started, Lt. Richard Doran of the University of Maryland Police Department drove to Driesell's home to determine exactly how Bias died. It was now three hours after Bias had expired and the media were asking the police questions they could not answer.

Driesell, Long and Gregg refused to talk with Lt. Doran.

Long and Gregg then left the meeting, on the advice of Driesell, and proceeded to the Hyattsville home of Robert Wagner without telling the police or anyone else where they were going. Wagner had coached Len Bias and David Gregg at Northwestern High School.

Later that afternoon, Driesell held a press conference back on the Maryland campus where he repeatedly denied that drugs were involved in Len Bias's death.

The next morning, June 20, on ABC's "Good Morning America," co-host Stone Phillips asked Driesell, who was standing outside Maryland's basketball arena, Cole Field House: "This is big-time college basketball and an athlete has died mysteriously, and there are a lot of reports today that drugs may have been involved. What can you tell us about that?"

Driesell replied, "Well, I would be very, very surprised, because Leonard just had an examination by the Boston Celtics and the Golden State Warriors and the New York Knicks, and you know, I'm positive there were no drugs in those examinations. It is completely out of character for him to do anything like that. That's one thing I told Red and all the teams that were interested in him, that they didn't have to worry about him with drugs and alcohol; he was a born-again Christian and a great person. And you know, I just—it would be completely out of character for him to do anything like that."[13]

Three hours later, Detective Carl Schallhorn of the University of Maryland Police Department discovered 11.1 grams of cocaine hidden under the dash board of Len Bias's Datsun 300ZX which was parked outside Washington Hall.

The following Sunday evening, 2,00 mourners waited as long as two hours to file past Bias's open casket at The Pilgrim African Methodist Episcopal Church in Washington, D.C.

The next day, 10,000 people filled Cole Field House at Maryland for a memorial tribute to Len Bias. At one point in the service, the crowd stood and cheered for three minutes. Jesse Jackson was the guest speaker. James Bias said, "As good a basketball player as Leonard was, he was even a better son."[14]

When Larry Bird of the Boston Celtics learned that Len Bias's life had been scythed away, he said, "It was the cruelest thing I ever heard."[15]

Instead of benefiting from the millions their son almost earned, James and Lonise Bias had to assume two loans amounting to $15,000 which Leonard had recently incurred. The Biases could not afford to put a marker on his grave. The Boston Celtics gave the Bias family $10,000 although no formal contract talks had ever begun.

Despite agreeing verbally to an endorsement contract which Bias already started to fulfill by appearing at the Reebok dealer party on June 18, Reebok gave the Biases nothing, not that they asked. "First, we invited him to the cocktail party. He didn't have to come," said Betsey Richardson. "Second, Reebok had no moral obligation to the Biases. Reebok is against drugs. We thought it would be hypocritical to give money to the Biases after Len actively took his own life with drugs.'' [16]

Paul Fireman personally earned $33.9 million as president of Reebok between 1986 and 1988.

State Attorney Arthur Marshall later said, ''Had Driesell told the truth right from the beginning, the case would have been over in ten hours. Instead, Driesell obstructed the police's inquiry, and we had to call in the Prince George's County Grand Jury to investigate the death.'' [17]

But the most damaging revelation came later.

''Driesell and his coaching staff knew that half the team [six of the thirteen players] used drugs, including Bias, on a consistent basis, and he condoned their use of it. It was more important to win a basketball game in Driesell's way of thinking than to try and correct the drug problem. In fact, there was no concern about the use of drugs by athletes, period. Campus police did not care, as long as it was inside the campus rooms. No one at Maryland cared about drugs, just about winning basketball games,'' Arthur Marshall said. [18]

Wayne Curry, attorney for the Biases, blamed Driesell, too. Curry said, ''The coaches knew half the team used drugs. That came out in the grand jury investigation. The law calls Driesell's tolerance of the team's drug problems 'passive consent,' which is a culpable offense.'' [19]

James Bias was even more embittered.

He said, ''Driesell was a what-you-call surrogate father to those boys. We trusted him to look out for them. Driesell looked the other way when he heard the players were taking drugs like he let them slide in their studies, so that Maryland could keep on winning. It's not about athletes getting an education at Maryland. It's about winning games, and making money, and getting television and shoe contracts.'' [20]

When asked if Driesell was guilty of a crime, Marshall said, ''No doubt about it. He should have been indicted for obstruction of justice, at the very least. But he appeared before the grand jury, and talked his way out of it.''

In a highly unusual move, Driesell's lawyer, E. Bennett Williams, was allowed to appear before the grand jury. Williams was a world-class litigator, one-time defender of Jimmy Hoffa, owner of the highly popular Baltimore Orioles, former owner of the Washington Redskins, and a Maryland legend.

Michael Ferriter, the police officer in charge of the Bias homicide, said, "In all my years I never met a man like E. Bennett Williams."[21]

Williams told the jury that Driesell was a very close personal friend of his, and while Driesett might be foolish, he never intended to do evil. Lefty was trying to preserve Bias's reputation, Williams said.

After deciding not to indict Driesell, the grand jury turned its attention to Maryland University.

The grand jury found that the university spent only $119,000 per year on drug rehabilitation out of an annual budget of $331 million.

The grand jury also discovered that there were no drug education programs for students like Len Bias other than the drug testing program, which was implemented haphazardly. Campus police were not allowed to enter a student's quarters in search of drug offenders, a policy that in effect turned certain dormitories and fraternities into dope dens.

The grand jury uncovered an even more telling disclosure—the campus police made only nine drug-related arrests in this five-year period, ". . .an incredibly low number considering the 35,000-plus student population at the University of Maryland, College Park, and the estimate that at least 35 percent of the students are frequent drug users."

But John Slaughter, chancellor of Maryland at the time, who also headed the NCAA's Presidents Commission, disagreed: "Maryland is no better or no worse than any other large university with respect to drugs. The basketball team, like our other varsity squads, were tested regularly for drugs. Rarely if ever did anyone test positive, and when that happened, we did something about it."[22]

But even Driesell publicly referred to Maryland's drug testing program "as a joke."

The grand jury had harsher things to say.

Its report said, "Based upon testimony presented, the voluntary drug testing program adopted by the university has been poorly managed and lacked adequate supervision to the point where the identity of an individual supplying the urine sample was not verified. The more serious concern, however, was the revelation that individuals responsible for the administration of the drug testing program refuse to believe or acknowledge the fact that a positive drug test result is substantial evidence that the individual from whom the sample was taken was at some recent point in time guilty of the possession of an illegal substance. The jury therefore finds that the current drug testing and counselling has been grossly inadequate and must be strengthened.''

When Dr. Margaret Bridwell, who still heads the campus unit that administered Maryland drug tests in 1986, was asked in March 1990 if there have been any improvements to Maryland University's drug testing procedures since Len Bias's death, she said, ''No, there is not that much different between what we do today and what we did back then.''[23]

The report of the grand jury went on to say, ''One of the most serious revelations presented during testimony was the fact that the University of Maryland-College Park dormitories are essentially off limits to the police. The jury understands the students' right to privacy but questions whether that right should include the use of illegal drugs at will, free from the threat of police intervention.''

The people of Maryland revered Charles Grice Driesell because he was a most persuasive recruiter who assembled winning basketball teams.

One of Driesell's recruits, Tom McMillan, went on to be All-America, a Rhodes Scholar, an NBA star, and a member of the U.S. House of Representatives from Maryland (4th Congressional district). McMillan said, ''Lefty was a good person and a good coach.''[24]

On the other hand, many people can't forget how Driesell acted when a Maryland co-ed accused one of his star players, Herman Veal, of assault with intent to rape in March of 1983. The victim dropped the police charges but did pursue the matter through a student judicial board. Driesell was incensed when the board suspended Veal for a crucial game against Virginia. He telephoned Veal's accuser three separate times, haranguing her for the action she had initiated. Many at Maryland, including the Women's Center, wanted Driesell fired. Instead, Chancellor John Slaughter issued a mild rebuke.

Former Secretary of State Dean Rusk, an alumnus of Davidson College where Driesell coached before coming to Maryland, said, "I heard Lefty Driesell give a speech in Washington one night when he was Davidson's basketball coach. He was frantic about winning. He was totally consumed by it, so much so that he was not the right person to coach at Davidson at all. His attitude was not congenial to a liberal arts college."[25]

In June 1987, one year after Len Bias died, Driesell astonished a coaches' clinic in Providence, Rhode Island, when he admitted, "I'm a firm believer that if you know how to use cocaine and use it properly, it can make you play better."[26]

Although the NCAA Manual requires coaches to "deport themselves with honesty at all times,"[27] neither the NCAA nor Maryland University ever admonished Driesell.

In fact, throughout the entire Bias affair, the NCAA was never even mentioned. When asked why the NCAA was not involved, Robert Minnix, director of enforcement, explained, "Len Bias was not a student-athlete when he died. Besides, it is not our place to pry when a university is conducting its own investigation which Maryland was doing at the time."[28]

Within weeks of the Bias death, Don Rogers of the Cleveland Browns and "Jeep" Jackson of Texas-El Paso, who came from Prince George's County, Maryland, died from cocaine intoxication as well. The nation was shocked to see cocaine could be that lethal. Headlines again heralded how the sport of track and field was rooting out drug offenders through the use of rigorous drug tests. Only later did people discover that many officials and federations aided athletes who used drugs by suppressing their positive drug test scores. *The New York Times,* for example, estimated that fifty percent of the 9,000 athletes who competed in the Seoul 1988 Olympics were on drugs.[29]

Carl Lewis insinuated that Ollan Cassell, executive director of The Athletic Congress, this country's track and field federation, regularly suppressed the positive drug test results of certain star athletes.

Charlie Francis, Ben Johnson's coach, said, "We are awash in a sea of denial."

The NCAA exhibited this same denial to which Francis alluded. In 1988, the NCAA executive director, Richard Schultz, said, "As far as drugs are concerned, we are no different than society is, as a whole. We tested several thousand athletes at championship events last year, and only two percent tested positive, and most of those were just for anabolic steroids. I'd compare that to any segment of society."[30]

But an expert disagreed with Schultz's conclusion.

Dr. Robert Dugal, the head of the independent laboratory that actually did the drug testing for the NCAA at the time, said, "The positive rate of two percent is by no means an accurate reflection of the extent of the drug problem in college athletics today. The NCAA testing program was so extensively advertised beforehand, it was easy for amphetamine and cocaine users to pass the test by simply abstaining on the day they were tested. The percentage would be far greater, maybe as high as fifteen times greater, if the tests were administered on a random, unannounced basis."[31]

Two years later, the same Richard Schultz, when announcing an expanded NCAA drug testing program, said that the association's old testing program, the one used where only two percent tested positive, "only caught the dumb ones."[32]

But Len Bias may not have died in vain.

A Michigan State survey reveals a substantial decrease in the usage of cocaine and marijuana among NCAA athletes in recent years. In 1986, seventeen percent of those NCAA athletes surveyed admitted to cocaine use. In 1989, the number had dropped to five percent.[33] Those athletes who continue to consume cocaine are using it more frequently. The survey showed that the number of athletes who take cocaine weekly doubled in the last four years.[34]

The Michigan State survey also showed that steroid use had leveled off at a low percentage of usage.

But Dr. Robert O. Voy, former head of drug testing for the United States Olympics Committee and now a member of the NCAA Drug Testing Committee, distrusts all drug survey results: "People don't tell the truth about steroids even when the survey is anonymous."[35] For example, estimates of steroid consumption in the National Football League have run as high as fifty percent overall, and seventy-five percent for offensive lineman. Yet only six to seven percent of those tested by the NFL in the last three years have tested positive for steroids. Estimates of steroid use among college athletes have ranged from fifty percent for football offensive lineman to close to ninety percent for power weight lifters. Yet, less that one percent of all the athletes tested by the NCAA since 1987 have produced positive steroid tests.

Notre Dame's varsity football team has demonstrated the same disparity between the number of steroid abusers detected through positive drug tests and the far greater number of actual steroid abusers who go undetected. Steve Huffman,[36] a former Notre Dame football lineman, wrote in *Sports Illustrated* that half the lettermen at Notre Dame used steroids, and that the percentage of usage among linemen was even higher. In denying this allegation, football coach Lou Holtz claimed that only five to six percent of the players had tested positive for steroid use in recent years, implying that that was the extent of the problem at Notre Dame.

Clearly, drug-testing technologies have not kept pace with drug-users' technologies.

In today's society, with its proclivity for anything that produces a younger, slimmer and more beautiful look, steroids represent the athletes' version of breast implants.

Steroids, a synthetic derivative of the male hormone testerone, pay a double dividend. First, they build muscle and tissue mass. Second, they increase a person's aggressiveness so that he or she may endure the pain and fatigue of strenuous exercise longer. The age-old question with anabolic steroids is, do they in fact directly build strength and endurance, or do they merely allow for more strenuous training which in turn produces additional strength and endurance?

Society, especially athletic society, is so competitive that if steroids did not exist, they surely would have been invented. Steroids were first given to the German infantrymen in World War II to make them more aggressive. Then the Russians and Eastern European nations used steroids for strength events. In 1954, after observing testerone's dramatic effects on Russian weight lifters, Dr. John Ziegler returned to the United States and invented Dianabol, the first American anabolic steroid. Dianabol built tissue and muscle mass without the negative side-effects of raw testerone.

When weight lifters and body builders started to "press" and "flex" more, shot putters, hammer and javelin throwers, and sprinters began using steroids to improve their performances too.

Football followed suit in the late Seventies, and an epidemic of steroid use broke out among professional and intercollegiate football players. A physician for an NFL team said, "When you see athletes in the showers with enormous bodies, but with testes the size of the tips of their little fingers, it's obvious they're on steroids."[37]

Eventually, steroids invaded high schools, and an estimated 500,000 teenage males now take steroids, a third of whom are nonathletes who take them to improve their chances with girls.

As the epidemic spread, athletes developed their own steroid technology which in some instances became quite advanced. Before going to jail for the illegal distribution of steroids, Dan Duchaine, former body builder and author of *The Underground Handbook on Steroids*, knew more about the drug than most physicians. Unfortunately, without doctors regulating the dosage, athletes began to take fifteen to twenty times the amounts Dr. Ziegler had originally intended.

Inevitably, these megadoses led to complications which included elevated blood pressure, weight gain due to water retention, acne, bad breath, enlargement of the prostate gland, liver cancer, anxiety depression, neurotic or psychotic bouts of hostility, heart failure and genital atrophy.

Just as Len Bias's death may have eventually contributed to the decline of street drug usage among athletes, two events in 1988 changed public opinion toward steroids which had been fairly benign up until then.

On September 24, 1988, at the Seoul Olympics, Ben Johnson ran the 100-meter dash in 9.79 seconds, the fastest ever. Twelve hours later, Johnson was stripped of his gold medal because of a positive drug test. Technicians at the Doping Control Center of the Korea Advanced Institute of Science and Technology had discovered stanazolol, an anabolic steroid, in Johnson's urine sample.

Then, a month later, in *Sports Illustrated,* University of South

Carolina football player Tommy Chaikin revealed to writer Rick Telander the horrors of his addiction to steroids.

Responding to the implied entreaty of a football coach to become bigger and tougher, Chaikin, a lineman, started taking steroids in his sophomore summer. The initial results were, in Chaikin's view, quite good. But then, responding to the inevitable drug-user's refrain of more is better, he went from a congenial, 220-pound teenager to a 280-pound gargoyle who came within moments of pulling the trigger of the gun he had placed in his mouth to end his steroid-induced agony.

Before the Chaikin article, the general public had always viewed steroids as a mysterious but innocuous elixir, like snake oil, that made already large athletes even larger and somehow pinker. Few recognized steroids' inherent addictive and destructive dangers. Fewer still recognized that steroid use in intercollegiate athletics involves a conspiracy of coaches, teammates, team physicians and college administrators.[38] As a result of the Chaikin article, three South Carolina football coaches were sent to prison for distributing steroids to members of the University of South Carolina football team.

Incredibly, a follow-up NCAA investigation of the University of South Carolina football steroid scandal failed to uncover any serious rules violations.

Shortly after the Chaikin article appeared, Congress passed the Anti-Drug Abuse Act which made the illegal distribution of anabolic steroids a felony.

Drugs in athletics dates back to the third century B.C., when Homer chronicled athletes taking mushrooms to make them faster and stronger. The next generation of Greek athletes relied upon root extracts to stimulate better performance. The Egyptians ground up rose hips. In the early 1900s, runners used nitroglycerine because it thinned the blood, thereby supplying more of it to the heart which increased the body's supply of oxygen. During the Depression, ether was dropped on sugar cubes. Scandinavian countries used extract from mushrooms that produced a hallucinogen called Berzelius, after a Swedish chemist, from which the word "berserk" is derived.

The first athlete to die from drugs was a cyclist from Holland who used a mixture of ethyl-ether and alcohol supplied by a bicycle manufacturer. The first Olympic drug death occurred in 1960 when Danish cyclist Kurt Enemar Jensen died after taking amphetamines to improve his performance in the 100-kilometer team cycling trials. As a result of Jensen's death, drug testing was instituted in the 1965 Tour of Britain Cycle Race and the 1968 Mexico Olympics. Initially, drug testing was conducted to detect those athletes who gained an unfair competitive edge by consuming performance-enhancing drugs. Drug testing then branched out to include street drugs because the increased use of cocaine and marijuana in particular was marring the image of athletics. The health and safety of the athletes remained a distant concern.

Because of indifference and legal challenges, it took almost twenty years before another sports federation followed the 1968 Olympics Committee's example. The NCAA, for example, did not institute its drug testing program until August 1986, and only then in championship events. Most athletic federations, including the NCAA, follow this drug testing procedure:

a) An athlete is selected by lot before the event. He or she is called to the drug testing facility and asked to sign a card agreeing to the test. The card is torn through the signature. Half is kept by the medical committee, half by the athlete.
b) The athlete then selects a sealed container and is asked to provide a specimen which must be witnessed or observed. From the container, the athlete selects a sealed pair of bottles. Half of the specimen is placed in each bottle by the athlete. The bottles are labeled "A" and "B" with a diamond-tipped pen and placed in a locked case. A forwarding agent delivers the case to the laboratory.
c) The lab analyzes the "A" bottle twice. All specimens are identified by number to insure confidentiality. No specimen is ever identified by name.

The actual drug testing procedure is a three-level process.

Immunoassay, the first level, screens large numbers of urine samples and detects the presence of broad categories of drugs. It can not detect anabolic steroids.

If a positive immunoassay occurs, i.e., the test detects the presence of a drug in the urine sample, the next level of testing, gas chromatography, is implemented. Gas chromatography identifies the specific drug which the immunoassay had indicated might be present.

Upon a positive gas chromatography, the next level of testing, mass spectrometer, is invoked. An electron beam explodes the drug molecules into smaller particles, called molecular fingertips, which also confirms the presence and the identity of the drug.

Only two things can go wrong in drug testing: a false positive where an innocent person is accused of using drugs; or a false negative, when a guilty person goes undetected. False positive errors are rare because the multi-level system of testing confirms three times the presence of a drug, and then detects and confirms, either two or three times, the identity of that drug. Whenever a sample tests positive, the entire multi-level testing procedure is repeated on the ''B'' portion of the same urine sample.

In fact, false positives are so rare as to render all appeals virtually meaningless. ''Positive urine is positive urine,'' says Dr. Robert Voy, a member of the NCAA's Drug Testing Committee.[39] Blaming positive test results on birth control pills or the devil may extend the appeal process, during which the athlete usually competes, but it rarely results in reversal.

Unfortunately, athletes are always a step ahead of the testers, using newer performance-enhancing drugs for which no test procedures have been determined yet.

For instance, athletes discovered that water-based steroids flush out of the system quicker than oil-based steroids, thereby enabling a user to take these steroids right up to a few days before the test. The side-effects of water-based steroids, however, are more harmful than oil-based steroids. Cocaine also flushes from the system quickly, which enables the majority of cocaine users to go undetected in announced drug testing programs.

Desperate for an edge, some athletes have gone to extraordinary lengths to elude drug testing detection. Weight lifters Paramjit Gill, David Bolduc and Raphael Zuffellato testified to the Canadian Drug Inquiry that they regularly collected drug-free urine specimens from their coaches and injected them into their own bladders via catheters inserted up their penises.

Masking agents, or chemical agents that block the detection of drugs, especially steroids, are the most popular means to avoid drug test detection. Dr. Jamie Astaphan, Ben Johnson's physician, who uncovered carinamide, "the golden boy of masking agents," became wealthy and notorious by inventing agents that stymied drug testers.

Dr. Robert Voy resigned from the United States Olympics Committee after its president, Robert Helmick, refused Voy's request of $16 million to finance research that would leapfrog the USOC's drug testing technology beyond that of the drug-using athletes. "They were always one or two very big steps ahead of us," Dr. Voy said.[40] Mr. Helmick, when denying Voy's budget increase request, said, "Every department head wants me to increase his budget."[41]

Each NCAA championship event is subject to testing at least once every four years. In the 1987 men's basketball championship, for example, the NCAA tested the first round (thirty-two) winning teams by selecting six players from each team, the five who played the most minutes and one additional squad member selected randomly. The NCAA also tested the four losing teams at the regional level of the tournament, and the players were selected purely on a random basis.

At the 1990 NCAA Convention, the association adopted a new drug testing procedure for major football programs. The football drug test will be year-round and announced, but no athlete will know if he is to be tested until the day of the test. A sample of thirty-six players from each of 192 Division I schools, 6,912 athletes, will be tested randomly at least once and possibly twice a year.

The 1990 NCAA Convention also tightened the penalties of drug use. A first positive test for any banned substance will bring the loss of one year's eligibility. A second positive test for street drugs, like cocaine or marijuana, will bring the loss of another year's eligibility. A second positive test for performance-enhancing drugs, like steroids, would result in a lifetime ban from NCAA athletics. Al Witte, president of the NCAA, said, "Compared to the street drug-user, we want to be harsher on the steroid-user because he is attempting to gain an unfair competitive edge."[42]

Even with the expanded NCAA drug testing program, less than 10,000 athletes out of the association's total of 250,000 athletes will be tested each year.

In addition to the NCAA's national drug testing program, only thirty four percent of all colleges and universities—sixty percent in Division I—have their own drug testing procedures.

In the 1989 Michigan State study, three out of every five athletes favored drug testing, a substantial increase over the 1984 number.

The study also showed that drug usage patterns are the same for race and region of the country. The incidence of drug use among black athletes is neither more nor less than what it is among whites. And the same holds true for New York collegiate athletes versus Iowa collegiate athletes. There are no geographic biases.

Drug testing on college campuses, as in professional sports, has stirred a storm of suits. Many of the rulings have favored the litigants who claim drug tests violate their right to privacy.

In 1986, the Attorney General for the State of Oregon ruled that the University of Oregon's mandatory drug testing policy violated the state constitution.

In 1987, the State Supreme Court in Washington ruled that a track athlete could not be tested on campus.

In 1987, Simone Levant, a diver at Stanford, won an injunction against the NCAA's testing her.

In November 1988, two other Stanford athletes—a soccer player and a football player—joined the suit and the Santa Clara County Superior Court ruled in their favor.

In January 1990, the eight members of the Ivy League opposed the NCAA's expanded drug testing program. They claimed drug testing in general discriminated against the athlete because the normal student population is not subjected to drug testing. The Ivy League contends that athletes should be representative of the overall student population and should not be singled out.[43]

Others who are against drug testing believe it is a "warrantless search" without probable cause, which is a violation of the Fourth Amendment: "The right of the people to be secure in their persons, houses, papers, and effects, against unreasonable searches and seizures, shall not be violated, and no warrants shall issue, but upon probable cause, supported by oath or affirmation, and particularly describing the place to be searched, and the persons or things to be siezed."

Still others maintain it is not unreasonable to search the Maryland, Oklahoma, Nebraska or Notre Dame football teams. They say history has shown that big-time college football players demonstrate probable cause since they have an inordinately high incidence of drug usage, especially steroid consumption. "Suburban housewives do not take anabolic steroids to perform their responsibilities better. Football linemen do," said an NFL physician who asked not to be identified.

The Ivy League also objected to the regulation of observing athletes urinate into sample bottles. As embarrassing as this regulation may be to some, proponents of drug testing believe it is necessary. "We must sacrifice the delicate feelings of a few Ivy League athletes to protect the NCAA's 250,000 athletes," said the same NFL team physician.

But *New York Times* columnist Tom Wicker [44] argues against random, mandatory drug testing. Wicker believes that the incidence of drug use is so low, less than ten percent, that the rights of the majority should not be sacrificed to detect the abuses of a distinct minority.

Mr. Wicker notwithstanding, the United States Supreme Court handed down two pertinent decisions regarding mandatory drug testing in the spring of 1989.

In *National Treasury Union v. Von Raab,* the Court ruled that employees who apply for certain drug-enforcement jobs can, mandatorily, be drug tested. And in *Skinner v. Railway Labor Executives Association,* it ruled that the Federal Railroad Administration may drug test railroad crews after accidents occur.

Universities, bastions of civil libertarians, will always oppose drug testing, and, somewhat surprisingly, so will professional players unions.

In August 1987, Richard Dent, Chicago Bears defensive end, drug tested positive and traces of marijuana were found in his urine. According to NFL policy, Dent was placed on the "watch" list and scheduled for testing again in August 1988. When the time came, Dent refused to be retested, which, according to the NFL's policy, was tantamount to a positive test result. Since his refusal constituted Dent's second offense, an automatic suspension was imposed. With the aid of the NFL Players Union, Dent took the league to court, which ruled in his favor. He was reinstated after talking with Pete Rozelle, the NFL's commissioner at the time. When Dent got off, there was widespread elation among Chicago fans—even though illegal drugs were involved.

When the NFL suspended two dozen players who had tested positive for steroids in August 1989, the players' union tried unsuccessfully to get a federal judge to issue a restraining order against the league implementing its penalties.

However, Steve Courson, who played nine seasons for the Pittsburgh Steelers and the Tampa Bay Buccaneers, wishes the NFL was even tougher against drugs now that he has only five years to live. Courson attributes his heart ailment, cardiomyopathy, to the megadoses of Dianabol, Anadrol-50, Anavar, and Winstrol he took to make him stronger, faster and meaner. Steroids, Courson believes, made him have a standing heart rate of 150 beats per minute when the average is fifty to seventy-five.

In May 1989, appearing before the Biden Senate Committee, Atlanta Falcons' Bill Fralic testified that "steroid madness pervades most NFL locker rooms, and that seventy-five percent of today's NFL linemen use steroids. It's rampant in the NFL, it's rampant in college and it's rampant in high school."[45]

Fralic also observed that "thirty-day suspensions are a joke. We're talking about serious addictions that can last a lifetime. Giving someone thirty days for a drug addiction is like applying talcum to cancer."

He was equally critical of the NFL Players Union's assertion that drug testing violates civil liberties. He told Senator Biden: "There should be no civil liberties where drugs are concerned. Drugs are illegal."

Fralic continued, "The NFL should choose a different topic than drug testing to flex its muscles over. We players should welcome testing. We should submit to drug testing because it is a deterrent against shortened careers, life-long addictions, shattered lives, serious injury and death."[46]

New York Representative Charles B. Rangel, chairman of the House Select Committee on Narcotics Abuse and Control, assumes an even tougher stance. He has proposed to the commissioners of all professional sports that athletes who test positive for drugs, even for the first time, should be banned for life from the sport. "There is a lack of seriousness in society today about the drug problem, especially when it comes to sports figures. Drug testing should become even more extensive, and lifetime bans for offenders would help convince youth that drugs kill, even our athletic heroes,'' Rangel says.[47]

William Bennett, the drug czar, called all the professional sports commissioners and their players union heads to Washington, D.C., in May of 1989, urging them to ban for life all second offenders of drug abuse.

But the NCAA did have the courage to suspend Brian Bosworth and twenty other Division I football players, after he tested positive for steroids in January 1987. All but five of the suspensions were for steroid use. Since then the NCAA has not come close to matching this number or celebrity of drug offenders which some suspect might stem from the association's inherent conflict of interest.

Both Jack Scott, the controversial sports consultant and one-time athletic director of Oberlin College, and Dr. Robert Voy believe that the organization that stages the event should not be the organization that drug tests the event. ''You can't have a sport test itself,'' Dr. Voy said. ''It's like the fox guarding the hen house.'' The NCAA, for example, has too much riding on the event not to be tempted ''to muzzle positive test results.''[48]

CHAPTER 3

100 Years Ago

On August 3, 1852, when Harvard beat Yale in crew on gleaming Lake Winnepesaukee, James Elkins, superintendent of the Boston, Concord & Montreal Railroad, was ecstatic. Although the race was the first intercollegiate athletic event in the United States, it was neither its historical significance nor its winner that made Elkins so happy. Unlike western railroads that prospered from gold rushes and land booms, eastern railroads had to dream up reasons for people to travel by rail. Elkin's scheme of pitting Harvard against Yale in a rowing contest proved to be just the attraction to draw more than a thousand people, including presidential hopeful General Franklin Pierce, to use the Boston, Concord & Montreal that day.

Elkins had to lure the Harvard and Yale teams to the wilds of New Hampshire with promises of lavish prizes and unlimited alcohol. In fact, both crews spent so much time drinking it was a feat they were able to compete at all. After Harvard's shell, the *Oneida*, crossed the finish line ten lengths in front of Yale, General Pierce presented the winners with gold-leafed oars and jeweled trophies from Tiffany's valued at over $500, prizes that compromised Harvard's and Yale's amateur standings, though no one cared a whit.

Thus, contrary to most people's innocent beliefs that a rosy-cheeked purity surrounded intercollegiate athletics in the 19th century, the first college sports contest was staged for the same shrill reason United Airlines promotes Hawaii today—tourism and money.

The commercialization of the first intercollegiate athletic event was a minor indiscretion compared to the other problems that plagued college sports in the 1800s. Although most people refuse to believe it, death, cheating, lying, bribery and cowardice were all integral parts of intercollegiate athletics one hundred years ago. What is even more difficult to believe is that 19th-century Harvard and Yale were the worst offenders.

Although 1852 marked the first intercollegiate athletic event in the United States, intramural sports were an essential, but controversial, part of college life dating back to the early 1700s. Most colleges established before the Revolutionary War were founded by militant Protestant groups. Only Columbia and Pennsylvania were non-sectarian. The rest—Harvard (Puritanism), William and Mary (Church of England), Dartmouth (Congregationalist), Brown (Baptist), Rutgers (Dutch)—were founded by clergymen who, if alive today, would rival Jerry Falwell in religious zeal. These schools were established to spread the word of God in the new colonies. Secular education was an unessential afterthought.

Unlike the great universities of continental Europe that were built in teeming urban centers to stimulate learning, American colleges were placed in somewhat remote locations to limit student distractions. Believing that college students personified the biblical aphorism, "The mind is willing but the flesh is weak," Cotton Mather and his fellow clergymen watched over their students' every waking moment, waiting, perhaps hoping, for the first signs of drift from the Puritan way of life. The religious atmosphere at American colleges before the Revolutionary War was only slightly less feverish than the Salem witch trials. Activities that favored the flesh, like athletics, were replaced by mandatory chapel twice a day, every day.

The war changed all that. After withstanding the horrors of combat, the returning veterans would no longer tolerate suppression, no matter how well-intentioned or religiously motivated. In 1784, once back at college, the Revolutionary War veterans could play games to relieve the tedium of Greek, Latin and Bible studies.

The returning veterans introduced football to college life, a game that had amused them in the slacker moments of the war. Football harkened back to 13th-century England where, as part of the annual fall harvesting rituals, medieval farmers would kick the inflated bladder of a pig from one meadow to the next, enthusiastically hurdling, swamping or crushing anything that stood in their way.

Even back then, football was such a violent sport that King Edward II banned it in London in 1312, and King Henry III extended the ban to all of England in 1349. But James I formally reinstated the game in 1622 because the ban had been largely ignored anyway.

For 200 years, the British working class placed great importance on playing football to escape the dreariness of their daily lives. And for 200 years, association football satisfied this desire, proving which town was better each time a match was won.

In 1822, Dr. Thomas Arnold introduced the game to the Rugby School, a British upper-class boarding school famous for its character-building cold showers.

Over the centuries, the term "association football" was shortened to "soccer" denoting a version of the game where kicking was the only acceptable means of advancing the football. But in 1823, an impatient Rugby School soccer player, William Webb Ellis, anxious to finish the game before the afternoon tea chimes rang, picked the ball up and tried to score by running over the goal line. The opposing team, startled only for a moment, caught and tackled Ellis before he reached the goal line, thereby winning the first "rugby" football game ever played.

But while rugby-style football remained the football game of choice in the British Isles, the United States favored the soccer-style version.

On the first Monday of every fall term, Harvard College sophomores played the Harvard freshmen in a soccer-style football game aptly named Bloody Monday. The game consisted of two opposing gangs of as many as 100 boys alternately rushing toward or running away from one another with no thought in mind other than to injure the opposing class as much as possible. In those days football lacked rules, a scoring system and tactics, which made the game boring to watch but exhilarating to play. Thirty years later, Bloody Monday had become so vicious that Harvard finally banned the game. But as the medieval English monarchs had discovered, it was impossible to sustain.

Harvard and Yale looked to Oxford and Cambridge for tradition. That's why the schools began their fierce rivalry in crew in the 1860s. As many as 25,000 spectators would watch a Harvard-Yale race, many of whom, following the British example set at Henley, would be drunk and disorderly before the day was over. Games that were once played for student enjoyment were now turned into intense spectacles staged more for fan gratification than for participant amusement.

America was too free-wheeling and too competitive for its colleges to continue the chivalrous British tradition of playing sport for fun. The strides America had made, when applied to intercollegiate athletics, meant an all-or-nothing preoccupation with winning. The Harvard-Yale competition, for example, determined far more than which school had the fastest shell. Judging from the intensity of the spectators and the participants, the stakes included which school had the more beautiful campus, the smarter faculty, the brighter student body, and the more successful alumni.

The ever-increasing emphasis on winning required athletes to be better conditioned and disciplined. If a school's reputation and honor were at stake, there had to be such things as practice, training regimens, tactics, and someone to make sure all these things happened.

In the first intercollegiate baseball game, when Amherst defeated Williams, 73-32, in 1859, a student leader, John Claflin, was responsible for Amherst's conspicuous superiority. Claflin was the first student-captain to function like a present-day coach.

In 1864, the Yale crew went a step further and hired college sports' first professional coach, William Wood. A physical therapist, Wood introduced a rigorous fitness program consisting of gymnasium work and running. Wood also invented the "training table" where specially prepared menus were served to the crew. As a result of Wood's efforts, Yale beat Harvard by the widest margin ever in 1865.

Yale hired Wood for only one reason—to win. And how many

times Wood won, especially against Harvard, determined how long he kept his job. With professional, paid coaches, winning was no longer desirable. It now became obligatory. Since their security depended on winning, college sports ceased being fun and became a business. John William Heisman, a famous paid football coach, exhibited this business-like attitude every fall. On the first day of practice, holding a football aloft, Heisman would say, "What is it? It's a prolate spheroid. It's an elongated sphere. It's a football. You will do better to have died as a small boy than to fumble it."[1]

Although it was never acknowledged, when Yale hired the first professional coach, amateurism in collegiate athletics ended. David Roberts, a former Cambridge oarsman, said, "In the 150 years of British public school competition, we have never had anything but students as team captains or coaches. You Yanks don't seem to understand that paid coaches is an inherent contradiction of amateurism."[2]

Roberts failed to add that amateurism is a sham purposely created by the British upper-class to exclude the working class from the sports of the privileged. In his recent book, *Sports and Freedom*, Professor Ron Smith, Penn State's eminent sports historian, revealed that the aristocratic British Rowing Association defined an amateur as someone who is not "or ever has been by trade or employment for wages a mechanic, artisan, or labourer, or engaged in any menial duty."[3]

Needing a veneer of legitimacy to make this hoax more plausible, the British fraudulently attributed amateurism to the Greeks. But a search of the literature of Pindar, the Greek poet, reveals that all four Greek games—the Olympian, Pythian, Nemean, and Isthmian—were populated by professional athletes who competed for prizes of considerable monetary value. The Greeks valued winning too much—to win was akin to meeting God—to ever have entrusted their athletics to amateurs.

Since British mechanics and laborers did not read much Pindar, no one challenged the notion of amateurism. It seemed plausible enough, at least to the gullible United States.

But amateurism was a concept far more suited to Britain and its upper-class citizens. Particular emphasis was always placed on an Oxbridge student maintaining a dignified sensibility. Oxbridge students were gentlemen first, and students and athletes only incidentally. They played sports as an avocation. And they were taught that although winning in sports was important, what was even more important was the process of occupying leisure time with a genteel, engrossing activity that could be enjoyed for a lifetime. To engage in sports too intensely would provoke anxiety which British gentlemen simply could not withstand. Also, the very people British gentlemen competed against at Oxford and Cambridge were the same select class with whom they spent their lives after university. To defeat them too soundly would surely alienate relationships that, by social necessity, had to endure.

On the other hand, American college athletes were not encumbered by such constraints. Despite the elitism of Yale and Harvard, the United States had no upper class. There was a meritocracy, to be sure, but it was based on achievement, not ancestral lineage. People were hungry for recognition, and it was accorded to those who won, and to those who had the money to prove it.

Winning in American college football meant the chance to prove something: virility, social worthiness or elitism. Even Harvard's philosopher, George Santayana, espoused a philosophy that placed extreme importance on winning. "In athletics, as in all performances, only winning is interesting. The rest has value only as leading to it or reflecting it."[4]

Winning at Cambridge and Oxford was far less important. It constituted an amusing but fleeting diversion from the mission at hand, which was to enrich the mind, body, soul and character of a gentleman. Winning at a continental university was never an issue because art, music and theater, not athletics, diverted students.

As the United States changed from an agrarian frontier to an industrial society during the second half of the 19th century, people feared a decline in personal bravery and ruggedness. Capitalizing on this fear, Rough Rider Theodore Roosevelt gained the White House by exhorting the nation to "hit the line hard."[5] No other activity could counter the image of a bookish and effete college student better than football, a real man's sport. No other activity could bolster a nation's vitality.

But English mores encouraged a gentleman to be sensitive. No matter how many times he won at a rugged sport, he never attained the glory his American counterpart did simply because the Brit did not need this artificial boost. By virtue of being born to the privileged class, an Oxbridge gentleman already had more than enough honor. In fact, the 19th-century British gentleman regarded accomplishment quite differently than his colonial counterpart did. The Brit reveled in self-effacement whereas the American reveled in heroism.

In the mid 1860s, baseball was the favorite recreation of both Union and Confederate soldiers, and when these young men returned home, baseball took hold on college campuses the same way football did seventy-five years before. The game's popularity was due to its accessibility. Unlike rowing or football, baseball could be watched by a vast number of people, crowds often numbered over 10,000 fans. And because colleges had an extensive athletic network already in place, complete with playing fields, college baseball in the 1860's held the same prominence as today's major leagues. Back then, college sports, like state fairs, were a form of public entertainment. Harvard, for example, exploited the public's interest in baseball by charging admission. By 1868, to keep up with the spectator demand, Harvard doubled the number of games it played to fifty, extending its season from April to August.

The clamor for college baseball also caused certain schools to look the other way as the game stole time away from the players' classroom duties. Nor did the colleges seem to care that they regularly competed against professional teams, and, worse, staffed their teams with professional players.

In 1878, Brown beat Yale, 3-2, for the national collegiate baseball championship. Lee Richmond, who was the college and professional baseball player of the decade, led Brown to the championship on the days he was not getting paid to play for the Worcester Sentinels, New England's pro team.

Harvard's Walter Clarkson, also a talented baseball player, was yet another example of how institutions—prestigious, world-famous schools—got caught up in the intensity of intercollegiate athletics and substituted the lofty principles of higher education for the glory and money of athletics. Only after he had helped beat Yale five consecutive times did the Harvard Athletic Committee throw Clarkson off the team.

Preoccupation with winning led many colleges to recruit the best athletes regardless of their academic fitness. Once they were on campus, these athletes were harbored in "scientific schools," euphemisms for enclaves that protected the playing eligibility of athletes with easy courses. Clarkson, for example, was a student of Harvard's Scientific School which, compared to Harvard's regular undergraduate colleges, had a far less demanding curriculum.

It was not until the 1920s, when professional baseball finally replaced college baseball as America's game, that the question of professionalism in college baseball was finally resolved. Before that date, proponents on both sides of the issue cited arguments that are still used today when examining the question of whether college football and basketball players should be paid. In *Sports and Freedom*, Professor Ron Smith cites one such argument when he quotes the president of Clarkson University, G. Stanley Hall, who said in 1900, ''I'm not only saying it is right for a man to play summer baseball for money, but I am going further than that. He is failing in his duty to himself and to the world if he does not take advantage of his God-given talent to use it to the best of his ability.''

The first intercollegiate soccer-style football game took place on November 6, 1869, when Rutgers defeated Princeton, 6-4. Each team was limited to twenty-five players who averaged five-foot-eight, 150 pounds, which was considered enormous in those days.

In 1872, Harvard played McGill University in the first American collegiate game of rugby-style football. The game also marked the first time football players wore uniforms. Harvard sported bandannas around their heads and sweaters, hence the tradition of varsity sweaters. McGill wore white duck trousers and turbans which eventually became helmets.

In 1873, the first soccer-style football game in the south was played between Virginia Military Institute and Washington & Lee University. Both teams had fifty men on a side.

On July 20, 1873, Cornell, Amherst and McGill staged the first intercollegiate track meet. It featured a two-mile run which was patterned after a game called the hounds and the hares—thus the term ''harriers'' to describe cross-country runners—that originated at Eton and at Rugby.

Intercollegiate soccer-style football spread to the Midwest in 1879 when the University of Michigan played Racine college (later the University of Wisconsin) in Chicago. Michigan won, 1-0.

But in those early days, Michigan and other neighboring colleges had a difficult time enticing eastern teams to brave the wilds of the Midwest. According to *The New York Times*, Cornell's president, Andrew D. White, answered Michigan's invitation by saying, "I will not permit thirty men to travel four hundred miles just to agitate a bag of wind."

The late 19th century's version of the Super Bowl always took place on Thanksgiving Day in New York City. More often than not, Princeton and Yale played each other before 40,000 fans at the Polo Grounds.

Because it was usually an exciting game to watch, the annual New York Thanksgiving Day Game became one of the social occasions of the year. The games themselves almost became incidental, overshadowed by the promotion and deviltry they provoked. Finally, things got so much out of hand that in the early 1900s colleges and universities started to build their own campus stadiums to control the environment of their football games better. Harvard was the first to erect a 30,000-seat stadium in 1903. Four years later, Yale built the Yale Bowl which held 80,000.

Following the custom established in baseball, colleges charged admission to football games, which meant that gate receipts influenced football in the early 20th century just as powerfully as television money does today. Yale, for example, played six home games in 1907, and all were sold out. Yale grossed $16,000 for the season which is equivalent to $1,245,117 in 1989, more than Michigan received from CBS for winning the NCAA's 1989 Final Four.

College football's commercialization, and its attendant brutality, raised the age-old question of whether or not colleges should be sponsoring football. Some felt that football had no place on a campus designed to enhance man's knowledge. People asked, why doesn't Heidelberg, or the Sorbonne, or even Cambridge and Oxford, for that matter, stage events like our Thanksgiving Day game? In fact, it was difficult at times to reconcile Harvard's axiom, "In Veritas," with the violence and occasional death of a Saturday afternoon football game.

Although football was thriving in the stadiums, a certain order and coherence were still needed on the playing field. Some schools began playing rugby-style football while others were still playing soccer-style. Eligibility rules varied expediently by the school, the

Hank Gathers's last shot of his life. Seconds later, he crumpled to the floor and died. Gathers had a heart disease that required him to take drugs to play. Photo: AP/Worldwide.

After Gathers died, his coach, Paul Westhead, said, "Nobody ever asked me to make sure he took his prescription." Photo: AP/Worldwide.

Walter Byers, the NCAA's first executive director, ruled the association with an iron fist from 1951 to 1987. Photo: AP/ Worldwide.

NCAA executive director Richard B. Schultz recently negotiated a $1 billion contract with CBS to telecast The Final Four. This money will tempt tournament semi-finalists with purses as high as $3 million. Photo: AP/ Worldwide.

UNLV routed Duke, 103-73, for the 1990 NCAA Final Four title. Six months later, the NCAA banned UNLV from defending its crown for recruiting violations. Photo: AP/Worldwide.

Three University of South Carolina football coaches received prison sentences after pleading guilty to distributing steroids to their football players. Yet, an NCAA follow-up investigation failed to uncover any violations. Photo: the State, Greenville, S.C.

Hours after signing a $1.6 million deal with Reebok, Maryland's Len Bias, the Celtics's #1 draft pick, died from cocaine. Larry Bird said, "It was the cruelest thing I ever heard." Photo: AP/Worldwide.

A tearful Lefty Driesell denying cocaine caused Len Bias's death. Later, Driesell told other coaches, "I'm a firm believer cocaine can make you play better." Photo: AP/Worldwide.

The Bias grand jury condemned Chancellor John Slaughter's reign at Maryland. Five years later, Maryland still spawns scandal. Photo: AP/Worldwide.

Georgia's Dr. Jan Kemp was fired when she accused the school of exploiting football players. She later sued the university and won $2.57 million. Photo: AP/Worldwide.

Herschel Walker was not yet admitted to Georgia but he played against Tennessee anyway. Photo: AP/Worldwide.

The University of Georgia's president, vice president for academic affairs and the assistant vice president for Developmental Studies all lost their jobs after Kemp won her suit. But the Bulldogs' football coach, Vince Dooley, remained an untouchable. Photo: AP/Worldwide.

Arthur Ashe claims blacks provide the thrills in college athletics, but only 10% graduate. Photo: AP/Worldwide.

There were forty-seven black football players on the 1988 Georgia football team. Only one out of nineteen coaches was black. Photo courtesy, Univ. of Georgia.

sport, and sometimes by the game. To ensure a reasonably level playing field of competition, students from Harvard, Yale, Princeton and Columbia formed the Intercollegiate Football Association in 1876 which adopted rugby-style football as the game of choice.

Yale dominated the association, and no one personified the Yale athletic persona better than Walter Camp, the father of American football.

Bandbox handsome Walter Chauncey Camp played football for Yale from 1875 through 1881, four years as an undergraduate and two as a medical student. The most notable in a long line of Yale football luminaries that included Amos Alonzo Stagg, Pudge Heffelfinger, Frank Merriwether and others, Camp built a football dynasty at Yale that has never been equaled. From 1875 through 1909, Yale won 280 games and lost only fourteen, which is the best record in intercollegiate athletic history. The 1888 Yale football team, the greatest college football team ever, amassed 698 points while shutting out all its opponents.

In 1882, a knee injury ended Camp's playing career. Rather than pursue medicine, Camp took a job with a local business firm so that he might remain involved with Yale's football team. While Camp was at work every day, his wife "Allie" scouted Yale's weekday afternoon practices. Every evening, the Yale captain, who was the team's field leader, Camp and his wife would gather in the Camp home and review that day's progress with an eye towards Saturday's game.

Besides being the winningest football coach in history, Walter Camp was responsible for creating this country's unique version of football. Unlike William Webb, who spontaneously but thoughtlessly invented rugby sixty years before him, Camp was always thinking, always scheming, trying to make the game more exciting. His concern, however, was not the welfare of his players. Camp wanted to attract more spectators, and to appease those people who wanted to ban football because of its violence.

Camp introduced two innovations: the line of scrimmage and the down system.

First, Camp eliminated the "scrum," the key stratagem in rugby where each play begins by both teams fighting for possession of the ball within a circle or "scrummage" that resembles a swarming, massive amoeba. Camp replaced this boring and brutal tactic with "the line of scrimmage" which arbitrarily awarded possession of the ball to one team. Next came the down system that gave a team three tries to advance the football five yards towards the opponent's goal. If the team was successful in gaining this yardage, it retained control of the ball. Falling short of the mark meant relinquishing the ball to the other team.

By inventing the line of scrimmage, Camp reduced the size of the football squad from upwards of twenty-five all-purpose players to eleven men playing specific positions with predetermined roles. Seven players occupied the line of scrimmage, and four men lined up behind in the backfield. The center would snap the ball to the quarterback who would hand it off to one of three backfield players who in turn would attempt to bull his way towards the opponent's goal. To keep track of progress, Camp marked the playing field with lime stripes every five yards to denote the downs, which gave rise to the word "gridiron."

The down system introduced the necessity for set plays which increased the responsibilities of a coach substantially. Someone had to create the plays and then make sure they were executed properly. No longer a spontaneous frolic, football became a discipline not unlike a military exercise, requiring both intelligence and brute strength.

With the onset of strategic plays came specialized duties for every member of a team. Some were more glamorous than others, but all had to be executed for the greater good. Unlike rugby, the importance of the team was greater than the fun of an individual.

Camp also invented signals to announce the plays, as well as a scoring system so that people on the sidelines could follow the game more easily. The scoring system motivated football players to improve their skills because, now, good performances were immediately recognized with quantifiable rewards—points. No longer was vigorous, fresh-air exercise the goal of football. Now it was scoring more points than an opponent to win the game.

Walter Camp, then, took the spontaneous fun of football away from the players and gave it to the fans. To compensate the players for their loss of innocence, Camp gave them far more important reasons to play the game—winning, and being named an All-American, an honor he also invented.

To gain five yards within three attempts, mass plays were developed in which a formation of offensive linemen would surround the man carrying the ball and advance, cluster-like, toward the opponent's goal, mowing down solitary defenders along the way. One particularly hazardous variation of this maneuver, the flying wedge, was invented by a Boston businessman who applied to football the Napoleonic military strategy of mobilizing a concentrated mass. Harvard was the first college to use the flying wedge against unsuspecting Yale in 1892.

Since the flying wedge was adopted from battlefield tactics, it sometimes produced the gruesome effects of death and injury. In 1894, *The Boston Globe* reported twelve fatalities for the season, up from the previous year's seven deaths.

By the mid-1890s, football was played at over 120 colleges and universities. Like boxing and bull fighting, football appealed to peoples' morbidity, offering the ever-present possibility of bloodshed. The violence of the gridiron became such a concern that in 1894, a committee consisting of representatives from Harvard, Yale, and Princeton were charged with researching just how damaging and dangerous college football had become. Similar to asking a wolf to guard a chicken coop, the committee appointed Walter Camp its leader. When Camp published his findings, he stressed only the merits of football and concealed any evidence to the contrary. He failed to include, for example, the well-documented facts that at least one in five college football players was permanently maimed by the game, or that an average of twenty-two players were killed on the field each year. Most college administrators knew the Camp report was a whitewash, but both the man and the game had grown so popular they went unchallenged.

Senator Henry Cabot Lodge likened football's deaths and injuries to the inevitable hardships the English-speaking people had endured while conquering the world. Football bonded together the university community: students, faculty, alumni and the general public. It also fulfilled a deep-rooted human need to view physical struggle as war, mankind's venue for winners and losers, heroes and cowards.

Every American college and university in the 19th century, including Harvard, Yale and Princeton, used football as a publicity device to enhance its overall reputation. As the historian Frederick Jackson Turner said, "It is an absurd idea that football has become the test of excellence of a university and the proper means of advertising it as well.'' The enhancing effect of football explains why so many college administrators, despite statements to the contrary, did so little to curb or root out the game.

True reformers, however, wanted football banned because it killed people. From 1880 to 1905, according to *The Boston Globe*, 330 deaths and 1,149 serious injuries occurred as a direct result of college football. It was an outrage, people argued, for universities to sponsor, much less condone, such a savage activity. Even the President got involved. Grover Cleveland banned the annual Army-Navy football game in 1893 because of excessive football injuries sustained by the Naval Academy.

One reaction to the outrage was the formation of faculty committees to wrest control of college athletics from the students. Princeton became the first college to form such a faculty committee in 1881, headed by William Milligan Sloane, a future organizer of the Olympics. The faculty athletic committee prevailed but not without considerable resistance. After managing intercollegiate athletics for the better part of fifty years, students were too entrenched to give up their role easily.

Shortly thereafter, Harvard established a faculty athletics committee, too. But it soon became embroiled in a controversy that mirrored the wars still being waged today. The regular faculty felt the faculty atheletic committee was entirely too sympathetic towards football.

Three years later, in 1887, Harvard's Board of Overseers instructed the committee to ban the game. Aided by many influential alumni, including President Theodore Roosevelt, the faculty athletics committee successfully conspired to keep the game intact. It was the third time in six years that a powerful segment of Harvard University, such as the Board of Overseers, wanted football banned. It was the third time in six years that even more powerful forces, such as the alumni who were responsible for Harvard's endowment fund, defeated that movement.

To compensate for losing much of their freedom in managing athletics, students began to encourage alumni to join the faculty athletic committees. In the late 1890s, wealthy Dartmouth alumni gained control of the school's athletics, and, overnight, Dartmouth went from perennial loser to powerhouse because the old grads spent their own money fielding winning and pride-restoring teams.

The Dartmouth situation also showed how football continued to thrive even through control of the game passed from students to faculty and then to alumni. Later, a few more parties were added to the game's power chain, i.e., coaches, athletic directors, conferences and, ultimately, a national confederation. But football had a life of its own and flourished irrespective of who tried to control it.

Investigative reporters of the day uncovered a secret $100,000 slush fund that Yale maintained to meet extraordinary expenses of its football team. One such expense occurred when Walter Camp gave James Hogan, Yale's football captain, a two-week, all-expenses Caribbean vacation.

Walter Camp's excesses were becoming intolerable. By 1892, Yale and its traditional Thanksgiving Day rival, Princeton, were the only two remaining schools in the Intercollegiate Football Association. The other seven institutions had quit to protest Yale's unwillingness to reform its football program. In fact, from 1880 through 1909, Yale refused to agree to any of the reform measures other schools had adopted.

As the need for football reform mounted, the most logical people to lead the reform—college presidents—were, too often, guilty of fiery rhetoric and inaction.

Towards the end of the 19th century, the job of operating a college had become so complex that many schools established boards of trustees to oversee finances and establish policies. For the most part, trustees were business leaders, men of action who were more concerned with money and fame than with the ephemeral ideals of education. These business leaders viewed football as an excellent training ground to acquire the competitiveness and the occasional brutality needed to succeed in a free enterprise society. Used to getting their own way, trustees often treated presidents as employees. And those presidents who were politically astute did not resist. When it came to football, most presidents were caught between their own educational ideals and the need to keep their jobs. Perhaps even more to the point, the presidents were caught between a faculty who sought to ban the game and a board who sought to glorify it. Usually, as the only way out of this quandary, presidents talked as if they agreed with their faculties, but acted as if they agreed with their boards.

To demonstrate concern, college presidents pressured faculty athletics committees to make football safer. But the committees had to gain the agreement of other schools before these safety measures could be adopted. Even in the face of death, schools were loath to cooperate for fear of forfeiting an advantage to a competitor and thereby jeopardizing their own chances of winning. As a result of these political machinations, few rules were ever actually adopted. No other college and its president demonstrated this problem, or its sleight-of-hand solution, better than Harvard and Charles Eliot, who spoke as if he were a fearless reformer but acted as if he were a see-no-evil-hear-no-evil enabler.

Like students who appeared reluctant to give up their freedom in managing athletics, colleges were reluctant to offer up a portion of their own independence so that a common rule for the greater good might be adopted. This short-sightedness led to chaos because rules pertaining to amateurism, academic standing, professionals, freshmen ineligibility, and upperclassmen eligibility varied widely from institution to institution. For example, some schools allowed seven years of eligibility, permitting graduate students to play alongside undergraduates. None other than John Heisman played football for five years from 1886-1891, three years at Brown as an undergraduate and two at Pennsylvania as a law student. Walter Camp played six years for Yale, and Amos Alonzo Stagg played four for Yale and two for Chicago several years after he left New Haven.

At the time, graduate education was a recent innovation consisting mainly of medical and law schools that did not require undergraduate degrees for admission. Thus, Harvard, which had the most well-established graduate school system, believed it was perfectly acceptable to draw athletes from all of its graduate schools and undergraduate colleges.

Hiring or recruiting football players by offering them money was also a common abuse, and Yale and Harvard competed fiercely in matching each other's offers. The same James Hogan who vacationed in Cuba at Yale's expense took a pay-cut when he graduated from Yale at the age of twenty-nine. Hogan's compensation consisted of a two-cent commission for every pack of American Tobacco Company's cigarettes sold in the greater New Haven area and a generous portion of the advertising revenues derived from Yale's football and baseball programs. Harvard was just as bad, but more discreet.

In the absence of universal rules, colleges had no residency requirements, which gave rise to "tramp athletes," mercenaries who roamed the country making cameo athletic appearances, moving on whenever and wherever the money was better. Perhaps the most famous tramp athlete was Fielding H. Yost, a third-year law school student at West Virginia University who, in 1896, transferred to Lafayette as a freshman just in time to lead his new teammates to victory against its arch-rival, Penn. A week after the game, Yost was back at West Virginia's law school. Yost later went on to be a legendary football coach at the University of Michigan.

In an attempt to neutralize his rivals, Walter Camp drafted an eligibility rule for the American Football Rules Committee which stipulated that an athlete must be in residence at a college for an entire year, and attend at least five classes per week. The athlete also could not receive financial aid for his athletic participation. The measure passed despite Harvard's objections due to its distrust of Camp. But rather than abide by the will of the majority, Harvard resigned from the Intercollegiate Football Association for the fifth time in twenty-two years.

Allowing freshmen to participate in athletics, either on the varsity- or freshmen-team level, was a serious concern even in the 19th century because both tiers of competition took time away from a freshman's studies. Freshmen competition began in the 1870s and soon became infected by the must-win syndrome. The fiercer the competition, the more tempting it was for colleges to bend the rules to ensure a winning season. For example, the 1888 Harvard freshmen football team was captained by a third-year Harvard Law School student.

Many presidents spoke out against the evils of freshmen eligibility, citing studies and statistics that proved freshmen were better off in the classroom, and not on the playing field. Also, freshmen ineligibility was cited by the presidents as a partial answer to recruiting abuses. They believed that if an athlete had to sit out a year before playing a sport, the interruption would be a strong reminder that he was in college primarily to be educated. Despite these posturings, the presidents merely sat on their hands waiting for other schools to adopt the freshmen ineligibility rule first. Of course, this never happened because each school was fearful that if it did adopt the rule, star freshmen athletes, anxious to play, would simply attend those rival colleges that did not adopt the rule. It was another Mexican standoff. The presidents sought to improve freshmen academics, but they knew that fielding winning football teams would preclude it.

Finally in 1895, just when there seemed no end to the short-sightedness of colleges, the Big Ten Conference was formed with Michigan, Wisconsin, Chicago, Minnesota, Illinois, Northwestern and Purdue. Unlike the elite eastern schools, these schools cooperated and adopted rules for the good of the group. The Big Ten's original charter contained twelve rules, eight of them pertaining to eligibility, including the clear-cut ban of freshmen and graduate students.

One of the Big Ten's guiding lights was Amos Alonzo Stagg, whose collegiate football career spanned seventy-four years before he retired from the game in 1960 at the age of ninety-eight. Stagg played for Walter Camp at Yale from 1886 through 1890 where he earned All-American honors as an end. After graduation, Stagg went to Springfield College in Massachusetts to coach football for two years, and then moved on to the University of Chicago where he stayed until 1932 as its football coach and a tenured member of the faculty. For his first two years at Chicago, besides being the coach, Stagg played left end.

Amos Alonzo Stagg was known for his clean living. He did not abide smoking, drinking, swearing or professional football, although when he first arrived at Chicago, Stagg used a war chest established by the Rockefellers to hire Chicago's early football teams. Like his former coach at Yale, Stagg was a brilliant student of the game, and he introduced many breakthroughs—the spiral pass, the huddle, diagrammed plays, playbooks, reverses, and the on-side kick—that forever changed and improved football.

Although the Midwest colleges had the Big Ten, and the South now had the Southern Athletic Association, the Eastern elite colleges still could not coalesce and play under a uniform set of rules.

Problems only got worse until finally, in 1898, Brown University called a summit meeting. Every school in today's Ivy League, except Yale, went to Providence eager to meet the challenge.

After painstaking and somewhat idealistic deliberations, the Brown Conference Report cited the Oxbridge tradition—sheer fun, free of the obsession with winning—as what the ideal objective of college sports should be. The Brown Conference Report proclaimed: "We should not seek perfection in our games, but, rather, good sport." The Conference also recommended a number of rule changes pertaining to eligibility and amateurism.

The Brown Conference Report participants were naive in thinking their rules would be ratified. In fact, the rules met the fate of past reform attempts. Since Yale, through its absence, had already declared it had no intention of playing by these rules, Harvard would not ratify them because that would mean certain loss to the dreaded Bulldogs of New Haven. Thus, the Ivy league was still not able to forge a federation.

Basketball was invented in the fall of 1891 by James Naismith at the Young Men's Christian Association School in Springfield, Massachusetts, an institution that trained executive directors and athletic directors for America's vast network of YMCA's. Having graduated from McGill University in 1887 with a degree in Divinity Studies, Naismith had come to Springfield to combine his vocation with his athletic skills so that he might become a chaplain to athletes.

Even back in the 1890s, Springfield was known for its excellent physical education training. The school had patterned its curriculum after the Swedish method which placed heavy emphasis on calisthenics and gym routines. Springfield students, however, regarded the mandatory gym exercises as dreary, especially during the winter months when they could not play football or soccer for fun.

Finally, Naismith and a group of students approached the head of Springfield's Physical Education Department, Dr. Luther Gulick, and complained about the onerous calisthenic drills required of them each day. The professor responded with a challenge. He would suspend the push-ups if Naismith would invent an indoor game that developed the body the same way calisthenics did.

At first, Naismith tried football, but tackling on a hard gym floor proved to be too much even for the toughest of Naismith's class-mates.

Undaunted, Naismith then thought of a softened hybrid of both football and soccer.

The game's objective was to pit two teams of indefinite number against one another in throwing a soccer ball through one of two peach baskets affixed to poles at either end of the court. To make the game more challenging, since floor-level baskets would allow too many easy goals, Naismith suspended the peach baskets ten feet off the gym floor. And for safety's sake, Naismith replaced kicking or carrying the ball with passing it as the means to score a goal. Also, since the entire court could be covered in a matter of a few strides—goals, not downs—became the means of determining pos-session of the ball. The team that scored the most baskets or goals after two fifteen-minute periods was the winner.

Because the action was fast, and the small gymnasium amplified fan enthusiasm, basketball at Springfield became popular imme-diately. Within a year, calisthenics were a thing of the past and Naismith had refined the game to include dribbling, backboards, and the game's namesakes were replaced with iron rims and cotton nets. Later, each team was restricted to five men on the floor, and the courts were enclosed in chicken wire to protect the players from the frenzy of fans.

The first intercollegiate basketball game occurred on February 9, 1895, when Minnesota beat Hamline, 9-3. Basketball gained a permanent foothold in the Midwest when Stagg became the Univer-sity of Chicago's football coach. Three years after he made the move, the first five-man game was played between Chicago and the University of Iowa. A year later, Yale trounced Penn, 32-10.

Following Stagg's example, Naismith headed west and ended up in Kansas where he enrolled in medical school. To make ends meet, Naismith took a job with the University of Kansas, and later became the head of its physical education department, a position he held for forty years. While at Kansas, Naismith coached Forrest C. ''Phog'' Allen and Adolph Rupp, both of whom would eclipse Naismith as men of importance in basketball.

In 1905, in the Union College-New York University football game, Harold Moore, a Union halfback died of a cerebral hemorrhage after a mass play involving every player on the field had senselessly crushed him. Moore was just one of eighteen to die on the college gridiron that year, and there were 149 serious football injuries in 1905 as well.

An incensed NYU chancellor, Henry MacCracken, summoned the leaders of thirteen colleges to New York on December 8, 1905, to decide yet again if football should either be abolished or reformed. In doing so, the MacCracken Group intentionally bypassed Walter Camp and the American Football Rules Committee because MacCracken and his associates knew all too well that Camp could be counted on to do nothing but preserve the status quo of football, deaths and all.

Nicholas Murray Butler, the president of Columbia University, made an eloquent plea to ban the sport nationally. but the representatives from West Point and Wesleyan University were even more eloquent in convincing their associates to give football one last chance. Another meeting was called by MacCracken for three weeks later so that each school, in the interim, could work out its own reform suggestions.

When it reconvened on December 28 in New York City, the MacCracken Group had swelled to sixty-eight schools. The first order of business was to establish formally the organization that would later be called the National Collegiate Athletic Association. The MacCracken Group (NCAA) then formed a rules committee which spent the better part of the day adopting far-sweeping reform measures.

Most, if not all, of the NCAA reform measures were proposed by Harvard in the last-ditch effort to save football once again in Cambridge. The Harvard Board of Overseers had already declared that if the rules were not adopted by both the new NCAA group and the American Football Rules Committee, football would be banned forever, irrespective of its rivalry with Yale.

The Harvard reform consisted of these rule changes: prohibiting the practice of heaving or hurdling an offensive player over the line of scrimmage to advance the ball; establishing a neutral zone on the line of scrimmage, equivalent to the length of a ball, that neither side could penetrate until the ball was snapped back to the quarterback; requiring six men on the line of scrimmage to preclude tackles and guards from lining up in the backfield to form mass wedge plays; outlawing tackling below the knees; increasing the number of referees to four; imposing stiffer penalties for infractions; and initiating the forward pass in an attempt to bolster the advantage of the offense over the defense.

Toward the end of the evening, the NCAA Rules Committee voted to join forces with Walter Camp's American Football Rules Committee which, coincidentally, was meeting in Philadelphia the next day, December 29. Detractors who still wanted the game banned were skeptical that Walter Camp and Yale would agree to accept the reform measures. Harvard's Charles Eliot said, ''It is childish to suppose that the athletic authorities who have permitted football to become such a brutal, cheating, demoralizing game could be trusted to reform it.''[6]

The NCAA Rules Committee proceeded to Philadelphia and encountered a resistant Walter Camp and his American Football Rules Committee. Besides being reluctant to share the limelight, Camp did not want to agree to the upstart's rules because they would severely hamper the way Yale played football. In the next three weeks, sixteen meetings between the two groups were required before Camp would agree to merge with the fledgling NCAA Rules Committee, and adopt its rules.

Through an astute demonstration of political skill, the Harvard football coach, William Reid, replaced Camp as head of the merged committees, ending Yale's and Walter Camp's forty-year dominance over Harvard and the rest of the collegiate world.

When the NCAA's reform rules went into effect in the fall of 1906, they immediately reduced football-related fatalities and injuries. But as beneficial as the NCAA's rules proved to be, colleges were still reluctant to demonstrate support for the new organization. As established, the NCAA was merely a federation issuing guidelines with no authority to enforce them.

To this day, NCAA members have a love-hate relationship with the NCAA which means they have a love-hate relationship with themselves. When attending the annual convention, members' feelings toward the NCAA are temporarily buoyed, influenced no doubt by the camaraderie that comes from working intensely with colleagues during the convention's four-day, no-nonsense agenda. A member can't help but assume a broader perspective during these conventions. But when he returns home, the narrower perspectives of his daily life often conflict with the national issues. And then, in this different setting, far from the eyes of his NCAA colleagues, the member favors his own immediate and selfish agenda, often contradicting the national rule he just fought so hard to get passed.

Once back on his own campus, the member acts as if the NCAA is made up of "those other people" and that they are the ones responsible for the organization's flaws. Oftentimes, the press picks up on this distancing technique, creating the erroneous impression that the NCAA is indeed a wholly independent organization from the person being quoted. Ambivalence and denial are the by-products of all these evasions.

The NCAA's founding tradition of allowing its members to determine their own policies concerning an athlete's admission and eligibility, commonly referred to as "home rule," became its rock of Sisyphus. Home rule enabled, almost encouraged, the NCAA member-schools to agree to disagree, a paradox that now has stunted the association for eighty-five years.

There is a deep-rooted predilection to believe that the college athletics of one hundred years ago were conducted in an environment reminiscent of Tom Brown's School Days at Rugby, where sports were played for the sheer joy of sweat and a quickened pulse. But, college athletics of olden times were just as bad as they are today. In fact, they were probably worse because at least today the flying wedge is not systematically killing big-time college football players.

CHAPTER 4

Academic Fraud

At 4:48 P.M. on February 13, 1986, a clamorous six-week trial that pitted a lowly remedial English professor against the vaunted University of Georgia's football program finally came to an end.

The professor, Dr. Jan Hammock Kemp, claimed she had been illegally demoted and then fired for accusing Georgia of coddling semi-literate athletes, most of whom were black.

Her superior, Dr. Leroy Ervin, head of Georgia's Developmental Studies Program, maintained he terminated Kemp because she had an abusive and disruptive personality which seriously impaired her teaching effectiveness.

After reading the three-page verdict carefully, Judge Horace T. Ward handed it to the clerk of the court. The plaintiff, defendants, and various attorneys all came to their feet.

Curiously, the verdict consisted of a series of questions and answers which, when he read them, made the clerk appear as if he were playing two roles simultaneously in a one-act play. There was not, however, the slightest suggestion of inflection as he delivered his lines.

"Was Jan Kemp's demotion a violation of her right to freedom of speech?"

"Yes."

"Was Jan Kemp's termination a violation of her right to freedom of speech?"

"Yes."

"Is the plaintiff to be awarded damages by the defendants?"

"Yes."

The courtroom began to stir.

"What are the nature and the amounts of these damages?"

"The plaintiff, Jan Kemp, shall receive punitive damages from defendant Virginia Trotter, Vice President of Academic Affairs, The University of Georgia, in the amount of $1.5 million dollars."

One woman exclaimed, involuntarily: "Oh my god!" The Clerk hiked his holster, signaling for quiet.

"The plaintiff, Jan Kemp, shall receive punitive damages from defendant Leroy Ervin, Assistant Vice President of Academic Affairs, The University of Georgia, in the amount of $800,000."

"The plaintiff, Jan Kemp, shall receive back pay from The University of Georgia in the amount of $79,687, and she shall be restored to her position as English coordinator, Developmental Studies, The University of Georgia."

"The plaintiff, Jan Kemp, shall receive $200,000 for the pain and suffering she endured by The University of Georgia."

All told, the jury awarded the astonishing sum of $2.57 million to Professor Kemp.

When the governor of Georgia, Joe Frank Harris, learned of the verdict, he fainted dead away.

The *Kemp vs. University of Georgia* case began in December 1981. Nine football players enrolled in the university's remedial education school, Developmental Studies, accomplished the impossible. They flunked the same high-school-level English course for the fourth time in a row.

University policy dictated that these football players should be automatically dismissed for a minimum of one year. But Dr. Leroy Ervin, head of the Developmental Studies Program, and his superior, the university's highest ranking academic officer, Dr. Virginia Trotter, employed a bit of bureaucratic legerdemain to keep the football players eligible for the upcoming Sugar Bowl. Despite the players' dreadful academic records, Drs. Trotter and Ervin promoted all nine football players out of Developmental Studies and into Georgia's undergraduate colleges.

Later, when asked why she took this course of action, Dr. Trotter explained, "I would rather err on the side of making a mistake."[1]

A tenth student in the same Developmental Studies Program class, a non-athlete, also flunked English for the fourth consecutive time. She was expelled.

In February 1982, Professor Kemp and several of her associates composed a letter to the university's president, Dr. Fred Davison, protesting Ervin's and Trotter's actions. The letter said, "It was important for the faculty and the other students to realize that if a student did not make an effort, did not try, then the student could not remain at the university."[2]

Moreover, since over sixty percent of the athletes who came into the Developmental Studies Program were black and underprivileged, few realized that what appeared to be preferential treatment was in fact "plantation kindness."

Kemp observed, "Rather than be thankful for being exempted from academic responsibilities, Georgia's black athletes should be demanding more of 'the right stuff.' Not Recreation and Leisure Studies, or Industrial Arts Education, but meaningful courses, liberation courses that will set them free."[3]

Two days after Professor Kemp composed the letter, Dr. Ervin demoted her from head of the English Department in Developmental Studies. During the meeting, Dr. Ervin screamed, "Who do you think is more important? You, or a Georgia football player?"

A faculty grievance committee hearing followed several weeks later. While testifying, Dr. Ervin called Professor Kemp "a liar and a bigot."[4]

One month later, in March 1982, Dr. Ervin informed Professor Kemp, by letter this time, that her contract would not be renewed when it elapsed several months hence.

In August 1982, one month after the birth of her first child, Will, Professor Kemp attempted to commit suicide by stabbing herself in the chest with a butcher knife sixteen times. Shortly thereafter, Professor Kemp swallowed a bottle of Haldol pills, an antipsychotic drug.

Three years later, after she had put her life back together with the help of the Church of the Living Faith, a born-again Christian sect, Professor Kemp sued the University of Georgia for damages and her old job back.

On the day she filed her action, Professor Kemp said, ''All that's necessary for the triumph of evil is for good men to do nothing.''

Only certain sections of Texas, and possibly parts of Oklahoma, rival Georgia for its adoration of football. From September through much of November, Friday evenings are reserved for high school football. Saturdays are spent in either Athens or Atlanta, cheering for Georgia or Georgia Tech, respectively. Sundays are devoted to all-day television sessions, watching the National Football League.

Athens, Georgia, is a surprisingly lively town. A certain dynamism pervades, as if to announce this is the home of the University of Georgia, an important school with an even more important football team.

The town has also spawned a surprising number of rock and country bands, including the Allman Brothers. Country star Kenny Rogers maintains a residence in Athens.

The Athens Chamber of Commerce claims that because the town is located amidst rolling hills, the town's climate is the best in Georgia. It would have visitors believe that when it snows in Atlanta, the sun shines in Athens, forty miles to the northeast.

The University of Georgia's campus is like a 1940s movie; all 26,000 students seem so wholesome and earnest. The men wear short-sleeved, dress shirts. The women wear bobby sox, cradle their books, and have hats with veils in their closets. Although the Georgia campus lacks one, unifying architectural style, the polyglot theme is not unpleasant. The buildings are on top of one another, creating a compactness that adds to the swirl of students and activity.

Sanford Stadium, Georgia's football facility, is located right in the heart of the campus, the perfect metaphor.

Georgia's Professor Kemp said, ''If Jesus Christ were to land in a helicopter in the middle of Sanford Stadium on a fall Saturday afternoon, He'd have to get out of the way and wait until the final whistle blew before anyone would notice Him.''[5]

Grantland Rice described the games played in Sanford Stadium as "those played between the hedges," referring to the privet hedges that rim the stadium's playing field.

If Sanford Stadium celebrates Georgia football, Butts-Mehre Heritage Hall celebrates the man behind Georgia football, Vince Dooley, former head football coach, athletic director, and president of the Georgia Athletic Association, Inc.

Located in isolated splendor in a remote corner of the campus, Butts-Mehre Heritage Hall, 78,000 square feet, was conceived by Vince Dooley to house Georgia's football program. It headquarters sixty-four adults and 125 football players who play, on average, eleven games each year for an annual take of over $7 million.

Butts-Mehre Heritage Hall is a black, four-story cube of glowering smoked-glass, with a domed roof and a glossy orange-colored marble entrance plaza, complete with a moat. If buildings were aircraft, Butts-Mehre would be an alien spaceship.

Because the building's entrance is situated on the rise of a slight hill, visitors enter Butts-Mehre on the third floor, and walk into the atrium courtyard which is Heritage Hall, a museum that contains some nineteen different lucite and chrome cubicles that commemorate Georgia's former football greats, including "Pop" Warner, Grantland Rice, Frank Sinkwich, Charley Trippi, Fran Tarkenton, Herschel Walker and Vince Dooley.

The Butts-Mehre elevator has buttons labeled "Hunker Up" and "Hunker Down."

The first floor houses two racquetball courts, a weight training room, medical training room, sauna and jacuzzi, classrooms, lockerroom, and an auditorium. The second floor is where the offices of Georgia's twenty-man football coaching staff are located: Assistant Head Coach, Offensive Coordinator, Quarterback Coach; Defensive Coordinator, Secondary Coach; Defensive Assistant, Outside Linebackers; Offensive Assistant, Running Backs; Defensive Assistant, Line; Offensive Assistant, Wide Receivers; Offensive Assistant, Line; Kicking Coach; Defensive Assistant, Inside Linebackers; Offensive Assistant, Tight Ends; Director of Strength and Conditioning; Administrative Assistant to the Athletic Director; Director of Departmental Recruiting; Assistant Strength and Conditioning Coach; and five graduate assistants.

The second floor is also where Vince Dooley has his office, which is too large and too splendid even for Ivan Boesky. And, as planned, Dooley can walk onto a private patio that directly overlooks the football practice field.

The anteroom to Dooley's office is usually filled with TV cameras, reporters and well-wishers, including men who have first names like "Hardrock," waiting patiently to have their pictures taken with "Coach."

On the third floor is where the ticket, sports information, marketing and promotion, business, and *Georgia Bulldog* magazine offices are located.

The fourth floor of Butts-Mehre houses Heritage Auditorium, the offices for the Athletic Director, the Associate Athletic Director, the Building Manager, and the Coordinator for Academic Standards and Eligibility. It also houses the Georgia Bulldog Club, the boosters organization that raises $4.5 million from over 12,000 alumni and benefactors each year.

Butts-Mehre is also the headquarters of the Georgia Athletic Association, Inc., a corporation established to separate the Athletic Department from the rest of the university so it can operate autonomously. Vince Dooley explained, "Because we're a state university, there was just too much red tape to go through every time we wanted to do something. This way, we are totally independent of the state financial commission."[6] In 1988, the GAA, Inc. earned $14.6 million in revenue, and had net assets of $33 million.

When asked about the appropriateness of an independent athletic department, Dr. Charles Knapp, president of the University of Georgia, said, "I believe in delegating, and if the Athletic Department feels it can function better as a separate corporation, that's fine by me."[7]

In his senior year at Johnson County High School in Wrightsville, Georgia, *Parade* magazine named Herschel Walker the most outstanding high school football back in the nation. Georgia coach Vince Dooley, never one to use hyperbole, made an exception and said, "A player like Herschel comes along once in a lifetime."

At six-foot-one, 218 pounds, Walker could run the 100 yard dash in 9.5 seconds which, ten years ago, would have been a world

record. Instead, Walker compiled these national high school football records: forty-five touchdowns in one season, and eighty-six
touchdowns throughout his high school career.

Dooley deployed Georgia's considerable resources to convince
Herschel to enroll at Georgia and play for the Bulldogs. Even Dean
Rusk, former Secretary of State who now teaches at the university's
Law School, helped recruit Walker. Rusk said, "I spent an hour
talking with Herschel. At that time, he was interested in the law."[8]

In his first college football game against Tennessee, it was apparent to the 95,288 in the stands and the hundreds of thousands of
television viewers that Herschel would be Georgia's greatest player.
Singlehandedly, he beat Tennessee by scoring both of Georgia's
touchdowns in a come-from-behind victory. The second score came
eleven minutes into the fourth quarter when Herschel, dragging four
Tennessee would-be tacklers, ran nine yards around left end to win
the game, 16-9.

Herschel led Georgia to its first undefeated season in the school's
ninety-year football history. The Bulldogs then beat Notre Dame in
the Sugar Bowl, January 1, 1981, and were named national champions. Vince Dooley became the NCAA Coach of the Year, and
Herschel won every honor worth mentioning as a freshman.

Georgia almost repeated as national champions in 1981 and 1982.
At the end of his junior year, Herschel won the Heisman Trophy.

When Herschel first applied to the university in the spring of
1980, he was rejected. But the admissions people referred him to
the university's Developmental Studies Program, a remedial program that prepared aspiring but academically-weak prospects for
Georgia's regular undergraduate courses.

It was not until September 10, 1980, four days after the Tennessee game, that Trotter, Georgia's Vice President of Academic
Affairs, and Ervin, Dean of Developmental Studies, nervously
explained to Dooley why Herschel Walker had yet to be admitted
into DSP. Although the two educators were quite accustomed to
granting admissions exceptions to athletes, Herschel Walker, they
explained, posed a challenge—even to them.

A product of a segregation-ravaged high school, Herschel Walker's grades were good but his SAT score was abysmal, signaling to
Ervin and Trotter he would have serious problems doing college-
level work. According to Ervin, after listening politely to what

Trotter and Ervin had to say, Dooley said quietly, "'I'm sure there's a way for the two of you to work this out. If you can't, Fred Davison [president of UGA] will.' "[9]

Not surprisingly, shortly after the meeting, Trotter and Ervin, invoking their "special admit exceptions," admitted Herschel Walker into Developmental Studies Program.

In the fall of 1979, Landy Ewings, six-foot-two, 250 pounds, and a senior at Tift County High School, was the best lineman in Georgia. Although overshadowed by Herschel Walker, Landy Ewings was recruited by Clemson, Florida, Tennessee and Auburn.

But Ewings had only one college team in mind, the Bulldogs.

Thrilled by the chance to block for Herschel Walker, Ewings accepted the Georgia recruiter's invitation without a moment's hesitation.

But for all his excellence on the football field, Landy Ewings never did well academically. Although innately intelligent and a natural leader, Ewings was just another high school athlete shielded from the responsibilities of a classroom.

The average SAT score for incoming freshman at Georgia in 1980 was 940. Landy Ewings scored a fraction of that, and his high school grades were not that much better.

As a scholarship athlete, Ewings had to live in McWhorter Hall, a dormitory that houses all of Georgia's scholarship athletes, with no exceptions.

Located ten minutes by foot from the nearest other dormitory, McWhorter's grille-like facade and guard rails makes it look like a cell-block. Fully self-sustaining, McWhorter has its own dining room, activities hall, and academic staff to tutor its athletes.

Because of injury, Landy did not play much during his freshman year in 1980. Despite this disappointment, his life on campus was still good. Being a student at Developmental Studies gave Ewings the sense he was a bona fide undergraduate of the University of Georgia. He attended classes, carried books and looked like everyone else. Only Landy knew that he was taking only high-school-level courses, a fact that did not concern him a bit.

Ewings was accustomed to being relieved of academic responsibilities. It was part of the preferential treatment teachers had accorded him since the seventh grade. Besides, he reasoned, "I felt pretty sure I was going to land in the pros anyway, so what did I care about school."[10]

Ewings's chances of making the pros were about the same as his chances of graduating from the University of Georgia.

The grades Landy Ewings achieved in Developmental Studies did not count towards a degree, but they did allow him to play football. Thus, Ewings and his teammates could be in the Developmental Studies program for two years, never pass a remedial course, never take a college-level course, and still maintain their playing eligibility.

Shortly after his eligibility elapsed, the University of Georgia dismissed Ewings.

He then tried to turn pro, but he returned to Athens, humiliated. "They were just too good, and there were just too many of them," Ewings said.

It was difficult finding work, and Ewings first had to settle for riding shotgun on a garbage truck. He then repaired sewer pipe, and later became a stock boy at the Piggly Wiggly.

In his opening remarks at the *Kemp vs. University of Georgia* trial, Hale Almand, defense attorney for the university, alluded to Landy Ewings. Almand said, "We may not be able to make university students out of them. But maybe they can work at the post office rather than as garbage men when they get through with their athletic careers."

Dr. Kemp was one of the first to testify. When she took the stand, she evoked great sympathy. "I knew I was doing God's work, and all of it was for His glory," she told the courtroom and the smitten media.

Like a Faulkner heroine, Jan Kemp masks her zealous nature behind a milkwood and magnolia demeanor, tarnished only slightly by the Satin cigarettes she chain-smokes.

Raised in Griffin, Georgia, a small town forty miles south of Atlanta, Jan Kemp's most striking attribute is her height. She is six-foot-two, and from some angles, looks like an uncertain ostrich. But from other angles, she can appear quite attractive, even pretty.

Kemp began her testimony by relating a series of confrontations between her and her boss, Dr. LeRoy Ervin, head of Developmental Studies.

In the fall of 1980, Dr. Ervin asked Jan Kemp to persuade one of the professors she supervised to change the failing English grades of five athletes to "incompletes." Kemp refused.

Six months later, Kemp received a late-night phone call from the son of a wealthy contributor. He became abusive and profane. When Kemp brought the matter to a campus grievance committee, Ervin strongly urged her to drop the charges. But she persisted, and the student in question was found wanting. Months later, at a parent-teacher conference, in front of several faculty members, Kemp witnessed Ervin accepting a donation from the student's father.

Kemp then related what her life was like after being fired. Estranged from her husband, she had a difficult time finding work and finally had to accept a part-time position at Southern Technical Institute in Marietta for $297 per month. She had been making $1,869 per month at Georgia. As a result of these circumstances, Kemp testified, she suffered bouts of severe depressions which led to her suicide attempts.

Asked about her teaching methods, Jan Kemp said, "I taught liberation literature. I would quote certain passages from works by Maya Angelou, Shakespeare and Richard Wright that showed the black athletes in my classes they were being disenfranchised by the university. Through these great authors, I wanted them so see that education was their true opportunity, and that they had to fight to seize it, to set themselves free."[11]

Kemp went on to testify that Georgia used the athletes only to generate football and basketball revenues. It never made a genuine effort to educate them.

"It's too bad about Herschel," Dr. Kemp told the courtroom. "Most people think he has it made now. But I think he should have stayed at Georgia and graduated. He had a photographic memory, and his poetry was beautiful. He could have done something with his life."[12] Herschel Walker dropped out of Georgia during his junior year to play pro football for Donald Trump for $8 million.

Many people in the courtroom snickered at Kemp's remark, but she continued: "We let Herschel come and play football for us so we could be the national champs. And when he left, we all said, 'Who could blame him, all that money.' But deep down, we were relieved. We never let Herschel and other blacks have what we have, a degree. We keep Herschel out of our board rooms, our operating rooms, our courts and our executive suites. We only let them into our living rooms, via television, to amuse us."[13]

Kemp's attorneys then called several witnesses who attested to her competence as an educator. They portrayed her as a conscientious teacher, willing to do anything to help her students. According to Ronnie Stewart, who played in the backfield with Herschel, Kemp once spent thirteen consecutive hours reviewing *Othello* with him, line by line. "Day or night, she would drop anything and come to my dorm to help me," Stewart added.[14]

But several people scorned Kemp.

Mrs. Barbara Carson, a professor in the university's College of Arts and Sciences English Department, said, "Jan Kemp stirred everything up. It was a tempest in a teapot, a tissue of lies. Jan Kemp is to be pitied. She's not mentally right."

When cross-examined, Mrs. Carson revealed a curious view of her own role as an educator. She cheerfully admitted to changing a grade for Herschel Walker's sister, Veronica, so she could compete in an important track meet. "I did it to help that poor child. She wanted to make the Olympics."[15]

Mrs. Carson also saw nothing wrong with allowing the nine football players to play in the 1982 Sugar Bowl. "Why should we bother about it? Such picky stuff! Let the boys have that much more exposure to the pro scouts."[16]

Another Kemp detractor was Kenny Sims, a former football player who had flunked out of the university. Sims wrote a letter to the court, criticizing Dr. Kemp's classroom demeanor. Frequently he and other classmates were distracted, Sims wrote, by Kemp's illustrating a point by alluding to her own sexual experiences.

During cross-examination, Kemp's attorney asked Sims if he would read aloud the letter he sent. A mortified Sims admitted he was unable to comply because he cannot read. He further admitted the letter was written by Ervin's secretary which he agreed to sign in exchange for being readmitted to Georgia.

A dapper, if not delicate, black man, Dr. Leroy Ervin sported a beard, designer eye glasses, and highly-polished shoes. The holder of a doctorate in Black Studies, Ervin came to the University of Georgia from Oberlin College, the Ohio liberal arts school which was the first college in America to accept blacks in the early 19th century.

As a witness, Ervin evoked none of the sympathy and support Jan Kemp did because he could barely conceal his rage. He resented being forced to justify why he granted so many admissions and promotion exceptions to athletes who attended Georgia's Developmental Studies Program.

It took three years, long after Ervin had left Athens and was heading a non-profit foundation at Georgia Tech, before he would admit certain things. Ervin acknowledged exploiting young men who came from the same background as he did.

Ervin said. "It was all true. Football players were treated preferentially, and had been for years. Many of them read on second- or third-grade levels. I felt guilty being part of the conspiracy to exploit the black athlete. I was poor, I grew up in south Georgia, and I lived with sharecroppers. The university promised to educate these poor players but that was a sham. It never wanted to. It only wanted to win with them."[17]

But the star of the trial was Vince Dooley.

Dooley, a native of Mobile, Alabama, comes by coaching naturally. A high school all-state football and basketball player, Dooley went to Auburn University on a football scholarship where, as captain and quarterback, he led the Tigers for three seasons.

After college, Dooley served two years in the Marines as a first lieutenant at Parris Island before he returned to Auburn as an assistant coach. He became Georgia's head football coach in 1964, a controversial choice since he had no head coaching experience.

A devoted husband and father, according to most Georgia media guides, Dooley has been married for thirty years. He has four children: Deanna, Daniel, Denise, and Derek. Dooley's family-man image was muddied momentarily when, in January 1987, a Georgia Bureau of Investigation undercover officer, an attractive woman, claimed that Vince Dooley approached her in a lounge in the Mariott Hotel near the Atlanta airport and offered her "coke and reefer."[18] The Georgia Bureau of Investigation subsequently dropped the investigation because it could not prove Dooley actually possessed the drugs.

But the incident only added to Dooley's celebrity which, arguably, ranks second to Alabama's Bear Bryant as the South's most venerable football coach.

Dooley can be remote, especially to his own football players. Dean Rusk, former Secretary of State who has known Vince Dooley for nineteen years, said, "As a football coach, he's really the chairman of the board of all the coaches, of which he seems to have a coach for every facet of the game, a tight end coach, a strength coach, and a kicking coach. A lot of the actual work is done by his staff, although he's still in charge." [19]

Chance Dobbs, a member of Georgia's 1989 football team, who lives in the athletic dormitory and practices with the team every day, said, "I have never met Coach Dooley. What am I supposed to do? Walk up and say, 'Hello, legend, I'm you're red-shirted freshman punter'?" [20]

Dooley began his Kemp trial testimony by portraying Georgia's athletes as good students. He claimed thirty-seven percent of black male athletes and 100 percent of black female athletes had graduated from Georgia between 1974 and 1984.

But Kemp's attorney, Hue Henry, immediately disproved Dooley's statistics when he named two prominent female black athletes who did not graduate. Dooley then explained his figures did not include athletes who were dismissed for academic reasons.

When asked if semi-literate athletes were admitted to Developmental Studies Program, Dooley answered, "I would be absolutely shocked if that were the case." [21]

But when pressed, Dooley admitted that over the span of his twenty-year career at Georgia he interceded for maybe seven or eight outstanding athletes, and got them in as "special admits."

The results of the special audit ordered by Georgia's Board of Regents revealed Dooley grossly understated his interventions.

In the fall 1982, alone, twenty-three athletes were admitted into Georgia's Developmental Studies program as "special admits." [22]

The audit described how these "special admits" actually occurred.

Dooley delegated the task of obtaining exceptions to Georgia's golf coach, Richard Copas, who also doubled as head of the Georgia Athletic Association's academic counseling unit.

Whenever Copas presented exception requests to Drs. Trotter and

Ervin, the audit revealed, Dr. William Powell, the Faculty Athletic Representative, would accompany him.

The audit report also revealed that whenever Trotter and Ervin considered rejecting a special admit request for an athlete, Copas would threaten to persuade Dr. Davison, president of the university, to reverse their decision.

Well over six feet tall, bespectacled, and partial to tropical, seersucker suits, Dr. Fred. C. Davison was born with a flattering tongue, an easy smile, and a cowlick that makes him boyishly appealing.

A native of Marietta, Georgia, Davison graduated from the University of Georgia in 1952 with a doctorate in Veterinary Science. After graduation, he practiced for six years before returning to academe to earn another doctorate in biochemistry and pathology from Iowa State University. "I was restless, and I loved school,"[22] Davison explained.

In 1967, Davison became the University of Georgia president at an annual salary of $104,000 and set out to improve the school.

Davison acquired two "super computers" enabling Georgia to become the number one university in the country for computer retrieval capacity. Also, after bolstering its faculty with a few key hires, Georgia's Biological Sciences college became internationally prominent, and the school was accorded national seagrant status in recognition of its marine research and educational reputation.

The arts flourished under Davison, as well. *The Times* of London named *The Georgia Review*, winner of a national magazine award for fiction, the best college literary magazine in America.

The Law School improved when Davison recruited Dean Rusk, a native Georgian, to head its International Law and Diplomacy branch. And finally, through acquisition, the university's library now ranks thirtieth in the country in total volumes.

Throughout this ten-year period, the university's undergraduate enrollment went from 15,600 to 25,000 students, and the graduate student population doubled to 6,000. During the same time, Georgia's operating budget went from $73 million to $375 million, and its research grants tripled.

These feats contributed to Davison's tendency to underestimate the import of Kemp's accusations. He told a press conference before testifying, "I doubt if the Jan Kemp suit is going to affect the scholarly reputation of the university."[23]

As Dooley had done before him, Davison blamed the NCAA for the deterioration of academic standards for athletes. Davison said, "Back in 1971, the NCAA asked us to do away with our separate admissions standards in favor of a national standard, a 2.0 high school grade point average, which is so low it's ridiculous. Since so many schools we compete against were admitting players with this low standard, Georgia had no choice but to do the same thing. We could not unilaterally disarm."[24]

Davison then implicated other schools, as well. He said. "Places like Georgia Tech and Indiana would be just as embarrassed as we are if they had to undergo the scrutiny that the Kemp trial has put us through."[25]

Bobby Knight, Indiana's basketball coach, disagreed, "That's bull! Davison does not know what the hell he is talking about if he thinks Indiana would be as embarrassed as Georgia is."[26]

So did Georgia Tech's athletic director, Homer Rice. "I don't understand Dr. Davison's thinking. At Georgia Tech, we have a few remedial courses, but if you fail one of them, you're gone. You don't have a second chance, or a fourth chance as is the case at Georgia."[27]

Davison then told the courtroom how concerned the athletic department was for the academic life of its athletes. Davison said, "The GAA pays for the bulk of the athletes enrolled in Developmental Studies."

The Georgia University System Board of Regents audit confirmed, as Davison said, that the Georgia Athletic Association, Inc., had donated $245,678 to Developmental Studies Program. But the audit revealed the GAA attached unprincipled strings to this seemingly generous donation. The money was used to establish a special "laboratory" within the Developmental Studies Program which was open only to athletes. This special lab had its own faculty who were paid by the GAA, not the University of Georgia. The mission of the special lab's faculty was to preserve athletic eligibility, not to educate. In effect, the audit said, the GAA founded its own school within a school so that athletes could play football without being burdened by normal or even remedial classroom responsibilities.

Three years later, Ervin, former Developmental Studies head, finally admitted, "The GAA paid us hush money to get us involved in their scheme. What they were doing was establishing their own little college within the university, a place where the dumb jocks could hide and play until their eligibility ran out."[28]

Davison denied admitting athletes into Georgia who did not meet the entrance requirements, explaining he never got involved in admissions. "I left those decisions up to Virginia Trotter. That's what she was getting paid $90,000 per year for."[29]

But Dr. Trotter told the auditors, beginning as early as 1980, both she and Ervin tried to convince Davison that too many academically weak athletes were entering the university via Developmental Studies.

Trotter also said that all exceptions to Developmental Studies' admissions policies were discussed with Dr. Davison who, although never rendering the final decision, always conveyed his tacit approval for these exceptions by saying "do the right thing." Trotter added that on one occasion, Davison said, "What do you want us to do? Play high school football?"[30]

Later, Davison said Dr. Virginia Trotter was incompetent. Many others share the same opinion. Dr. Ted Hummock, a former Dean of Students at Georgia, said, "Virginia Trotter was way over her head. Here was a woman who was Under Secretary of Education in President Ford's administration before she came to Georgia, and she was the most disorganized, emotional and scatterbrained person I've ever met."[31]

But when asked why, if she were so incompetent, he kept Trotter as the university's highest ranking academic officer for seven years, Davison said he had no choice but to retain her because she was a woman. The hue and cry in getting rid of her, Davison added, would have been too great. Others said Trotter kept her job because both Davison and Dooley needed a weak personality they could control.

Although the Kemp trial was an athletic scandal of the highest magnitude, the NCAA was never involved.

Early on, the NCAA assigned Robert Minnix, Director of Enforcement, to investigate the case.

Minnix attended Notre Dame on a football scholarship and played first-string running back for Ara Paraseghian in the same backfield as Joe Theismann. After being graduated from Notre Dame, Minnix returned home to attend the University of Seattle Law School. Upon receiving his law degree in 1977, Minnix went to the NCAA as a field investigator.

When asked about the Georgia-Kemp case in May 1989, Minnix said, "I started with Virginia Trotter and worked my way all the way down, and then all the way back up again. I did not find anything contrary to NCAA regulations. I came away with a positive outlook towards Georgia's remedial program. I knew Ervin and Kemp were going at each other, and that's what I thought the whole issue was about, that personality conflict."[32]

Jan Kemp thought Minnix was rude and inept. Kemp said, "First, he came to my house, unannounced, and demanded to speak with me. Then he just kept asking me if there were illegal payments being made to the football players, or if they had fancy automobiles, or some other fool such thing. When I tried to tell him about the academic fraudulence, he ignored me."[33]

Shortly after the audit confirmed to the public what the trial had revealed, namely that Davison violated the very rules he was supposed to uphold, the Board of Regents wanted Davison to resign gracefully. But he resisted the board's wishes for a few months, all the while claiming his innocence. Finally a compromise was struck. There would be a Fred C. Davison Day in the Georgia General Assembly, in exchange for him stepping down. Six months later, Davison assumed the presidency of the National Science Foundation in Augusta, Georgia.

Nothing ever happened to Vince Dooley.

Since the Kemp trial in February of 1986, many things have occurred at the University of Georgia.

Dr. Charles Knapp, 41, attractive and personable, replaced Fred Davison as president of the University of Georgia on July 1, 1987. A former Deputy Assistant Secretary of Labor, and executive vice president of Tulane when that school dropped basketball to solve a point-shaving scandal, Charles Knapp was recruited by the professional head-hunting firm of Heidrick & Struggles largely because he had the experience of dealing with an athletic-related scandal.

Like all college presidents, Knapp likes to think he, not the football coach, runs Georgia. Right from the start, Knapp tried to establish himself as the boss. Knapp said, "I told the Search Committee that I was not a follower. If they were looking for that type of person, I was not their man."[34]

One year into the job, Dr. Knapp contradicted that statement.

In December of 1988, Tim Worley, an outstanding All-America who placed second only to Herschel Walker in scoring the most points in a season, and Keith Henderson, also a gifted player, flunked out of the university in much the same manner as the nine football players did in 1981. A rival coach alleged, "Worley never even darkened the doorway to a classroom in the fall of 1988." But both Worley and Henderson were allowed to play for Georgia in the Gator Bowl against Michigan State on January 2, 1989, a game which Georgia won 34-27.

When asked why he allowed this situation to occur, Dr. Knapp thought for a moment and said, "Coach Dooley and I sat down and we both agreed if an athlete makes no effort, if he performs poorly, he should not be given a second chance, and he should become ineligible the moment he receives his notice of dismissal. But when we felt there was a bona fide effort, then we would let them play. In the case of Worley and Henderson, we believed they should play."[35]

In April 1989, three years after she won her suit, Jan Kemp met with Dr. Knapp and charged that the counselors employed by the Georgia Athletic Association were not tutoring athletes, but actually doing their work.

Kemp also alleged that she was the victim of four different acts of "retaliation" since being reinstated in February of 1986.

After a two-month investigation by several different faculty and administrative committees, Dr. Knapp publicly conceded that certain Georgia Athletic Association academic counselors were indeed engaged in "excessive tutoring." Knapp also confirmed Kemp had been victimized by university personnel.

The investigations also recommended the abolition of the Developmental Studies Program which Knapp rejected out of hand.

CHAPTER 5

The Black Gladiator

For an awkward moment, National Basketball Association Commissioner David Stern looked blank, as if he did not hear the question. Then, ever so slowly, he said, "So what if our black players don't have college degrees? Is that the worst thing that can happen to them? The degree may turn out to be less important than the education."[1] Stern was responding to why less than twenty-eight percent of the NBA black players graduate college.

Many people like Commissioner Stern do not appreciate the problem of the black athlete in collegiate athletics today.

They fail to realize less than one out of six big-time black football and basketball players graduate. They further do not realize that although black males account for only four percent of the student population at these big-time institutions, they make up sixty-five percent of the NCAA big-time football and basketball squads.

They also are unaware of the Faustian agreement between black athletes and big-time colleges. Black athletes go to college to become pros. Colleges, in turn, admit black athletes so they might win and reap the winner's share of revenues. Both parties view education as an obstacle, something to be overcome.

For blacks, the goal of graduating from college is overshadowed by the glamour and money of professional athletics. But the odds of making it to the pros are so slim that no one should consider professional athletics a viable career alternative.

Today, there are just 1,500 black athletes making a living in professional football and basketball. If you include baseball, major and minor leagues, and all the trainers, coaches, and physicians associated with the three professional sports, the number is still less than 2,600 black people who are employed by professional sports. When you compare the number of these opportunities with the three million black youngsters between the ages of twelve and eighteen, it is difficult to fathom why blacks, by a five-to-one margin, believe athletics, not education, offer the best routes for success for their children, according to a 1980 survey conducted by *The Miami Herald*.

The problem of the black collegiate athlete is less than twenty years old.

Georgia's Vince Dooley did not go from being a Jim Crow coach to recruiting sixty-five percent blacks because he believed in moral imperatives. More than likely, Dooley followed the example set by Bear Bryant at Alabama. In 1970, USC beat Alabama 42-21. USC was led by Sam "Bam" Cunningham, a black, who scored three touchdowns that day. Cunningham so impressed Bear Bryant that the very next year, Alabama had the Deep South's first black football player.

As race consultant Dr. Harry Edwards put it, when a few schools discovered "that the brothers can run down the sidelines like hot oil on a slanted pane of glass,"[2] other major colleges quickly followed suit.

By the mid-Fifties, because every inner-city or rural playground had a basket, and because the sport could be played without equipment, organization or a coach, basketball became the black man's game of choice. Bill Russell was the black trailblazer in college basketball, leading the University of San Francisco to back-to-back NCAA titles in 1956 and 1957. Wilt Chamberlain, playing for the University of Kansas, reached the NCAA western championships in 1958 where he saw the Klu Klux Klan set a cross on fire across from his Dallas hotel. Texas Western University, now University of Texas at El Paso, won the NCAA title in 1966 by beating Kentucky 72-65 with an all-black starting five who were part of the university's 250 blacks out of a total student population of 10,000.

Today, blacks so dominate football and basketball that, according to Arthur Ashe, "Thousands of white kids have been brainwashed. They can't be sprinters, wide receivers, or guards in the NBA. They've been told, over and over, 'You're not black, do something else.' "[3]

But even if the black athlete has been allowed to dominate the big-time college sports scene because of his athletic superiority, he has never been allowed to dominate the big-time graduation scene.

Dr. Richard Lapchick, head of the Center for the Study of Sports in Society, said, "The University of Houston went twenty-five years without graduating a black basketball player until Elvin Hayes, after he finished his NBA career, went back and got his degree in 1987. Memphis State wasn't that much better. It didn't graduate a black basketball player for twelve straight years."[4]

Referring to the problem of major college black athletes who never seem to graduate and who fail to turn pro, Dr. Harry Edwards said, "The black athlete's role in college sports today is rooted in the legacy of slavery and one hundred years of segregation."[5]

The blacks themselves have exhibited a certain selfish passivity about low graduation rates. Black stars, such as Herschel Walker, have great sway over a university, but they don't seem to leverage it. Jan Kemp said, "Had Herschel Walker, not Jan Kemp, raised the issue of black athletes never receiving a degree at Georgia, no doubt the university would have done far more to improve those graduation rates."[6]

Moreover, the public is diverted by other discriminations against black athletes that, although worrisome, are not nearly as destructive as low graduation rates.

Jimmy the Greek set off the biggest diversion when he told a Washington D.C., television station several years ago:

"The black is a better athlete to begin with, because he's been bred to be that way, and because of his high thighs and his big thighs that go up into his back. This goes all the way back to the Civil War when during the days of slave trading the slave owner would breed his big black to his big woman so that he could have a big black kid, see? I mean, that's where it all started."[7]

In April of 1989, Tom Brokaw, in an NBC show entitled "Black Athletes—Fact & Fiction," which some fifteen million people watched, tried to answer the implied questions contained in Jimmy the Greek's intemperate remarks. Is there such a thing as black athletic supremacy? And if there is, is it innate or acquired?

The show touched upon the fear most blacks harbor, expressed by Arthur Ashe: "Black dominance over certain sports reinforces the false notion that the only things blacks can do well is sing and dance, run and jump. We're fearful of admitting any athletic superiority lest it also makes us admit we are intellectually inferior."[8]

To resolve whether blacks are intrinsically superior athletes, and then to determine why they are, is to tilt at sociological and physiological windmills. Noting the racial composition of any championship football or basketball team answers the question of black athletic superiority convincingly.

The empirical evidence indicates blacks perform certain athletic functions—running and jumping among them—better than whites. If they didn't, blacks would not be playing because the virtually all-white coaching establishment is persuaded by only one argument: the player who helps us win, plays.

Another factor contributing to the low black athlete graduation rate is the lack of reliable statistics on the subject.

The NCAA publicizes certain graduation figures as Executive Director Richard Schultz did in May 1989 when he appeared before the U.S. House Subcommittee on Postsecondary Education. With pride, Schultz compared the graduation rates of all student-athletes, forty-seven percent, to the graduation rates of the nation's general student body, fifty percent.

But Schultz failed to reveal that black big-time football and basketball players graduate at the rate of 26.4 percent and 17.1 percent, respectively. Schultz also failed to reveal that zero to twenty percent of the NCAA's Division I basketball players graduate. The graduation rates for NCAA Division I-A football players are only slightly better.[9]

To avoid this type of deception from continuing, Senators Kennedy and Bradley drafted a bill, the Student-Athlete's Right to

Know Bill, which would require all universities and colleges receiving federal funds to publicize their five-year graduation rate by race, sex and sport.

But Schultz appeared before Congress to convey his personal misgivings about disseminating this information. First, he said, the term "graduation rate" has many definitions, and most schools choose the one that best portrays their rates, which invariably are misleading.

Senator Bill Bradley openly smirked as Schultz articulated his concern. Finally, Senator Bradley said, "What we want to know is very simple, Schultz [the Senate's form of addressing a witness]. We want to know if a university awarded 100 athletic scholarships in 1980, how many of the recipients graduated in 1985?"

Then Schultz expressed his grave concern that the disclosure of specific graduation rates would risk violating the Buckley Amendment, the law that safeguards a student's privacy.

Senator Bradley again interceded and persuaded Schultz to admit that if athletes were to agree to a disclosure waiver, the Buckley Amendment's integrity would remain intact.

At the January 1990 convention, the NCAA passed the legislation to disclose graduation rates. It then hailed the new regulation as another reform step initiated by the NCAA.

Even though it was against the Bradley Bill, the NCAA decided to publish graduation data to keep the Federal government out of its territory. According to Robert Atwell, president of the American Council on Education, "The NCAA is mortally afraid the federal government will meddle in its business."[10]

Today, the two principal defenders of the black athlete are Dr. Harry Edwards, sociology professor at the University of California-Berkeley, and Arthur Ashe, Hall of Fame tennis champion.

Edwards is a descendant of the extremist, Malcolm X, and Ashe champions the more moderate views of Dr. Martin Luther King, Jr. Edwards is a firebrand who masterminded the protest of the 1968 Summer Olympics at Mexico City that produced the indelible picture of Tommy Smith and John Carlos receiving their medals with downcast heads and raised fists.

Not surprisingly, in the Sixties, Edwards wore the uniform of the Black Panther: black beret, beads, black sunglasses, dashiki, and an open book of matches pinned to his black leather jacket presumably as a symbol for the slogan, "Burn, Baby, Burn."

Although very much a soulmate of Bobby Seale, Huey Newton and other revolutionaries, Edwards still sought a mainstream identity as well. He graduated from San Jose State and then obtained a doctorate in sociology from Cornell via a Woodrow Wilson Fellowship.

Today, Edwards continues to lead his life in two, disparate camps. He is a race consultant, espousing many of the militant attitudes of twenty-five years ago. He also earns $400,000 per year working in three-piece suits for such establishment institutions as Major League Baseball.

The other great advocate of the black college athlete today is Arthur Ashe, former U.S. Open and Wimbledon winner. Ashe is a somewhat fragile man who, because of his world-champion status and soft-spoken demeanor, always attracts an admiring and respectful crowd.

Ashe grew up in a well-regulated and proud family in Richmond, Virginia.

"Precious few had the father I had, or attended the schools I did," said Ashe in describing his childhood. "I was taught to aspire to be one of the sacred six: doctor, lawyer, teacher, mortician, preacher or professor."[11]

As a junior tennis champion in Virginia, Ashe received his share of discrimination, but he always emerged stronger for the experience. "I was raised on the beliefs of my father, my uncle, and Dr. Martin Luther King which, in essence, are 'Don't do me any favors. Just let's agree on what the rules are, and then judge me fairly.' "[12]

The willowy, bespectacled Ashe went to UCLA on a tennis scholarship, and won the U.S. Open as an amateur in 1969 when he was still a lieutenant in the U.S. Army.

Then Ashe hired former Davis Cup captain, Donald Dell, as his agent. Through Dell, Ashe has earned millions from endorsements for tennis equipment and apparel manufacturers.

Both Ashe and Edwards joined other leading educational and sports leaders at a seminar entitled "First Black Athletes in America Forum: Implications for the 21st Century," which was held at the University of the District of Columbia on April 7, 1989.

The first agenda item was the discussion of the just-released NCAA research study entitled "The Experiences of Black Intercollegiate Athletes at NCAA Division I Institutions," which prompted Ashe to say, "It is ironic our athletes, our idolized black warriors, are now simultaneously the object of our proudest moments and the subject of our greatest worries."

The study quantifies the disproportionate number of blacks on big-time college football and basketball teams versus total black student population.

Referring to this imbalance, Arthur Ashe said, "Clearly blacks are providing the fun and games for the nation on Saturday afternoons. However, eighty to ninety percent of these black football and basketball players never graduate."

Reacting to the same overrepresentation, Harry Edwards said, "America has this head-lock on us through sports. We've simply moved from the cotton fields to the football fields."

In addition to dominating big-time football and basketball teams through sheer numbers, blacks are overrepresented in the "star" category, and underrepresented in the "mediocre" category, which is a lingering effect from the days when black athletes had to be truly exceptional to break the collegiate athletics color barrier.

In perhaps its most sobering revelation, the NCAA study revealed that nearly half (forty-nine percent) of all black football and basketball players came form the lowest socioeconomic quartile, the mean family income was less than $17,500 per year, where females were the most likely head of household. Completion of the eleventh grade of high school was the median level of education, and the occupations were virtually all either unskilled or clerical. In sharp contrast, only thirteen percent of the white football and basketball players came from this lowest socioeconomic group.

Integration, according to Edwards, is why so many black superior football and basketball players come from the lowest socioeconomic quartile.

Integration was a black civil rights movement which relied on the white Establishment to provide equal opportunities because it was the ethical thing to do. Edwards said, "But nobody does something because it's right, despite what Dr. King and others told us. Morality never solves anything for us. We've got to help ourselves."

Initially carried away by the promise of integration, blacks—

specifically, the black middle class—discarded their own cultures and identities in pursuit of the white way of life. A classic but little known example occurred when Jackie Robinson integrated major league baseball on April 17, 1947. That celebrated day also marked the demise of the Negro Leagues, a mainstay of black pride and tradition never acknowledged or appreciated by white America.

Integration, then, had a decidedly white tinge to it which Edwards and his fellow militants regarded as a modern version of Uncle Tomism.

Integration opened the doors of racial equality just wide enough for the black middle class to dribble unobtrusively into the periphery of white society. Black lawyers, doctors, teachers and other professionals were quietly assimilated into the white suburban society while the inner-city neighborhoods were left with only the black underclass.

"Black middle-class creep was what really hurt the black community," Dr. Edwards said.

The black inner-city conclaves then became entrenched political, social, economic and cultural vacuums where only single-parent households remained. Black women, supporting their children either through welfare or a minimum wage job, had neither the tradition nor the inclination to stress the importance of education, much less a college degree.

The black underclass, according to Edwards, produces superior athletes because it is the only socioeconomic stratum which allows its children to put in the time required to be outstanding by the age of seventeen.

Not many people in the black underclass are inclined to acquaint their youth with the odds—one in 12,000—associated with becoming a professional athlete because, regardless of the chances, the ambition of doing so keeps many black youth gainfully occupied. As Arthur Ashe said, "Often black athletes play sports as a means to stay alive."

The NCAA study also showed that almost two-thirds of the black football and basketball players had $25 or less each month for personal expenses. This means, of course, that blacks have a serious problem paying for the incidentals of college life: clothing, dates, laundry, travel to and from the university.

Unlike Edwards, Arthur Ashe felt that the black athletes' social and academic problems documented by the survey were more the responsibilities of blacks to correct, regardless of how underprivileged their surroundings were.

"As blacks we've been caught up in the affirmative action plan since the mid-Sixties, and many of us have continued to lean too much on set-asides, or special dispensations. I personally don't like being thought of as an exception. If I know what the rules are from the start—which for black athletes today starts in the eighth or ninth grade—and I don't measure up, then I don't collect my reward.

"As blacks, we should not be seeking opportunities by qualifying for exceptions. We should just try harder next time. Where I live now, in New York, the number one basketball prospect is Kenny Anderson of Archbishop Malloy High School. Kenny Anderson, like so many others, took the standardized test early in his junior year. He didn't score 700. So he had to sacrifice some of the time playing basketball to study. He really buckled down and the next time he took the test he passed it way beyond the minimum."

Ashe continued, "No matter how poor or disadvantaged a high school might be, if that high school and its coaches have the organizational skills to produce first-rate athletes, well, then I say they can use the same organizational skills to produce second-rate scholars. It's just a matter of summoning the will to do it. One can not send third-rate students to first-rate schools where they spend more hours on their sport than they do in class and expect them to get by academically, let alone graduate. Seventy-four percent of all black athletes in the survey said that tutoring was easy to get. If it is so easy to get, and if it is unlimited and free, why are black athletes still not doing well academically?"

But many other seminar participants disagreed with Ashe, claiming that the high schools most black student athletes come from are so inept their grades are virtually meaningless.

Ashe responded by saying: "After visiting literally hundreds of black high schools across the country, black athletes think they can slide by academically. It's evident they think the world owes them a living when they say, 'I don't need to study. Even if I am a senior, I can still get my scholarship. And when I get to that Division I school, they're going to cheat to make me eligible.' "

Unlike Ashe, Harry Edwards thinks high schools and colleges are responsible for much of the black athletes' academic plight.

"High schools can't produce first-rate scholars because they are not the institutions producing the first-rate black athletes. The streets are doing that. And, anyway, these black athletes don't go to first-rate universities. They take their first-rate athletic skills into first-rate athletic programs and the student in them is utterly ignored by the universities. And the NCAA and its constituent institutions have done absolutely nothing to deal with this fact. If the black kids think their academics are going to take care of themselves, well, so do the universities. They think the black athletes' academics are going to take care of themselves, too.

"I just left the University of Michigan which, as everyone in America must know by now, just won The Final Four. It's the only school ever to win the Rose Bowl and The Final Four in the same year.

"Michigan has what it calls 'Athletic Dormitories.' I call them slave quarters."

Edwards continued, "I walked into one of the kid's room who brought the national championship in basketball to Michigan. This kid didn't have a book on his shelf. I said, 'Young man, where's your books?' 'We can't keep our books,' he said. 'We have to give them back. The books are actually on loan to us. Besides, we all take the same easy courses to keep us eligible, so this way, next year, other guys can use these books and the athletic department doesn't have to buy anymore.' This was from a kid who just put $1.2 million into the coffers of the University of Michigan."

Regardless of whether Ashe or Edwards is right in explaining why black college athletes are such poor students, the NCAA study did irrefutably document that black athletes are significantly less academically qualified than their white counterparts.

The survey showed close to sixty percent of the blacks scored in the lowest quartile of both standardized tests, while only six percent of black football and basketball players scored in the highest quartile of these tests. The mean SAT score for blacks was 740, and the mean score for whites was 890. Significantly, close to forty-five percent of the black football and basketball players scored below 700 on the SAT's. The high school and college grades of black athletes paralleled their SAT scores. Blacks constituted forty-eight percent of the lowest quartile for high school grades and sixty-one percent of the lowest quartile for college grades (1.99 gpa or below), while whites made up only twenty-five percent and thirty percent, respectively, of these quartiles. The survey's average grade point average for black athletes was 2.16.

The academic problems of black athletes are exacerbated because they spend more time on their sport than they do on their studies. The survey showed that black football and basketball players spend twenty-eight hours per week practicing for and competing in their sport, and twenty-three hours either preparing for or attending class. And the black athlete misses two classes per week during the season, and one class per week off-season—which means the black athlete attends classes only three-fourths of the time, something he can ill afford to do.

Perhaps the one positive academic development that the study unearthed—which debunked a popular belief—was that only a small portion of black football and basketball players major in physical education. Today, blacks are enrolled in business administration courses.

Ironically, the survey indicated that although black athletes placed great value on the ideal of obtaining a degree, their primary purpose for going to college was not to obtain an education. The black athletes admitted that if it were not for being recruited they would never have attended college.

Black athletes' lassitude towards academics usually begins in the eighth or ninth grade when well-intentioned but misguided parents, teachers, coaches, playground instructors and peers begin to allow them to avoid classroom responsibilities. Landy Ewings, the Georgia football player, said, "As soon as I picked up a football, I put down my books,"

By the time these superior black athletes have become high school seniors, they have been recruited by an average of fifteen schools. In the fierce competition of courting these players, recruiters do little to disabuse them of their dreams of becoming pros. Nor do the recruiters dwell on the academic work that should be required. By the time they actually attend college, these black athletes have been coddled throughout most of their junior high school and high school years.

"The black athlete's sense of responsibility has been removed by his parents, coaches, counsellors, teachers and the media," said Dr. Lapchick of the Center for the Study of Sport in Society. "In the process, his sense of self-worth off the field has become virtually non-existent.''[13]

Texas, where over half of the high school football stars are black, provides an example of how black teenage athletes can study, if forced to.

At the suggestion of billionaire, H. Ross Perot, the Texas legislature adopted the no pass-no play law that mandated a student must receive a passing grade of seventy or better in every class before he or she could participate in extracurricular activities. Failure to achieve this standard resulted in the student automatically being suspended from participating in any and all extracurricular activities for six weeks.

Initially, high schools lost, on average, close to twenty percent of their athletes because of the no pass-no play law, seventy-five percent of whom were black. But the following year, apparently having learned their lesson, the number of students declared ineligible was halved. The number of black athletes declared ineligible had been lowered to forty-five percent of the total.

Possibly because of their underprivileged backgrounds, black college athletes exhibit alarming tendencies to entertain unrealistic goals, a fact borne out by the NCAA study which concerned Arthur Ashe greatly.

Ashe said, ''Our kids—forty-four percent of them according to the NCAA survey—think their academics are going to take care of themselves, and that they are going to turn pro. Only twenty percent of whites held that aspiration. What are we teaching our kids? To have so many black college athletes holding on to those delusional goals is scandalous. You can't blame the white man for that.''

More than eighty percent of black football and basketball players placed the greatest importance on receiving a college degree, yet almost fifty percent of the black athletes who stated this belief had gpa's of 1.99 or less, indicating they were not likely degree candidates. Of those black athletes who said they were going on to graduate or professional school, thirty-five percent had gpa's of 1.99 or lower.

There was a similar inconsistency between classroom performance and the amount of income these black athletes expected to be making when they reached forty.

Black athletes regularly experience pronounced feelings of isolation, depression. This is especially true for black athletes attending predominantly white institutions. One-third of the respondents claimed they experienced at least six separate incidents of racial discrimination on campus. And they sense the rest of the university community perceives them as necessary but not entirely welcome components of campus life whose main purpose is to win football and basketball games.

Out of necessity, black athletes rely almost solely on coaches to show them the way. Oftentimes, the quality of that relationship is in inverse proportion to the success of the team. The more a team wins, the more preoccupying pressure there is to continue winning, a pressure that blocks a coach's ability to care for his players in a genuine manner.

As important as it is, a black athlete's relationship with his coach is fraught with the potential for discord since both come from entirely different backgrounds. The black athlete is a seventeen-year-old teenager, away from home for the first time, who has abruptly entered an unfamiliar world. His coach is a white male, forty to fifty-five years old, whose $200,000-a-year income depends on one thing only, winning. Add to this circumstance the black athlete's naïve belief that he should be on next week's cover of *Sports Illustrated* and there could be a lot of trouble.

The black athlete's problems are further aggravated by the shortage of black college coaches. Harry Edwards, when talking about the shortage of black coaches, said, "We have only four head football coaches and twenty-five head basketball coaches in the NCAA's Division I, clearly a racist situation when you consider how many black athletes [approximately 8,000] there are. And the NCAA is the worst racist of all because it has yet to address the discrimination that it and its constituent members have been practicing for eighty-five years. And I don't mean bringing in some 'head negro' and making him head of 'Negro Affairs.' The NCAA has negative feelings towards blacks. No blacks are being hired for head coaching positions, but when you watch The Final Four, it's like watching Nigeria play Ghana in basketball."

John R. Gerdy, a representative of the NCAA, defended the NCAA's racial attitudes by saying:

"I think Dr. Edwards makes a very valid point, but I also think it bears mentioning that we at the national office are making strides.

We've instituted a minority intern program, and this is the first year we've done it. Each year eight interns are hired for athletic administrators. So we are beginning to open the doors in this regard.''

Dr. Richard Lapchick of Northeastern University's Center for the Study of Sport in Society agreed with Edwards. "Collegiate hiring of blacks is worse than the pros. Blacks are simply not represented," Lapchick said. "There are 1,000 athletic programs in the U.S., each supporting, on average, twenty different sports. That means there are 20,000 head coaching positions, 40,000 assistant coach positions, 10,000 athletic department positions.''[14]

In 1970, there were no black head coaches in Division I football or basketball. In 1980, 5.4 percent of the schools had black coaches, a figure which increased to 8.4 percent in 1985. But there appears to be a positive trend developing on the assistant coach level. In 1970, 2.1 percent of the Division I institutions had black assistant coaches. In 1985, that figure had jumped to 25.1 percent.

Harry Edwards introduced the seminar's next topic of discussion when he said, "The racist media portrays black as athletes, buffoons, and criminals.''

In the spring of 1987, after the Detroit Pistons beat the Boston Celtics for the Eastern Division crown of the NBA Championships, the Detroit Pistons' Dennis Rodman said, "If Larry Bird was black, he'd be just another good guy.''

Rodman's remark provoked a bristling response from sportswriters everywhere because Bird, most everyone believes, is truly one of the game's greatest players ever.

In the absence of any black sportswriters leaping to Rodman's aid, Isiah Thomas, Detroit's superstar teammate, assumed that role. In explaining what Rodman meant to say, Thomas laid bare what apparently frustrates most black athletes about the media's portrayal of their roles. "When Bird makes a great play, it's due to his thinking," Thomas sighed. "All we do is run and jump. We never practice or give a thought to how we play. It's like I came dribbling out of my mother's womb.''

Two years later, Thomas's assertions were confirmed by a reporter of *The Boston Globe*, Derrick Z. Jackson, who studied the media's coverage of two seasons of NBA and NFL action, including post-season bowls and tournaments, and the NCAA's Final Four.

Jackson found that television commentators, virtually all whom were white, praised black athletes for their brawn and animal grace, and never for their intelligence or hard work. Blacks, according to television, are "natural athletes" and are "strong and fast." Whites, on the other hand, "work hard" and "hustle" to achieve their talents. But more importantly, because they are determined and smarter, whites are "the brains behind the outfit," "the natural leaders" both on the field and on the coaching sidelines.

The University of the District of Columbia seminar then heard from James Brown, the black CBS Sports basketball commentator and former basketball standout at DeMatha High School and Harvard College. Brown related his frustration over still being relegated to a minor role after five years with CBS. Brown conceded there are a number of black analysts, people who fill in the blanks for, but are far less important than, play-by-play announcers.

"And once you're an analyst, he said, "you tend to be pigeon-holed at that level. Also, an analyst is forever vulnerable to being replaced by next year's retiring superstar like Magic Johnson or Julius Erving."

Brown then described a CBS meeting held for its on-air sports talent to enhance their awareness and sensitivity when commenting on black athletes. The meeting was CBS's response to an editorial of *The New York Times*, entitled "CBS, The Network of Impaired Vision" which pointed out that in the 1988 NBA playoffs, CBS had four broadcasting teams covering the NBA playoffs, and not one black among them.

CBS sportscaster James Brown said, "Billy Packer and Tommie Heinsohn got upset at CBS's management for not backing them up after being criticized by Derrick Jackson's study. But based on what they said at that meeting, it was apparent Billy and Tommie still thought of blacks as brutes while still regarding whites as the smart guys who actually ran things."

Brown ended his seminar speech by stating that his experience as a student at Harvard taught him that "progress is not made without protest. And I am tired of listening to white men describe how blacks play football and basketball."

CHAPTER 6

Proposition 48

Freshmen Eligibility, and Satisfactory Progress

First, there was the pathetic newspaper photograph of the six-foot eight-inch former college basketball star, Kevin Ross, twenty-three, sitting at a third-grade desk with his knees around his ears, baffled by an illustrated primer. The photograph's caption explained that five years after leaving Creighton University without a degree, Ross was forced to return to a Chicago elementary school to learn how to read.

Then, there was all-Pro Washington Redskins lineman Dexter Manley, who had attended Oklahoma State for four years, confessing to *People* magazine's twenty-seven million readers he could not read.[1]

Appalled, people asked, how could anyone attend a university and not know how to read?

The answer lay in the history of the NCAA's attempts to effect academic reform in intercollegiate athletics. For the first 100 years of college athletics, most major colleges and universities maintained a separate admissions standard for athletes. If a high school football lineman could run the forty-yard dash in under five seconds then normal admissions requirements somehow were waived. And if an athlete exhibited future all-America possibilities, his ability to read was considered non-essential.

After World War II, the NCAA tried to curb preferential treatment for athletes by adopting the Sanity Code. The code required, among many things, that athletes possess similar academic credentials as the rest of an institution's student body. Although a big improvement, the Sanity Code's admission standards still varied widely by institution. The Ivy League's standards, for example, were difficult when Georgia's were too easy.

Then, in 1965, the NCAA created a national admissions standard, the "1.600 Rule," that applied to all NCAA member-schools. It required an incoming high school athlete to achieve a predicted first-year college grade point average of at least 1.600 (C – minus) before he could receive financial aid. Predicted first-year college grade point averages were determined by comparing an athlete's high school class rank and SAT scores with an expectancy table comprised of the same statistics for 40,900 students at some eighty different colleges.

For the next six years, the 1.600 Rule noticeably improved the academic caliber of the NCAA athletes.

But in 1971, annoyed that it was bound to an inferior admission standard, the Ivy League prompted the NCAA to reexamine the 1.600 Rule. Anxious to make recruiting easier, not harder, certain athletic directors took advantage of the occasion and convinced the 1971 NCAA Convention to adopt the 2.000 Rule which, despite its title, was substantially more permissive than its predecessor.

Rather than focus on the more important area of predicting how an athlete would perform in a college classroom, the 2.000 Rule merely required an athlete to have graduated from high school with a C+ average in any course, including driver's education. Because the 2.000 Rule did not compel athletes to take college preparatory courses, the NCAA weakened rather than strengthened the academic standards of its athletes. Even a president of a big-time football power later admitted: "It's simply impossible to graduate from high school without achieving a 2.000 gpa.''[2] The Ivy League was later sorry for even broaching the subject.

Adopting the 2.000 Rule coincided with another signal event in college sports.

In the early Seventies, after years of observing how much more successful integrated teams were, coaches began recruiting black athletes by the score. Although good to superior athletes, most black teenagers exhibited academic wounds inflicted by segregation-ravaged elementary and secondary schools. The 2.000 Rule was the NCAA's answer to open admissions for these athletes.

Unconcerned university officials made no real attempt to educate these 2.000 athletes. Instead, some schools initiated courses that were little more than high school vocational classes. The following was excerpted from the University of Georgia's Undergraduate Bulletin—1989-90.

101. Industrial Arts Woodwork. 5 Hours. One lecture and four 2-hour lab periods.

A beginning course in woodworking where consideration is given to the tools, materials, processes, planning, and construction of wood products as they relate to industrial arts and our society.

300. General Shop. 5 Hours. One lecture and four 2-hour lab periods.

Prerequisite: Basic industrial arts courses or permission of department.

Practices of working with tools, materials, and methods of managing an educational workshop.

Thus, when the reasonably effective 1.600 Rule was replaced by the 2.000 Rule, the NCAA member-schools could recruit whomever they pleased. For the next fifteen years, from 1971 to 1986, every high school prospect who graduated with a grade point average of 2.000 in general shop was eligible to receive an athletic scholarship.

The 2.000 Rule provided a coach with the best of both worlds. He could justify recruiting semi-literate athletes and still boast of complying with the law. Vince Dooley, Georgia's athletic director, explained: "We recruited 2.000 athletes because other schools were doing it. Besides, we were all within the NCAA's regulations."[3]

Once enrolled at an NCAA member-school, these 2.000 athletes spent at least four and a half hours a day, seven days a week, practicing and competing in their sport. Since there was little time left for the pursuit of even industrial arts, an avalanche of academic scandals occurred throughout the Seventies and the early Eighties.

In 1982, dissatisfied with the NCAA's response to the mounting scandals, two separate groups of college educational and athletic leaders set out to reform college athletics.

The first group, led by Georgia's Fred Davison, met at Sapelo Island, Georgia, in the spring of 1982 to devise a replacement for the 2.000 Rule. The participants included Chuck Neinas, commissioner of the Big Eight Conference, Vince Dooley of Georgia, Joe Paterno of Penn State, Bobby Knight of Indiana, Dean Smith of North Carolina, and Don Canham of Michigan.

After non-stop deliberations, the Sapelo Island group drafted a proposal, later called Proposition 48, that required incoming high school athletes to achieve at least a 2.000 grade-point average (C+) in a college prep curriculum and a 700 on the SAT's before they could receive an athletic scholarship. It's important to note that athletic administrators, not admissions or standardized testing experts, devised these standards. The group had no scientific evidence to support its decision to use 700 as the minimum cutoff score, for example.

In September 1982, Fred Davison took the Sapelo Island proposal to the American Council on Education, a trade association of the nation's leading universities. The ACE had just established its own committee of reformers consisting of thirty-two major university presidents, headed by Harvard's Derek Bok. Included on the committee were Notre Dame's Father Theodore Hesburgh; Georgetown's Father Timothy Healy; Miami's Edward "Tad" Foote; and Robert Atwell, president of the American Council of Education; North Carolina's William Friday; and Donald Shields of Southern Methodist University.

The Bok Committee arrived at the 1983 NCAA Convention armed with several reform measures, the Sapelo Island proposal among them.

Many of the presidents were attending their first NCAA convention and they were not prepared for the NCAA old-guard's reception. Georgetown's Father Healy said: "We confronted political maneuvers that would have impressed even Niccolo Machiavelli."[4]

Knowing that SAT scores and college prep requirements would hinder recruiting, the entrenched athletic directors and faculty athletic representatives fought the Bok Committee's proposition vigorously. Proposition 48 eventually passed, but not without a debilitating compromise. Acting like the shrewd politicians they were, the athletic directors persuaded the convention to adopt a compromise that curtailed much of Proposition 48's power.

Using the objections of black college presidents as an excuse to meddle, the athletic directors and faculty athletic representatives tacked on a last-minute compromise amendment, the "partial qualifier." The amendment enabled high school athletes who failed either the SAT or college curriculum minimums to still receive an athletic scholarship. In exchange, the partial qualifier merely had to sit out his freshman year, presumably to establish a solid academic footing for his three remaining years of eligibility.

The athletic directors and faculty athletic representatives presented the partial qualifier amendment so skillfully that the Bok Committee did not realize it permitted the very recruiting practices Proposition 48 was supposed to stop to continue.

Commenting on how the partial qualifier loophole could slip by the Bok Committee, Robert Atwell, ACE president, admitted, "We just didn't understand it."[5]

That was not the only consideration that escaped the Bok Committee at the 1983 NCAA Convention.

Although it was clear from the start that academic reform would affect black athletes the most, both the Sapelo Island group and the Bok Committee failed to include black educators in their deliberations. Berkeley's Harry Edwards said, "Once again, blacks had to sit on the sidelines and watch whites determine the fate of blacks."[6]

As a result of being ignored, black college presidents arrived at the 1983 NCAA Convention seething, convinced that Proposition 48's real purpose was to stop black athletes from integrating big-time colleges further.

Dr. Jesse N. Stone, Jr., president of Southern University, said,

"The end result of Proposition 48 is the black athlete had gotten too good, and you are now saying, 'Let the white boy win once and awhile.' We're going to bring Jesse Jackson in on this one."[7]

Another black president, Grambling State University's Dr. Joseph B. Johnson, likened Proposition 48 to racial onslaught: "They came after the Jews and I said nothing; they came after the Catholics and I said nothing; they came after the Blacks and I said nothing. Then they came after me and there was no one there to say anything."[8]

What incensed the black presidents most was Proposition 48's reliance on arbitrary SAT minimum test scores which, they said, discriminated against culturally-deprived black students.

Of the 1.1 million high school students who took the SAT's in 1982, only seventeen percent scored below 700. But eighty-five percent of this group were black. The average SAT score of the 1982 Princeton freshmen class was 1342, while the national average for whites was 904. The national average for blacks was 712. (To score a combined 700 on the SAT's a person need only answer thirty-five out of the 145 questions correctly. One gets 400 points for signing his or her name.)

Black syndicated columnist Chuck Stone illustrated an example of the difficulties black youth experience when taking standardized tests.

SAT's are culturally biased, and you've heard that argument before, haven't you? But here's proof of what the psychometricians call "differential item functioning" or DIF. Try this question.
Runner is to marathon as:
(a) envoy: embassy
(b) martyr: massacre
(c) oarsman: regatta
(d) referee: tournament
(e) horse: stable
The correct answer is (c) regatta. Whereas 52 percent of white test takers get that question right, only 22 percent of

black test takers do. Suburban kids are just more familiar with regattas then ghetto kids.

Recruiting academically-sound athletes has always been a problem in college athletics. When Rutgers and Princeton played the first college football game in November 1864, ten freshmen played for Rutgers that day, three of whom were failing Algebra. Since that day, the question of freshmen eligibility has never been satisfactorily answered.

During the 1880's, Dr. Charles Eliot, president of Harvard, led a movement to abolish freshmen eligibility. Eliot observed that too many Harvard freshmen athletes did poorly in their studies.

Initially, Yale, not wishing to disrupt its athletic dynasty, resisted Harvard's attempt to abolish freshmen from varsity competition. But over time, Yale agreed that freshmen needed their first year on campus to adjust to college life. Soon thereafter, like-minded schools formed conferences that excluded freshmen from varsity competition. The Southwest Conference was established in 1916, followed by the Southeastern Conference in 1922, and the Atlantic Coast Conference in 1952.

But the temptation to use freshmen always lurked in the background.

World War II offered the perfect excuse for many institutions to reinstate the practice. Barely a month after Pearl Harbor, the Missouri Valley Conference allowed freshmen to play varsity sports again, claiming the war would greatly reduce its male student population.

After several more decades of vacillation, the NCAA restored freshmen eligibility for good in 1972.

Today, however, most college presidents believe the practice should be abolished. But few are willing to abolish it unilaterally. Reverend Timothy Healy, S.J., then president of Georgetown, said, "I'm dead set against freshmen eligibility. Freshmen need time to adjust to college. The biggest thing is, they don't go home at night. College is a twenty-four-hour place. But sadly, we could never stop freshmen eligibility on our own because then we couldn't recruit."[9]

Dr. John Slaughter, then chancellor of Maryland University, said, "Personally, I'm against freshmen playing varsity sports. But let's face it, if Maryland did not allow freshmen to play intercollegiate athletics, we wouldn't recruit. If that happened, we wouldn't win. And if that happened we might as well drop out of the ACC [Atlantic Coast Conference]."[10]

But in the spring of 1989, one big-time college president, the University of Iowa's Hunter Rawlings, did attempt to abolish freshmen eligibility on his own.

Humiliated after several Iowa football players admitted in a widely-publicized trial they majored in Water Coloring and Archery, Rawlings announced that if the NCAA did not adopt freshmen ineligibility within a year, he would do so on his own. Reactions to Rawlings ultimatum showed why other university presidents know better than to act so impulsively.

First, Iowa's football coach, Hayden Fry, who presumably works for Rawlings, called a press conference and threatened to quit. Then, three-fourths of the local newspaper's readers, when polled, said they opposed Rawlings' plan. And finally, Iowa's governor, Terry Branstad, accused Rawlings of being "insufferably naïve" for believing that the university's education reputation was more important than the entertainment value of Iowa football. "Hawkeye football," Branstad said, "is for all the people of Iowa, not just past and present students."[11]

More than a year has passed, and Rawlings "is still studying the question," as is the NCAA. Dr. Charles Young, chancellor of UCLA, and Dr. Thomas Hearn, president of Wake Forest University, debated the pros and cons of freshmen eligibility at the 1990 NCAA Convention but no legislative action was considered.

For three decades now, the NCAA has attempted to monitor the academics of incoming freshmen. But the association has done little to monitor the academics of athletes once they are in school. Throughout most of the Seventies, NCAA school officials looked the other way as academic counselors employed by athletic departments advised 2.000 Rule athletes to take easy courses that preserved their playing eligibility but seldom led to a degree.

Commenting on this inequity, Leo Miles, former football coach for Howard University, said: "There is such a contrast between getting into school and staying in school. The SAT makes it so hard for an athlete to get a scholarship now. But once he's in school, he's got a free ride."[12]

To correct the situation, the Bok Committee sponsored another reform proposal at the 1983 convention, the "Satisfactory Progress" proposition. Again, by the time the convention actually voted on the measure, Satisfactory Progress had been stripped of its potency.

Now Satisfactory Progress merely requires an athlete to be a full-time student earning at least twelve credits per semester in a program leading to a baccalaureate degree. He must also declare a major course of study by the beginning of his junior year.

When the measure was first considered, the Big Ten and the Mid-Atlantic Conference had proposed a schedule of specific minimum grade point average achievements: 1.600 for freshmen, 1.850 for sophomores, and 2.000 for juniors and seniors. Without this specific requirement, the Big Ten argued, it was entirely possible for an athlete to accumulate twelve credits each semester and still not graduate.

Today, after four years of being on the NCAA's books, Satisfactory Progress has failed to improve either the academic life or the graduation rates of big-time athletes.

On the other hand, the Bok Committee's Proposition 48 continues to provoke as much controversy and misunderstanding as it did at the 1983 NCAA Convention.

The measure received favorable publicity in 1989 when the University of Michigan, led by two Proposition 48 basketball players, Rumeal Robinson and Terry Mills, won The Final Four. Both players did not play their freshmen years because they failed to achieve 700 on the SAT's. To proponents of the measure, the fact that Michigan benched two stars for a year and then came back to win The Final Four is convincing proof Proposition 48 works. Detractors say the Michigan experience was merely fortuitous.

It is still too early to determine conclusively if Proposition 48 will work. But of the 2,500 athletes deemed partial qualifiers since the legislation went into effect in August 1986, over seventy percent have been black. Of this group, ninety percent have failed the SAT minimum requirement.

Disregarding widespread sentiment to make the partial qualifier loophole even more liberal, the Southeast Conference sponsored a measure, Proposition 42, at the 1989 NCAA Convention that would have eliminated the loophole entirely. If Proposition 42 were to pass, no longer would athletes who majored in vocational courses or who failed the SAT minimum be eligible to receive scholarships.

The Southeast Conference committed the same blunder the Bok Committee did. It failed to consult black college presidents beforehand. In turn, the black presidents reacted predictably. They came to the 1989 convention sounding cries of indignation. Sacrificing a year of eligibility was bad enough for black athletes to endure, they argued. Now, if the loophole were to close, the majority of black athletes would be precluded from college because few could afford to attend without an athletic scholarship.

In the fight against Proposition 42, black presidents joined forces with athletic directors who were also opposed to eliminating the partial qualifier, but for entirely different reasons. The athletic directors knew that without the partial qualifier, star athletes would be barred from big-time college athletics. As a consequence, black college presidents became allies with many of the same people who were exploiting black athletes through indiscriminate recruiting.

A furious convention floor battle ensued. Initially, the convention voted down Proposition 42. But within hours of the defeat, the measure, somehow, was reintroduced. This time it passed.

Three days later, Georgetown's basketball coach, John Thompson, who had not attended the convention, denounced Proposition 42 as "racist and unfair to poor students." Thompson then announced he would boycott his own coaching responsibilities until the NCAA changed the rule. No one, least of all the media, knew how to handle this unusual form of protest.

One week after his boycott began, Thompson flew to NCAA headquarters to confer with NCAA officials. Three hours later, the NCAA announced Proposition 42 would be reconsidered (for the third time) at the 1990 NCAA Convention.

It was the NCAA's way of saying Proposition 42 is dead.

Besides providing added entertainment for a confused public, Thompson single-handedly reversed what nearly 200 NCAA schools had approved just a week before. It was as if a private citizen had persuaded Congress to rescind an act the majority had just passed.

A year later, at the 1990 NCAA Convention, the elimination of the partial qualifier was reconsidered, as promised. To no one's surprise, the loophole was not only reinstated, but liberalized.

Under the old version of Proposition 48, a partial qualifier counted toward a coach's yearly allotment of scholarships. Because there are a limit in the number of scholarships available each year (twenty-five for football, five for basketball), a coach was careful not to squander too many on partial qualifiers, a caution that served as a quality-control check of sorts. Also, the old version required the coach to pay for the partial qualifier's scholarship out of his own budget.

But from now on, a partial qualifier will not count as a scholarship until the athlete starts practicing with the team after his freshman year. Also, the university's general fund, not the coach's budget, will pay for the partial qualifier's first-year scholarship. These two new provisions will now allow coaches to recruit an unlimited number of partial qualifiers, and then stockpile them during their freshman year as so much basketball or football inventory. The coaches may then pick the best of those who have survived their freshman year of classes.

And so, John Thompson did a great service for himself and his fellow big-time coaches in persuading the NCAA to keep and subsequently liberalize the partial qualifier. Big-time coaches still have the NCAA's approval to continue to recruit semiliterate athletes.

Did John Thompson manipulate the highly-charged accusation of racial discrimination to obscure his own recruiting motives? Or is he one of the truly thoughtful men of intercollegiate athletics who took a stand against something he believed was wrong?

Georgetown's former president, Father Tim Healy, regards Thompson as one of Georgetown's most valuable assets. Father Healy said: "John Thompson is a winner, and he's dragged us along with him. As one of our theology professors put it just the other day, 'John Thompson is no longer educating Georgetown, he's now educating America.' "

Father Healy continued, "He's so outstanding that if he ever left, we'd be through. He's a one-man program. Thomspon is like two other guys we have on our faculty. Mark Sutton has turned us into a leading cancer resource, as has Michael Lemp in ophthalmology. Both these men are like John in many ways. Tyrannical. Nice guys rarely get things done."[13]

But others wonder.

Ken Free, the black commissioner of the black college Mid-Eastern Athletic Association, pointedly said, "I'm inclined to do something to make him [Thompson] suffer. He doesn't care about any kid except the kid who can get him on television and keep Georgetown in the top twenty or thirty."[14]

According to Father Healy, Georgetown has always educated students who come from underprivileged academic backgrounds. Father Healy said, "Georgetown ranks second to Stanford in the percentage of minorities it graduates each year. We have a number of programs under the supervision of Bill Reid, our director of minority education, beginning with Saturday classes for inner-city high school students."[15]

But skeptics maintain Georgetown's minority program is a front for a special college within a college created so that basketball players might circumvent the rigors of Georgetown's regular under-graduate classrooms.

Georgetown's sincerity should not be measured by Thompson's boldness or Father Healy's rhetoric but by the graduation rates of its basketball players. If they are high, as Father Healy suggested, then John Thompson's stance was justified. But if they are low, then Thompson and Georgetown exploit its athletes just as Georgia did. They merely use the mantle of a scholarly reputation to cover it up better.

Either way, Thompson should not have quit his crusade until he persuaded the NCAA to pass legislation that is fair to minority athletes but still demands meaningful high school academic achievement before an athlete is awarded a scholarship. As it stands, there are roughly 1,000 athletes admitted each year as partial qualifiers who, some argue, have no business being in college. These are the athletes who will be exploited because precious few will graduate and even fewer will make it to the pros.

At the very most, only five of these partial qualifiers attend Georgetown. The remaining 995 are at the mercy of other, perhaps less ethical universities. In effect, John Thompson abandoned the very people he said he was trying to protect.

Perhaps without recognizing it, Thompson argues for open admissions, but only for outstanding athletes.

Open admissions for athletes are nothing new. They existed from 1971 to 1986 when the 2.000 Rule was in effect. During this fifteen-year period, only one in six black football and basketball players graduated, compared to one in three white athletes who graduated. During this same period, less than 200 athletes out of 7,850 made it to the pros each year. But big-time colleges grossed upwards of $50 million per year in gate and television receipts, and John Thompson became a millionaire.[16]

People wonder how John Thompson's basketball players, who rank in the lowest decile of their high school classes, can compete against the typical Georgetown undergraduate.

In a letter to the editors of *Sports Illustrated,* Collie F. James III of Plano, Texas, said, "My son—1360 on the SAT's, 3.5 grade point average, National Merit scholarship semifinalist, starting quarterback on the football team, starting pitcher on the baseball team—is one of 12,000 students who have applied for a spot in next fall's freshman class at Georgetown. Some 10,000 of those applicants, most of whom have impressive credentials, will be turned down. It it ludicrous to believe that a student with a 2.0 GPA and a 700 total score on the SAT's should be allowed to occupy a seat in the classroom when so many young people who have put great effort into their studies are told to go elsewhere."

Duke and Stanford Universities, two NCAA schools that prove an equilibrium between excellent athletics and excellent academics is possible, disagree with Thompson over the issue of admissions for athletes. In fact, both Stanford and Duke refuse to recruit athletes who can't measure up to the their normal admission standards which, among several things, require high school grades that rank the prospective student in the top five percent of his or her class and at least a 1300 on the SAT's. Dr. Chris Kennedy, Duke's head of academic counseling for its athletic department, said, "We don't recruit athletes who can't compete with our normal students. It makes them insecure. It's not fair to them and it's not fair to us."

Another basketball coach, Indiana's Bobby Knight, disagrees with Thompson's open admission stance for superior athletes, too. Knight believes athletes, regardless of how gifted they are, have to be academically qualified for college *before* they are admitted. Knight reportedly tells certain high school athletes, most of them black, "College isn't for everyone, and anyone who tells you otherwise is just trying to use you. Do something else with your life, but accept the truth about you and college now. It is never going to work."

CHAPTER 7

Beer

In the summer of his junior year in college, when he was practicing with the 1984 U.S. Olympic basketball team at Indiana University, Chris Mullin obliged an Indiana tavern owner by autographing a team photo with the inscription, ''If the beer is cold, we'll win the gold.'' The epigram revealed the passions of Mullin's life, beer and basketball, in the order of their importance.

As promised, Mullin did win an Olympic gold medal, as well as All-America status, the John Wooden Trophy commemorating the nations's best college basketball player, and a $600,000 yearly contract with the Golden State Warriors of the NBA.

But on December 10, 1987, at the beginning of this third season with the Warriors, Chris Mullin finally admitted he was an alcoholic and checked himself into a California alcohol rehabilitation center. Mullen's problem with beer had become so acute that his life had become unmanageable and neither he nor those around him could deny it any more.

Lou Carnesecca, his college coach at St. John's University, who knew Mullin since he was 14, told *The New York Times*, ''I'm shocked. I never knew he had a problem. I would see him take a beer or so at a social function, but it was no big deal.''[1]

But Don Nelson, the Warrior's executive vice president, knew better.

"Chris had a problem," Nelson told *The Sporting News*, "and I confronted him with it. He denied it, so I bet him he could not lay off beer for six months. Four days later, Chris lost the bet."

As of January 3, 1990, two years after he returned from the treatment program, Chris Mullin was the fourth best scorer in the NBA, averaging 26.6 points per game. His annual salary is now $3 million. Mullin credits Don Nelson for saving his life.

A native of Brooklyn, Mullin has been idolized by fans and coaches alike ever since he grew to be six-foot-seven and learned to shoot the lights out of any gym he played in. To many fans, Chris Mullin is the world's most unlikely alcoholic. How could someone that young, that good an athlete, who only drank beer, be an alcoholic?

First in 1985 and then again in 1989, the NCAA conducted two comprehensive surveys to ascertain the drug and alcohol use of a large sample of athletes. In the most recent study, nine out of ten athletes admitted they drank compared to only one in twenty athletes who admitted he used cocaine. Yet, most people focus on drugs while they regard such an inordinately high percentage of alcohol use as perfectly reasonable.

Like *Pravda, The NCAA News* can be mind-numbing in its insistence to present an NCAA news item in the most favorable light possible. In reporting the survey findings, *The NCAA News* neglected to emphasize to its readers how serious and widespread the problem of alcohol abuse in college sports really is.

But the person who conducted the study, Dr. William A. Anderson of Michigan State University, in a special interview, was far more forthright.

"Epidemiologically, alcohol is the gravest drug problem in college athletics," Dr. Anderson concluded. "And yet the NCAA chooses to focus on anabolic steroid abusers for the publicity value. What it really should be doing is concentrating on the alcohol abusers. And the NCAA could start by refusing to accept advertising from the breweries. But it's a matter of headlines and economics with the NCAA."

According to Dr. Anderson, close to twenty percent of the athletes surveyed drank three or more times per week, and nearly a third of these athletes consumed six or more drinks each time they drank.

Over forty percent of the athletes admitted that alcohol had a harmful effect on their athletic performances. Yet, only thirty-three percent of the schools represented in the survey had drug testing programs, and only a third of these tested for alcohol.

"The University of Colorado is the worst," Dr. Anderson continued. "Last spring I went to a football game at Boulder, and Coors threw a tail-gate party for the entire stadium, complete with a rock band. Coors was also being sold in the stands, and Coors sponsored 'Ralphie' the Buffalo, the team's mascot, trip to the Orange Bowl."[2]

As part of his many efforts to reduce drunk driving fatalities while Surgeon General of the United States, C. Everett Koop, wrote to Colorado's president, Dr. D. Gordon Gee, asking him to prohibit such promotions. There are an estimated 13,000 Colorado undergraduates under twenty-one for whom beer is an illegal drug.

Dr. D. Gordon Gee admitted receiving Koop's letter, but he doesn't think Colorado's problem is acute. "We value the Coors people. They are a big benefactor of the school, and they are helping us implement an alcohol abuse program on campus."[3]

Close to two dozen football players at the University of Colorado were arrested between 1987 and 1989 on charges ranging from rape to assault. By the team's own admission, beer drinking contributed greatly to its crime wave.

James Delany, commissioner of the Big Ten, offered one reason why the NCAA, the University of Colorado, and many other schools appear to be dragging their feet on the problem of alcohol in college lockerrooms. Delany said, "Many Division I schools have local beer sponsorships, including lucrative signage contracts, program ads, and TV-radio shows, which can amount up to thirty percent of a school's revenue. They can't afford to disrupt these relationships."[4]

Former U.S. Health Secretary Otis R. Bowen confirmed Delany's observation. Bowen said, "Beer distributors spend many millions each year on campuses, encouraging heavy drinking, and contributing to poor grades, excessive vandalism, many injuries, and not so infrequently, death."[5]

Drinking beer has always been a rite of passage that most athletes proudly brandish. In fact, there is such a disregard for the dangers of beer that the 1984 Olympics drug-testing procedure used beer to induce urination. Chris Mullin would joke with his teammates that he wanted to be drug tested so he could "drink four or five cold ones."

No recent sports figure portrays the alcohol-and-athletics affinity better than Lawrence Taylor, the New York Giants' All-Pro defensive end. In his autobiography, *LT: Living on the Edge*, Taylor depicted his North Carolina college experience as one long drunken siege interrupted by an occasional football game. Lawrence Taylor tells the story of his drunkenness as if it were necessary to sustain his virility and ferocity. Judging from the well-publicized difficulties Taylor has had with substance abuse throughout his professional career, not much has changed since his days at Chapel Hill.

Since the NFL, NBA or NCAA do not ban alcohol, to avoid the automatic suspension that comes from drug use, several prominent players, most notably Dexter Manley of the Washington Redskins and, many suspect, Lawrence Taylor, have confessed to an alcohol problem to mask their drug problems.

High school and college drinking among non-athletes are as widespread as they are with athletes.

According to an annual study commissioned by the National Clearinghouse on Drug and Alcohol Abuse, ninety-two percent of all high school seniors, 2.4 million seventeen-year-olds, drink beer. Nearly a third, one million seventeen-year-olds, are "binge drinkers." They drink at least five consecutive beers at one sitting at least every two weeks. General Koop said, "This much drinking can be deadly especially when it is combined with driving. And it's important to note these kids are all underage."

By a margin of two to one over distilled spirits and wine, beer is the beverage of choice for high school seniors and underage college students.

According to the same survey, five million college students are binge drinkers, 2.7 million of whom are underage. Dick Bast, senior technical adviser for the National Clearinghouse on Drug and Alcohol Abuse, said, "These numbers prove there's a nationwide epidemic of alcohol abuse among people for whom it is illegal to drink."[6]

A study of eighth graders, conducted by the Association for the Advancement of Health Education, found that one out of four

Nike's Sonny Vaccaro, an ex-gambler, pays over 60 college coaches, some upwards of $100K per year, to outfit their teams with Nike shoes. Photo: Sports Illustrated.

Georgetown's John Thompson earns $700K annually: $200K comes from Nike, $318K from Georgetown and $200K from camps and TV. Photo: AP/Worldwide.

Because CBS's Neal Pilson risked $1 billion to get The Final Four, he and the NCAA must now slake Anheuser-Busch's desires until 1997. Photo: AP/ Worldwide.

By virtue of Pilson's $1 billion gamble, CBS's CEO Laurence Tisch became the unofficial boss of the NCAA. Photo: AP/ Worldwide.

No one at Michigan wanted the Donald B. Canham Natatorium except Don Canham, the school's athletic director, who created a $2 million deficit to build this memorial to himself. Photo: Courtesy Univ. of Michigan.

While 100,000 cheer Michigan's football team, the athletic department's annual sales swell to $20 million. Photo: Courtesy Univ. of Michigan.

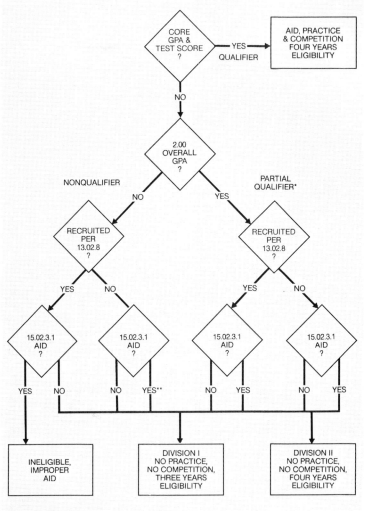

FIGURE 14-1

Relationships Between Academic Requirements, Recruitment,
Financial Aid and Eligibility in Divisions I and II (14.3)

CORE GPA & TEST SCORE ? — YES QUALIFIER → AID, PRACTICE & COMPETITION FOUR YEARS ELIGIBILITY

NO

2.00 OVERALL GPA ?

NONQUALIFIER — NO / YES — PARTIAL QUALIFIER*

RECRUITED PER 13.02.8 ?   RECRUITED PER 13.02.8 ?

YES   NO   YES   NO

15.02.3.1 AID ?   15.02.3.1 AID ?   15.02.3.1 AID ?   15.02.3.1 AID ?

YES   NO   NO   YES**   NO   YES   NO   YES

INELIGIBLE, IMPROPER AID

DIVISION I NO PRACTICE, NO COMPETITION, THREE YEARS ELIGIBILITY

DIVISION II NO PRACTICE, NO COMPETITION, FOUR YEARS ELIGIBILITY

*Effective August 1, 1990, the provision for a partial qualifier will apply only to Division II.

**Must be certified as not related to athletics ability.

This is a diagram of the NCAA's Proposition 48, a rule few members understand. To make matters worse, rules like this are subject to annual change. Reprinted with permission of the NCAA.

Former football coaches Barry Switzer of
Oklahoma, above, and Jackie Sherrill of Texas
A&M. Both almost kept their jobs despite
raging scandals because of powerful ties to
their governors and university trustees. Photos:
AP/Worldwide.

In 1983, Jim Valvano, North Carolina State's ex-basketball coach, won the NCAA Final Four. But in 1990, Valvano had to resign after ABC-TV alleged four of his players shaved points. Then, ABC-TV turned around and hired Valvano as a commentator for $300,000 per year for three years. Photo: AP/ Worldwide.

Texas Governor Bill Clements admitted that when he was chairman of Southern Methodist University, he authorized payments totaling $61,000 to SMU football players over a sixteen-month period. Photo: AP/Worldwide.

Eric Manuel, Kentucky
basketball star, was caught
cheating on his standardized
entrance exam Photo; Lexington
Herald-Leader.

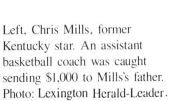

Left, Chris Mills, former
Kentucky star. An assistant
basketball coach was caught
sending $1,000 to Mills's father.
Photo: Lexington Herald-Leader.

surveyed indulged in a binge drinking episode two weeks prior to the survey.[7]

Everyone knows adolescents are not supposed to drink, and everyone knows they do it anyway. Despite alcohol being an illegal drug for people under twenty-one, there are too many signals encouraging underage drinking for society to admit it is a serious problem.

Underage drinking probably started when European immigrants permitted their children to drink beer or wine at the family dinner table, continuing the practices of the old country. Few realized that France, for example, a country most Americans believe has drinking well under control, has one of the highest rates of alcoholism in the world.[8]

Aided by states where the legal drinking age, until very recently, was only eighteen, adolescent drinking migrated from the home to the bars when teenage driving became widespread in the Fifties. Most adults continued to wink at the practice because they themselves drank as teenagers.

Then came the Sixties and Seventies when marijuana, amphetamines, cocaine and other hallucinogens became the primary targets in the war against substance abuse. In the meanwhile, beer came to be regarded as a welcomed alternative to drugs despite the well-known fact that teenage drug-abusers invariably were heavy beer-drinkers well before they started using drugs.

According to a 1988 study conducted for the New York State Office of Mental Health, fifty percent of those teenagers surveyed started to drink when they were 12.9 years old. They did not start to use drugs until almost two years later, at an average age of 14.6. The study also showed that when compared to a similar study done in 1983, while drug usage declined sharply, the drinking age and incidence remained the same.[9] Another study has shown that first drinking usually occurs at twelve, in contrast to ages thirteen and fourteen in the 1940s and 1950s.[10]

In the United States alone, alcoholism and alcohol abuse have been at epidemic proportions for quite some time, affecting 18.2 million men and women,[11] at an annual cost of $145 million.[12]

But mention the word ''alcoholic'' and the average American still thinks of a panhandler, sitting on a park bench, drinking wine out of a brown-paper bag. Possibly because Chris Mullin was not in rags and tatters, Coach Lou Carnesecca, conveniently or ignorantly, denied that Mullen had a problem. As all addiction experts know, denial is the single biggest reason why alcoholism is so virulent.

Another lethal form of denial is the widely held belief that beer is less harmful than distilled spirits and wine. The myth of beer's harmlessness begins with the oft-misinterpreted concept of alcohol content. Every fifth of 80 proof distilled spirits, for example, contains 10.27 ounces of alcohol, whereas a fifth of wine contains. 3.08 ounces of alcohol, and a fifth of beer contains a mere 1.21 ounces of alcohol. Thus, people assume that scotch is far more potent than beer.

But what most people fail to realize is that the amount of alcohol contained in each beverage's average serving size is precisely the same: twelve ounces of beer contain 0.564 ounces of alcohol; 1.41 ounces of distilled spirits contain 0.564 ounces of alcohol; and 4.7 ounces of wine contain 0.564 ounces of alcohol.[13] No doubt beer's comparative harmlessness is why it is advertised on television and distilled spirits are not.

But television advertising represents the most compelling reason why this country regards beer as a harmless alcoholic beverage.

Over the years, Madison Avenue has portrayed beer drinkers as young, attractive men who, after rising to some athletic or work-related challenge, cavort with Dick Butkus, win over hard-bellied, melon-breasted women, and drive Clydesdale horses, all in an atmosphere where beer flows freely without consequence. In the process, Madison Avenue has created television-beer, a miracle-drug that assures male sexual and athletic success.

When watching a beer commercial on television, it is impossible to associate what happens on the screen with what happens to 24,000 people each year who die in drunk-driving accidents,[14] the majority of whom are between the ages of fifteen and twenty-four, and drink beer.[15]

Television-beer is different from the beer that contributes to drunkenness and drunk driving being the most frequently committed crime in the United States, representing 19.6 percent of all arrests, a sum that is two and a half times greater than the number of drug abuse arrests.[16]

Television-beer is not the beer drunk by 4.6 million teenagers who have alcohol-related problems.[17]

Television-beer is different from the beer that provides riots, fights, public urination and vomiting, indecent exposure and verbal threats in baseball parks and football stadiums across the nation.

Television-beer is not what Chris Mullin abused.

Although most adult men accept the tongue-in-cheek beer commercials for what they are, research reveals that children and adolescents do not.

Bob Stratton of the AAA Foundation for Traffic Safety, alluding to "Myths, Men & Beer," a research report sponsored by his organization, said, "Our four researchers discovered that American kids, from two to eighteen, the period when children learn the most, are exposed to over 100,000 beer commercials. The kids drew such erroneous conclusions from the beer commercials that the researchers recommend they be prohibited."[18]

A survey conducted for the U.S. Bureau of Alcohol, Tobacco and Firearms revealed that eighty percent of those studied believed that beer advertising influences underage youth to drink. Teenagers who testified before the National Commission against Drunk Driving for its 1988 youth report corroborated this belief. The Commission reported, "With near unanimity, the youths themselves declared that advertising encourages adolescents to drink."[19]

Bubba Smith, the former NFL great, refused to appear in any more Miller "Tastes Great, Less Filling" commercials after seeing first-hand how they encouraged drunkenness at his alma mater, Michigan State.

Robert King, executive director of MADD, when asked about the effect of beer advertising on minors, said, "Despite their denials, beer companies advertise to males between the ages of fifteen and thirty-five, even though the legal drinking age is twenty-one. The breweries glamourize life through drinking beer. They advertise life-style, not the product, which is misleading to youngsters."[20]

The American Medical Association supports efforts to restrict the advertising of beer and other alcoholic beverages. "We want beer makers and distributors," said the AMA's Victoria Davis, "to stop their high school and college campus promotions, and to stop depicting beer as a social enhancer."[21]

Similar restrictions have been recommended by the Surgeon General, the American Academy of Pediatrics, and the American Academy of Family Physicians.

Even the television networks impose severe restrictions on alcohol. According to Christine Hikawa, ABC's Vice President, Broadcast Standards, East Coast, drinking beer in a commercial is strictly prohibited. When asked why, Ms. Hikawa explained, "We don't show people drinking because it leads to excessive drinking."[22]

Today, there are eighty million beer drinkers in the United States. All of them, it seems, are sports fans. Because of this proclivity, breweries have long been the number one sponsor, media advertiser, and event underwriter of sports.

Ever since 1881, the year Christophe Von der Ahe became part-owner of the St. Louis Browns so he could sell his beer inside the ball park, America has permitted beer to be a paradoxical partner of sport. Even with its far more entrenched beer-culture, Germany has never allowed breweries to be associated with sport. In 1953, August A. Busch, Jr., of Anheuser-Busch bought the St. Louis Cardinals. Twenty-five years later, Busch admitted just how much the baseball team helped Anheuser-Busch increase its sales six hundred percent during this period.[23] Today, Anheuser-Busch has advertising contracts with twenty-three out of twenty-six major league baseball teams which call for Anheuser-Busch to be their official beer.[24]

But as beneficial as beer is for owners' pockets, it can be menacing for fans.

Immediately after the 1989 Philadelphia-Dallas NFL football game, which was marred by drunken fans randomly beating up people, Eagles owner Norman Braman asked Mayor W. Wilson Goode to ban the sale of alcohol at Philadelphia's Veterans Stadium for all Eagles games, and to prohibit the possession of alcohol in the parking lots.[25]

Largely because the late baseball commissioner Bart Giamatti believed beer and alcohol were the root causes of fan misconduct, which he said had sunk to alarming depths, seven out of the twenty-six major league baseball teams stop selling alcohol in the seventh inning, seventeen offer alcohol-free sections, eight limit the number of beers that can be purchased to two, and nine stadiums do not permit beer vending in the stands.

The San Francisco Giants prohibited the vending of beer in the stands of Candlestick Park and lost $600,000 in the bargain, which was only partially recouped by increased food and non-alcoholic beverage sales. But attendance has since increased because fans, who approved of the beer-ban by a margin of nine to one, are grateful that the owners made Candlestick safer.

As an insight into the brewers' mentality, one local San Fransicso brewery official actually argued that if beer were banned, the fans would get drunk on hard liquor at nearby bars before the games and come to Candlestick even more drunk and unruly than had they been allowed to continue to get drunk on beer inside the park.

Other people are resisting the connection of beer and baseball, too. Houston's Glenn Davis, a non-drinker, and six other major league baseball teams, including the New York Yankees, refused to participate in an Anheuser-Busch promotion that heralds every home run with, "This Bud's for you."

Besides exploiting baseball teams as beer-selling devices, breweries rely heavily on television sports, a siren for tens of millions of young males who also happen to be inveterate beer drinkers. The beer sales generated from stadiums are infinitesimal compared to the sales generated from television homes and bars.

Anheuser-Busch spends $450 million, and Miller, Coors and Strohs, between them, spend another $300 million each year on televised sports.[26] All told, these four breweries account for a third of the $2.2 billion spent each year on televised sports which makes them forces to be reckoned with by the networks and cable people.[27]

Prior to 1978, Anheuser-Busch relied more on print advertising and word-of-mouth to sell Budweiser, Michelob and its other beers. But from 1978 to 1980, at the behest of a newly appointed marketing-sales executive, Michael J. Roarty, Anheuser-Busch experimented with television and increased its advertising budget by $100 million. The test proved successful as Anheuser-Busch's sales went from $2.7 billion to $3.82 billion, an increase of over forty percent. More importantly, Anheuser-Busch's profits increased fifty-five percent during this period. By 1988, Anheuser-Busch was spending $450 million on television advertising, and its sales had risen to $9.7 billion, and profits were $1.26 billion, six times greater than what they were in 1978.

Even more tellingly, before it came to rely so heavily on television advertising, Anheuser-Busch had thirty-one percent of the United States beer market in 1977, and Miller's had twenty-one percent.[28] In 1989, after it increased its television sports advertising expenditure five-fold, Anheuser-Busch had increased its market share to forty-two percent. Anheuser-Busch went from being a $2.7 billion company to a $9.7 billion company in ten years largely because of television advertising.

Some people are worried Anheuser-Busch has gotten too big, too powerful.

Francis X. Matt, president of Utica Club Brewery and also president of the Brewers' Association of America, told *Sports Illustrated* in 1988, "Anheuser-Busch has things its own way, and with that kind of concentration of power, bad things can happen. The federal regulators are afraid of them, afraid of their lawyers. Nobody should have unlimited power, but they are getting it. All sports are dominated by Mr. Big, all television, all markets."

The power of Anheuser-Busch, coupled with the power of Philip Morris, the makers of Marlboro cigarettes and Miller beer, are demonstrated in how beer is taxed.

First, beer manufacturers pay disproportionately far fewer taxes than distilled spirits manufacturers do. Despite beer's annual volume being a third more than distilled spirits', beer pays a federal tax bill of $1.57 billion, whereas hard liquor pays $4.84 billion.[29]

Second, the federal excise taxes on beer have remained the same for forty years. The reason behind the exceptional leniency reveals the power of the beer lobby.

Beer is an acutely price-sensitive product. Higher prices mean lower beer sales because beer's primary consumers, young people, can not regularly afford to drink the more expensive distilled spirits and wine everyday. Keeping the federal excise taxes low is one means to keep beer retail prices affordable and still preserve a profit for the breweries.

Two economists came upon an astonishing discovery concerning the relationship of beer's price-sensitivity and its deadly effect on young people. If beer had been taxed at the same rate as distilled spirits, and if beer taxes had kept up with inflation since World War II, the average retail price of a six-pack would have been $5.70 from 1975 through 1981, as opposed to $4.20, the actual price. The resulting decline in sales caused by this $1.50 variance, according to economist Saffer and Grossman, would have reduced the number of eighteen-to-twenty-year-olds killed in drunk driving accidents in this period by fifty-four percent. Some eight thousand teenagers, minimally, would still be alive if this country taxed beer more fairly.[30]

In the last several years, the beer industry has continued to lower retail prices significantly. It also conducted a nationwide petition to keep beer prices low.

Although still popular, alcoholic beverages have come under increased scrutiny in the emerging age of fitness.

Appearing trim and athletic has become the order of the day. Aerobics, running and Nautilus are *de rigueur,* and lunchtime martinis, tea-colored whisky, meat, cholesterol and fats are now passé.

Capitalizing on this new-found concern for wellness, grass-roots citizen activist groups have sprouted up all over the country. Mothers Against Drunk Driving, for example, developed the notion of the designated driver and, in so doing, increased the nation's awareness about alcohol-related problems. In turn, the federal government licensed nine thousand alcohol treatment centers, and, overnight, treatment for alcohol-related problems became available to everyone who wanted it.

This change in the nations's awareness of alcohol prompted some people to question whether beer advertising, like cigarette advertising, should be banned from television. If anti-drug advertising can help reduce the incidence of drug usage, people reasoned, then eliminating pro-alcohol advertising might help reduce the persistently high incidence of problem drinking, particularly among teenagers.

Nothing strikes terror in the collective heart of the beer and advertising industries more than to suggest the elimination of beer advertising on television.

If the beer industry is powerful when controlling its own taxation, it is warlike when controlling its own advertising and marketing destiny.

An example of how bellicose the beer industry can be occurred in 1988 when the surgeon general convened a Washington, D.C., summit meeting to discuss drunk driving. Fearful that a ban on beer television advertising might be recommended, the National Beer

Wholesalers Association sued unsuccessfully to postpone or cancel the meeting.

The meeting was attended by representatives of appropriate private and public agencies involved with the drunk driving problem, including several members of Congress and Health Secretary Otis Bowen. Invitations were also extended to John O'Toole, executive vice president of the American Association of Advertising Agencies; Dewitt Helm, president of the Association of National Advertisers; and Edward Fritts, president of the National Association of Broadcasters, three organizations who benefit directly from beer advertising. Messrs. Helm and O'Toole declined to attend because they "did not have the time to adequately prepare for the conference." Fritts was far more honest. In a letter to Dr. Koop, Fritts wrote, "At best, this workshop is designed to politicize the emotional tragedy of drunk driving. At worst, it is a total abuse of the policy-setting process."

The beer industry's first defense against a possible ban is to express bewilderment over why people are concerned about beer advertising since it has no effect on increasing sales.

"Beer advertising," says Jeff Becker, the youthful vice president of Alcohol Issues for the Beer Institute, "merely influences people who already drink beer to either switch brands or stay with their current one. It does not create or increase demand."[31]

But sales and population growth figures say otherwise.

Total annual U.S. beer sales have risen from 120 million barrels in 1975 to 195 million barrels in 1989 [32], an increase of 62.5 percent whereas the population, sixteen years old and over, has increased only 21.7 percent during the same period.[33]

No less than John Kenneth Galbraith repudiated this argument thirty years ago when the tobacco industry invoked it to ward off the threat of banning cigarette advertising. Professor Galbraith found that "advertising affects both brand preference and the aggregate level of consumption of a product or service."[34]

As the nation became more aware of the problems of alcohol, so did the NCAA.

"The abuse of alcohol is the most pervasive drug problem in the country, far graver than crack, cocaine or heroin," claimed an NCAA pamphlet on drugs and the athlete, published in 1986. "With the ingestion of three to four drinks per hour, the person will suffer impaired speech and coordination, diminished inhibitions and a loss of judgment. If more than three or four drinks are ingested in less than an hour, the effects become even more pronounced: slurred words, staggered gait, unpredictable emotions, mood swings, and inappropriate behavior . . . The combination of alcohol and depressants can lead to serious illness or even death."[35]

The NCAA also began to worry about beer advertising appearing on the NCAA's telecasts of The Final Four basketball tournament.

Realizing there is an estimated cumulative audience of some seventy-five million people under twenty-one who watch its Final Four telecasts each year, the NCAA was concerned that exposing these youth to beer commercials would contradict the association's anti-drug stance. NCAA executive director Dick Schultz said, "Beer is a legal product for those of drinking age. But beer is also an illegal drug for those below the drinking age. A large percentage of college students is below twenty-one, as are most high school students."

And to have the beer commercials appear side by side with the NCAA's own anti-drug commercials, Schultz added, made the contradiction that much more embarrassing.

When negotiating The Final Four television contract with CBS in 1985, Dick Schultz, who was then head of the Special Television Negotiating Committee, failed to persuade CBS to ban beer advertising. Schultz also failed to persuade the network to adopt a compromise position: reduce the number of beer commercials broadcast in a given hour from ninety seconds to sixty.

Some people believed Schultz only paid lip-service to the issue, that he had in fact compromised the ban of beer advertising when CBS offered him a seventy-six percent increase in rights fees for his cooperation on the beer issue.

But Schultz did vow to eliminate beer commercials from the NCAA telecasts in the next contract, three years hence.

In the spring of 1989, six months before the NCAA television contract was to be renegotiated, the matter resurfaced, along with Schultz's vow to eliminate beer advertising.

Predictably, the Schultz's position caused an uproar in the advertising industry.

"It is a very dangerous thing," according to David Martin, Vice President, Corporate Media, for Stroh's Brewery. "I hope that

CBS, ABC and NBC or whoever will be bidding on the tournament recognize that it isn't just college basketball or college sports or sports in general, but all television time slots, and it is not just the beer business that was threatened by this, but other major advertiser categories as well."[36]

Reactions like these apparently had an effect on Schultz because in its April 17, 1989, issue, *Advertising Age* reported that "Schultz appears ready to drop his ban of beer commercial in postseason tournament telecasts because of pressure from beer marketers. Industry sources say Schultz's about-face probably stemmed from opposition by the brewing industry and college athletic directors."

Several days after the *Advertising Age* article appeared, Schultz wrote a letter to Harold Shoup, executive vice president, American Association of Advertising Agencies, Inc., which is Madison Avenue's lobbying group. Schultz maintained, "To restate our position, we never said we were going to ban beer commercials from our telecasts."

But two weeks later, on May 3, 1989, in a front page article in *The NCAA News*, Dick Schultz again contradicted himself. "The NCAA will continue to seek a reduction, possibly leading to total elimination of beer commercials in its telecasts despite published reports to the contrary," he said.

On May 4, 1989, in his office at NCAA headquarters in Mission, Kansas, Schultz confirmed his latest position. "Alcohol is an illegal drug for people under twenty-one," he told the visitor. "And we have a lot of people in our television audiences who are under twenty-one. The NCAA also has an effective drug announcement, and we feel that beer advertising contradicts this drug message."[37]

The beer industry responded to Schultz's contradictions with trench warfare. It applied pressure to the NCAA's most vulnerable joint: the budgets of the NCAA's athletic directors. Despite the illegality of underage drinking, most big-time NCAA schools and local beer distributors have their own advertising and television contracts, some as high as $4 million per year. Anheuser-Busch, alone, advertises in more than 300 college athletic events.[38]

The breweries asked their distributors to deliver a clear message to the athletic directors: renewal of the local beer contracts depended solely on the NCAA not banning beer advertising in its Final Four telecasts.

The athletic director of the University of Pittsburgh, Edward Bozik, who chairs a special NCAA committee on drugs and who also is a member of the NCAA's executive committee, said, "There is no problem with beer advertising in The Final Four. It's just like advertising in the Super Bowl, as far as I'm concerned."[39]

The University of Pittsburgh is a member of the Big East Conference, along with Georgetown, Syracuse, Seton Hall, and many other powerhouse schools. The Big East Conference is famous for its lucrative television contracts with ESPN and CBS. It is estimated that Pittsburgh gains an incremental $2.5 million per year from these television deals, of which beer advertising contributes $700,000 annually.

The person responsible for the Big East's television contracts is Dave Gavitt, now of the Boston Celtics but former commissioner and founder of the conference, and also former basketball coach of Providence College in the Seventies. Known for his keen promotional skills, Gavitt had this to say about the appropriateness of beer advertising appearing on a college sports telecast. "We are certainly not insensitive to the issue of alcohol abuse among people who are under twenty-one. But we don't believe beer commercials make a difference, one way or another. Besides, we don't have the leverage to refuse the beer advertisers."[40]

In November of 1989, The Final Four television negotiations began and a month later, CBS agreed to a $1 billion deal, the first ever for college sports.

A few days after the excitement of the $1 billion deal had subsided, Schultz issued a prepared statement containing this explanation: "While the NCAA considered further restrictions with respect to beer advertising, they were deemed unnecessary upon learning of Anheuser-Busch's intention to institute a voluntary plan of educational advertisements on these telecasts."[41]

Apparently, at some stage of the negotiation, Anheuser-Busch agreed to show its "Know When to Say When" commercial, an attempt to encourage responsible drinking, with its regular beer-selling commercials at an undisclosed ratio. Former surgeon general Koop said of moderation commercials, "These messages are completely overshadowed by alcoholic beverage product advertising. They are not as slick, not as sophisticated, and not as frequently aired as the alcohol ones are.''

When informed of the NCAA's beer advertising compromise, Joe Anastos, executive director of the Students Against Drunk Driving (SADD), said, "The NCAA sold out for the dollar bill. 'Know When to Say When' suggests adults drink in moderation. There is no such thing as moderation for underaged kids. And weren't they the people the NCAA was trying to protect in the first place?''

The "Know When to Say When" campaign, according to Anastos, appeals to the universal teenage yearning to be grown-up. "Anheuser-Busch is saying to the kids in a stage whisper," Anastos speculated, "'Go ahead and drink. You're a man now. You can handle it.' But few teenagers handle beer responsibly. That's why the drinking age is twenty-one in all fifty states.''[42]

Attempts to ask Anheuser-Busch why its "Know When to Say When" commercial, earmarked for the NCAA Final Four, would not include a warning to youth under twenty-one not to drink were thwarted. Michael J. Roarty and Steven J. Burrows, the two Anheuser-Busch executives ultimately responsible for such matters, were protected by a battery of secretaries and public relations people.

Finally, Mark Abels, of the St. Louis public relations firm Fleischman-Hillard, responded on behalf of his client, Anheuser-Busch's Michael Roarty.[43]

Ignoring the question about the underage warning, Abels insisted on reading a statement which he had prepared for Roarty. "We wish to offer congratulations to the NCAA and to CBS for their new agreement for telecast of the NCAA basketball tournament. The sports fans and the schools are the big 'winners,' just as they should be.

"We are happy to see that this agreement was concluded without a ban of beer advertising. We are proud of our past association with the NCAA tournament, and we look forward to continued sponsorship, both through our beer brand commercials and through our 'Know When to Say When' campaign to promote responsible drinking.''

Coors Brewery was far more accessible and courteous.

Ben Mason, Coors's manager of Alcohol Issues, felt it was not necessary to include such a prohibiting warning to underage people because Coors only advertised on adult television shows. When asked what the specific age parameters of Coors's target audience is, Mason replied, "Men between the ages of twenty-one and thirty-five."[44]

Robert King, executive director of Mothers Against Drunk Driving, deplored this advertising practice. "Who are they trying to kid? Everyone knows it is virtually impossible for television to separate nineteen-year-old viewers from twenty-two-year-old viewers. If the beer industry is so sincere, why doesn't it just add the tag line, 'People under twenty-one should not drink?'" King asked.[45]

When this question was put to Jeff Becker, vice president of Alcohol Issues for the Beer Institute, he said, "Should car manufacturers tell kids under sixteen, 'Don't drive cars'? Should beer companies be telling people not to break the law? Kids know they are not supposed to drink."[46]

Jim Delany, commissioner of The Big Ten, and Judith Sweet, treasurer of the NCAA and athletic director of the University of California, San Diego, represent the new breed of athletic administrator. Both are in their early forties, attractive, and highly educated. Delany is a lawyer and Sweet has an MBA and a master's in physical education. Both are politically adept in the often treacherous politics of the NCAA, with Ms. Sweet being the heavy favorite to succeed Al Witte as the NCAA's president in January 1991.

Since Delany and Sweet are the future of the NCAA, both sat by Dick Schultz's side as he negotiated the CBS deal.

When asked what he thought about the "Know When to Say When" solution, Delany said, "We live in an imperfect world, and we compromised. The committee received a lot of pressure from the athletic directors. If the national NCAA television contract were to ban beer advertising, then the ban could jeopardize their local contracts."

Delany continued, "Also, the CBS folks claimed the NCAA's refusal to accept beer would raise issues pertaining to First Amendment rights."[47]

It's interesting to note CBS's regard for the rights of the beer industry in this situation. Yet, the First Amendment is never invoked when its own censors prohibit beer to be consumed in a commercial. Nor is the freedom of speech raised when CBS grants Anheuser-Busch product exclusivity for the Super Bowl, banning other breweries from advertising in the most important sports event of the year.

When Judith Sweet was asked about her views on the beer advertising issue, she paused for a long time, as if the question literally took her breath away. Finally, she said, ''The committee felt it was a First Amendment issue, meaning the NCAA could not dictate who could and could not advertise on television. We hope the public perceives it as an improvement. We did reduce the number of beer commercials from ninety seconds each hour down to sixty seconds. It is not the final step in the process. Also, Dick Schultz has been working closely with Anheuser-Busch. A-B will air those moderation and education spots in 1990 even before the new contract begins.''

Ms. Sweet then intimated that beer advertising would be eliminated or curtailed the next time the contract was negotiated, in 1997.

But this is unlikely since Anheuser-Busch's advertising dollars are why CBS can afford to pay the NCAA $1 billion from 1991 to 1997. By virtue of this agreement, CBS holds the NCAA's mortgage and Anheuser-Busch holds CBS's mortgage, a network badly in need of the St. Louis brewery's advertising dollars.

In August 1990, sports-bar owners proved just how much Anheuser-Busch dominates CBS.

The networks were going to cut-off the NFL telecasts sent to thousands of sports-bars because these establishments, which attract as many as 300 people to watch pro games, pay no rights fees.

Fearing a considerable loss of business, sports-bar owners, rather than appeal to CBS, went directly to Anheuser-Busch and threatened the brewery with a boycott. ''Who do you think supports you and buys your product? I have other beers to sell,'' Bill Rose, owner of the Sporting Club in New York City, told his Anheuser-Busch wholesaler.[48] Mr. Rose sells 75 cases of Budweiser each week.

Shortly thereafter, Neal Pilson announced CBS was postponing indefinitely its plans to scramble the signal to sports-bars, citing a lack of equipment.

If anything, the presence of Anheuser-Busch as the official brewery of the NCAA will be felt even more in the next decade, carefully packaged in the "Know When to Say When" campaign, a tactic designed to advertise Budweiser and keep critics at bay.

Similarly, the NCAA and Anheuser-Busch joint venture to fight alcohol abuse on the nation's college campuses, advertised with great fanfare during the 1990 Final Four, demonstrates why both organizations need watching.

After seeing Anheuser-Busch's spot and the NCAA's spot featuring President Bush during the 1990 Final Four telecast, viewers were persuaded to believe the joint venture's war against alcoholism in colleges would rival, as it should, William Bennett's war against drugs.

However, the NCAA, Anheuser-Busch and, unwittingly, President Bush were boasting about a phantom program.

More time, effort and money went into making the Anheuser-Busch-NCAA commercials then went into fighting the war against alcoholism.

On May 3, 1990, a month after the commercials aired, when asked if there was any material explaining the joint venture, Emmie Morrissey, the NCAA Foundation's program coordinator, said, "There are no brochures, no prepared materials as of yet. We haven't proposed a program to Anheuser-Busch yet, and they haven't given us any money, either. But Frank Uryasz might know more about it. Why don't you ask him?"[49]

The following day, Frank Uryasz, the NCAA's director of Sports Science and the man who coordinates the association's illegal drug activities, queried about shedding some light on the NCAA-Budweiser joint venture, said, "I have had no involvement with it. I didn't even know about it until I saw a release at The Final Four."[50]

Despite the U.S. Surgeon General's declaration that underage drinking is the nation's number one health problem, the NCAA conspires with Anheuser-Busch and CBS to stimulate minors to use an illegal drug, beer.

CHAPTER 8

Greed

" 'A fish stinks from the head down.' is an old Russian Jewish proverb that applies to CBS these days," said Werner Michel, senior vice president for Bozell, Inc., Chrysler's advertising agency. Mr. Michel was reacting to the $1 billion CBS-NCAA Final Four deal that stunned much of the sports, advertising and Wall Street worlds. Michel's proverbial allusion referred to Neal Pilson, head of CBS Sports, and to Laurence Tisch, CBS's chief executive officer and investor extraordinaire, who also owns Loews Hotels.

"Mr. Tisch is a hotel man," Michel continued, "who knows nothing about television. He can't see that Neal Pilson, in his quest to be CBS president, has sold him a bill of goods."[1]

Brandon Tartikoff, who brought "Hill Street Blues," "The Bill Cosby Show" and "Cheers" to television, told *The New York Times,* "CBS has no vision at the top. I don't think the guys running CBS have a clue."[2]

This marked the second time in eleven months that industry experts reacted harshly to sports deals negotiated by CBS's Tisch and Pilson.

In December 1988, when Peter Ueberroth announced that CBS

had wrested major league baseball's television contract away from NBC, Laurence Tisch's smile of triumph vanished into a tight-lipped frown as the business world groaned its incredulity.

CBS had agreed to pay $1 billion to broadcast a minimal number of regular season games, the All-Star game, the playoffs, and the World Series each season for four years. NBC had been broadcasting twenty-four major league baseball games per season. Somehow, Ueberroth had convinced CBS to reduce its number of regular season games to sixteen. By limiting CBS's telecasts, Ueberroth had a surfeit of games to sell elsewhere. ESPN bought 175 of them per season for a per game rights fee of $571,430, forty times less than CBS's.

In the past five years or so, CBS had been a company in deep trouble.

In its heyday, 1984 and before, CBS was as solid as the Federal Reserve: first in prime-time, news, sports and profits. But today, NBC leads the ratings by a wide margin, and CBS has fallen to a distant third.

CBS's slide began twenty years ago when CBS's larger-than-life founder, William Paley, neared retirement. When the CBS Board of Directors pressed for a successor, Paley had to go outside the company because his covey of lieutenants were long on compliance, but short on skill. Paley spent most of the Seventies recruiting a series of presidents who, after several years of enjoying the office, were terminated abruptly without explanation.

And then, in 1980, Paley hired Tom Wyman, whose most relevant experience consisted of working for a Minnesota concern that canned and freeze-dried peas. For five years, Wyman ran CBS by simply maintaining the forty-five-year momentum Paley had created. Then, in 1985, CBS began to unravel.

In April 1985, Ted Turner, flamboyant owner of Tuner Broadcasting, announced his intention to purchase a majority interest in CBS. Publicly dismissing Turner as a lunatic, but secretly terrified he might have to work for him, Wyman thwarted Turner by buying back 6.4 million shares of CBS stock, incurring $1 billion in debt in the process. With so much to repay—the interest alone was $400 million per year—CBS needed bold and innovative management, a challenge beyond Tom Wyman.

By this time, Laurence Tisch, owner of Loews Hotels, Lorillard Tobacco, and CNA Financial, had increased his CBS holdings to twenty-five percent, and gained a seat on the CBS board. Thinking Tisch was his "white knight," Wyman welcomed him to CBS enthusiastically.

A year later, Tisch fired Wyman, who departed CBS with a $4.3 million "golden parachute" severance package.

With Wyman gone, Tisch named himself CBS's chief executive officer and proceeded to terminate most of Wyman's forty-three presidents and vice-presidents.

One man who survived the purge was Neal Pilson, 42, a Hamilton College and Yale Law School graduate who headed CBS Sports. Tisch liked Pilson because he had this notion of how to restore CBS's lustre.

Because CBS's prime-time programming was in such a pitiful state, Pilson believed CBS should use sports as the magnet to attract viewers back to CBS. Pilson was able to persuade Tisch to finance a sports event shopping spree, with the World Series first on the list. By telecasting the World Series, Pilson suggested, CBS would gain the nations's attention during prime-time in October, the beginning of each new television season. In addition to boosting its prime-time ratings with the World Series itself, CBS could, via promotional spots, expose snippets of its new fall shows to the Series audience, people who otherwise would be watching ABC, NBC or cable.

Meanwhile, Dick Schultz and his Final Four television negotiating committee, aware that CBS was on a sports shopping spree, lay in the tall grass waiting patiently for Neal Pilson to happen by.

Jim Delany, commissioner of the Big Ten and a member of the committee, said, "We were extremely well-prepared. We also had the advantage of knowing CBS had just lost the NBA contract to NBC, and it wanted this one [The Final Four] badly."

The negotiations began by the NCAA encouraging ABC, NBC, ESPN and Turner Broadcasting to submit bids. The negotiations ended when CBS, nervous it might lose, preempted the competition with a $1 billion bid, the largest deal ever in intercollegiate athletics.

Stephen M. Leff, Vice Chairman, Backer Spielvogel Bates, the ad agency for Miller Brewery, said, "I'm good friends with Neal Pilson, and I don't think this billion dollar deal is his idea. It's

Tisch's. It's an extraordinary amount of money to pay for the NCAA men's basketball championship.

"I'll tell you one thing. Pilson did not take the trouble to check the advertising business to see if we will pay these high rates. We would have told him, 'No, we won't.' "

Leff added, "The ratings will never increase to the point where CBS can recapture these tripled rights fees. And there is no chance CBS can pass the increase on to advertisers by charging more for the advertising spots."[3]

Wall Street echoed the ad community's sentiments, alarmed by its estimate that CBS could lose $75 to $100 million on the first three tournaments of the new contract.[4]

Following on the heels of its $1 billion negotiations with major league baseball and the NCAA, Pilson agreed to broadcast the National Football Conference games of the NFL for four years for yet another billion dollars. Pilson's latest deal means that in 1992, CBS will pay $1.03 billion in rights fees, up from $281 million in 1990.[5] Madison Avenue and Wall Street fear that CBS will not be able to recoup from its advertisers this four-fold increase that Pilson has incurred as part of his "mosaic strategy."

Industry fears were justified. On October 10, 1990, after CBS announced its third quarter profits had decreased sixty-five percent because of its major league baseball telecasts, the broadcaster's stock fell twelve points.

Based on these numbers, it would appear Pilson's strategy is an abject failure. Now, to salvage his career, Pilson must do whatever is necessary to keep advertisers happy. No doubt this will mean cramming even more commercials into the NCAA telecasts.

Long-term, CBS's staggering losses make the NCAA dangerously vulnerable. The association's mortgage-holder—CBS provides $143 million of the NCAA's estimated $155 million annual revenues—has an uncertain future. Rumors abound Tisch will sell CBS to a foreign company who might be less sanguine about the $1 billion NCAA contract than Pilson is.

The first time a television camera panned a college football stadium, the NCAA lost whatever innocence it had. Using large sums of money as bait, television persuaded college football and basketball to leave the campus in favor of the Great White Way.

And in so doing, the NCAA shifted its allegiance from the ticket-buying college student to the commercial-buying advertiser.

It was simply a matter of numbers and economics. The shift in affection made perfect business sense because for every one dollar a fan paid, an advertiser paid twelve. Capacity crowds in the largest stadiums numbered 100,000 while television regularly drew hundreds of millions.

As the advertising dollars rolled in, so did the advertiser-induced accommodations. First came TV time-outs to broadcast the commercials. Then the World Series switched to prime-time since the networks could double the price of a spot to $250,000 because the television audience doubled going from afternoons to evenings. In 1973, the NCAA's Final Four final went from Saturday afternoon to Monday evening for the same reason the World Series did. Then came tie-breakers in tennis, golf's switching from match play to seventy-two hole tournament scoring and The Skins Game, and no zone defense and the twenty-four-second shot-clock in the NBA.

But these accommodations to television and its advertisers were worth it. Major league baseball players now earn $3 million per year, NBA players average $1 million per year, and the NCAA awards $3 million apiece to the universities that win four consecutive basketball games in its annual Men's Basketball Championship.

In the early years of televised sports, right after World War II, the medium concentrated on major league baseball, with Mel Allen's mellifluous drawl articulating the exploits of Joe DiMaggio, Mickey Mantle and other heroes.

When professional football replaced baseball as America's favorite television sport in 1958, the average pro football team was worth $600,000 and it received $45,000 annually from television rights fees. Today, the average pro football franchise is worth $128 million, and it receives over $34 million annually from television rights fees.[6]

In the late Fifties, hundreds of thousands of television viewers, inspired by Arnold Palmer winning four Masters titles in six years, enlisted in "Arnie's army" and took up golf themselves. Fifteen years later, NBC's "Breakfast at Wimbledon" and CBS's U.S. Open Tennis tournament featuring Billie Jean King, Bobby Riggs, Chris Evert, Rod Laver, John McEnroe and Jimmie Connors caused millions to flock to tennis as well.

In 1966, Pete Rozelle invented the Super Bowl which eventually would attract 125 million viewers and command $700,000 for one 30-second commercial. In the 1990 Super Bowl, CBS sold fifty-six advertising spots for $39 million.

Although a popular novelty throughout the Fifties and Sixties, sports still took a back seat to other forms of television programming until November 1968 when a pig-tailed young lady showed network executives how far sports had come.

At 5:58 P.M., Eastern Standard Time, the Jets were leading the Oakland Raiders 32-29 with only a minute left in the game. Rather than disappoint its prime-time Sunday evening audience waiting to see *Heide*, NBC abandoned the game and cut to the movie with virtually all of the game's viewers thinking the Raiders could never score two touchdowns in less than a minute to win the game. The Raiders, of course, did exactly that and beat the Jets, 43-32. The next day, when the fans learned the true outcome of the game, they overwhelmed NBC with protests.

And then, in 1972 at the Munich Olympics, ABC's Jim McKay calmly reported the triumphs of Mark Spitz and Olga Korbut, and the abomination of hooded Arab terrorists killing eleven innocent Israeli athletes.

In 1979, as a further indication of the country's increasing passion for televised sports, ESPN began broadcasting twenty-four hours a day, and the nation learned to love Canadian slo-pitch softball and ox-pulling.

The next year, it was ABC again, this time broadcasting possibly America's proudest Olympic victory, the United States hockey team defeating the heavily-favored Soviet Union squad, 4-3.

Then, in 1988, television captured perhaps the most impressive Olympics victory ever, Ben Johnson, his right arm raised in false triumph, crossing the 100-yard finish a full half-second ahead of the steroid-free Carl Lewis.

And, in 1989, no longer satisfied with professional and intercollegiate athletics, television invaded the nation's high schools. The cable network SportsChannel American and the National Federation of State High School Associations announced a five-year agreement to broadcast fifty to eighty high school football and basketball games annually for $250,000 per year.

The NCAA's involvement in television dates back to January,

1952, when Walter Byers, the NCAA's first executive director, negotiated a $1.2 million football contract with NBC. Because of the $1.2 million television pool, the NBC deal marked the beginning of the NCAA's and Byers's concurrent reigns of power. Heretofore, the association had always been a money drain. NBC transformed the NCAA into a money-maker, with attendant power and influence.

Byers gave most of the $1.2 million back to the member-schools, but not before taking twenty percent to finance a national office which he promptly moved from Chicago to Kansas City, his hometown.

Byers continued to negotiate the NCAA television rights for the next thirty years, securing contracts of ever-increasing size every three years or so. But as lucrative as these contracts were, a number of the more competitive big-time schools grumbled about their share. Their dissatisfaction blistered into rebellion in 1976 when sixty-six of the biggest football powers, not including the Big Ten and the Pac-10 Conferences, formed the College Football Association to serve as a shadow television negotiating body to the NCAA. Finally, in 1982, the Universities of Oklahoma and Georgia, acting on behalf of the College Football Association, sued the NCAA, alleging that Byers violated anti-trust laws insisting member-schools assign their television right to the NCAA as a condition of membership. Federal Judge Juan C. Burciaga decided in favor of the universities, stating that the NCAA had in fact acted like a classic cartel. Byers appealed, but two years later, the Supreme Court upheld Judge Burciaga's ruling.

Free at last to strike their own deals, big-time universities, through the College Football Association, flooded the networks with a wave of football that far exceeded demand. As a result, what was supposed to be a boom became a bust, and college football ratings and rights fees plunged. Four years after Oklahoma and Georgia won, college football rights fees totaled only $45 million, just half of what Byers had attained when he was the sole negotiator.[7]

In February 1990, Notre Dame startled the world of college athletics. It pulled out of the College Football Association-ABC television deal and negotiated its own pact with NBC for $30 million, three times what the school would have gained from the former one.

In essence, Notre Dame, once the mightiest symbol of rectitude, fell victim to greed and provoked other colleges to seek more lucrative television contracts on their own, as well. From the first deal with NBC, the NCAA's television money has always tempted big-time universities to act in an unseemly manner, a reaction that Water Byers refused to acknowledge. "To blame the NCAA for the few problems of intercollegiate athletics is like blaming the IRS for income tax fraud," Byers once wrote.[8]

But the Burciaga decision marked the end of Walter Byers's reign. After more than three decades of uncompromised rule, Georgia and Oklahoma, two of his own, humiliated the man who had made them all rich twenty-five years before. In 1987, five years before his employment contract was to expire, Byers announced his retirement.

The NCAA believes its NCAA Men's Basketball Championship is, unlike the Super Bowl and World Series, too exciting ever to be anti-climatic. Yet, through overexposure, any television event can lose its popularity. In 1979, there were 108 college basketball games on television. Ten years later, there were 345 televised college basketball games, an increase of over three hundred percent.[9]

The ever-increasing commercial clutter on the NCAA telecasts can also contribute to the public's potential disenchantment with The Final Four.

On the evening of April 2, 1990, in the final game of The Final Four CBS telecast, seventy-three different commercials appeared in a span of 146 minutes. The viewer saw one advertisement for every two minutes of game.

Televised basketball games can be maddening. It is not uncommon at the end of a tight game for coaches to call, say, three time-outs in a row. But the television viewer, rather than sharing in the excitement of these closing minutes, is forced to watch as many as thirty-two commercials over this six-minute span.

Next year, to pay for tripling the rights fees, CBS's commercial clutter will be even greater.

In 1979, sports fans had to wait until the end of March for The Final Four before they could see Magic Johnson square off against

Larry Bird, a delay that made the telecast that much more exciting. But by the end of January of the 1989-90 season, one month into the new season, fans had already seen two freshman sensations, Kenny Anderson of Georgia Tech and Bobby Hurley of Duke, play against each other twice on national television. Georgetown University, another perennial favorite, had appeared on national television four times by the end of January 1990. Eighteen of the top twenty teams appeared five or more times on television before the start of the 1990 Final Four tournament.

On Monday evenings in 1990, ESPN offered a college basketball avalanche. "Big Monday," as it was called, started at 7:30 P.M. with a Big East contest, shifted to the Midwest at 9:30 P.M. to a Big Ten contest, and concluded on the West Coast with a Pac-10 game that usually did not end until 1:30 A.M. the next day.

Dave Gavitt founded the Big East Conference in 1979 while he was the basketball coach of Providence College. Gavitt was struck with the commercial possibilities of forming a league of schools located in eastern television markets that comprised twenty percent of the nation's TV households. Thus, Georgetown (Washington, D.C.), St. John's (New York), Syracuse. Pittsburgh, Connecticut (Hartford), Providence, Seton Hall (New York), Villanova (Philadelphia), and Boston College, all basketball powers, came to be members of the Big East Conference.

Responding to ever-increasing fan interest piqued by television, many of the Big East schools moved their home courts off campus to huge basketball arenas normally used by the NBA and other professional sporting events and teams. The new and bigger arenas heightened the already intense level of competition and commercialism, similarly to what college football experienced at the end of the 19th century when it left the campus for the Polo Grounds and other civic stadiums.

Gavitt's handiwork has made the Big East schools rich from television and gate receipts, so rich that eventually the Big East could begin to encroach upon the popularity of The Final Four. But Gavitt does not believe the NCAA will be threatened. Gavitt said, "The Big East games, or all the other televised games for that matter, do not steal the thunder of The Final Four. On the contrary, they whet the public's appetite for it."[10]

Gavitt better not be wrong because the NCAA's Men's Basketball Championship feeds a lot of hungry institutional mouths.

If present distribution formulas hold, each of the sixty-four teams invited to the 1991 Final Four will receive $601,850. For every subsequent round gained in the six-round tournament, the payoff increases, culminating in $3.3 million apiece to the four teams that reach the semi-finals. In 1970, opening round teams received $8,000, and semi-finalists received $49,500.

Some schools, desperate for this kind of money, have lost their balance and have tried anything and everything to gain an invitation to The Final Four.

Andrew Gaze, an Australian transfer student, helped Seton Hall come within one point of winning the 1989 NCAA's Division I Men's Basketball Championship. Even though it lost the title, Seton Hall became richer by $1.3 million and it also gave the small college some unaccustomed acclaim.

Gaze arrived at Seton Hall's campus in South Orange, New Jersey, in October 1988, a month late, and enrolled in First Aid, Creative Motion, and Ethics.

As the season progressed, Gaze became the team's premier three-point shooter, averaging 13.6 points a game. With his help, Seton Hall eventually posted a 29-5 record and secured an invitation to the NCAA's Men's Basketball Championship.

For reasons that only the NCAA can fathom, Seton Hall became part of the tournament's West regional draw which caused the team to leave New Jersey on Tuesday, March 14, and return exactly three weeks later, on Tuesday, April 4. Because of this road trip, each team member missed, on average, twenty-four classes while wandering from Tucson to Denver to Seattle, before losing in the final game to Michigan, 80-79, in the last three seconds of overtime.

When the team returned to campus on Tuesday, April 4, Gaze did not unpack. On Friday, April 7, Gaze returned to Melbourne where he turned pro to play for his fathers' team.[11]

Seton Hall was not the only school besotted by the NCAA Men's Basketball Championship.

Illinois, another team that made it to The Final Four semi-finals in 1989, allegedly offered two Chicago high school stars $85,000 apiece and new cars for each year they played for Illinois.[12]

The University of Kansas, winner of the 1988 Final Four, was the previous year's egregious example of a Final Four team gone astray.

Although a good team, the 1987-88 Jayhawks were not expected to win the title because they had lost eleven games in the regular season, a disappointment for Larry Brown, Kansas's controversial coach, and Danny Manning, its six-foot-eleven megastar.

Coach Brown arrived at Kansas in 1983. Two years later, Brown lured Danny Manning, a North Carolina high school star, to Kansas by hiring his father as an assistant basketball coach.

By March 1988, although Kansas was not among the nation's top twenty teams, it received a bid to The Final Four on the strength of its showing in the Big Eight Conference. Once in the tournament, Kansas remembered its heritage and defeated Xavier, Murray State, Kansas State, Duke, and the heavily-favored Oklahoma for the championship. It was a victory that accorded Brown and Manning, who also won the College Player of the Year Award, the stature of other Kansas greats.

Shortly after winning The Final Four, Brown announced, as many had predicted, he was leaving the university to coach the San Antonio Spurs in the NBA for $3.5 million over four years.

On June 23, 1986, one week after Larry Brown left Kansas, the NCAA came to Lawrence to investigate alleged recruiting violations.

On November 1, 1988, the NCAA placed Kansas on probation, prohibiting it from post-season play for three years. It was the first time in the fifty-year history of the tournament that a school was barred from defending its title.

The NCAA investigation established that Larry Brown had in fact committed a flagrant recruiting violation. In the summer of 1986, Vincent Askew, a guard for Memphis State, let it be known he wanted to play for another school. In dire need of such a player, Brown attempted to hire Askew by giving him a sign-on bonus amounting to $1,427.12 for clothes, airline tickets and money to pay his grandmother's electric bill.

Askew took the money, but declined the offer and finished out his college career at Memphis State.[13] But The Final Four was not a total loss because Kansas's annual endowment drive garnered $2.5 million in 1988, up from $1.7 million 1987.

The 1990 Final Four champions, UNLV, are banned from defending their title in 1991 because of recruiting violations that occurred thirteen years ago. Thus, scandal has touched the winners and the losers of The Final Four for the last three years.

Winning in intercollegiate athletics is akin, financially, to a dog chasing its tail. The more a university wins, the more money it has. The more money it has, the more money it spends. The more money it spends, the more money it needs. The more money it needs, the more it must win. The NCAA's Men's Basketball Championship intensifies this tail-chase.

The universal complaint among major college athletic officials these days pertains to the difficulty of operating athletic programs without incurring significant financial deficits caused by, so the athletic directors say, the rising cost of education. The rising cost of education provides the big-time athletic departments with the perfect excuse. To the unsuspecting, it allows athletic departments to distance themselves from the problem.

The excuse also permits the NCAA to justify the huge payoffs of the NCAA's Men's Basketball Championship and other post-season tournaments. It suggests this money is the only way a big-time athletic department can operate in the black. Thus, the ever-increasing NCAA purses are actually a service, not a temptation, to all of higher education.

The NCAA's Dick Schultz said recently, "The truth is more athletic departments operate in the red than in the black. True, the schools who sell out large football stadiums do all right, for the most part. But then you have a Michigan, which has a 103,000-seat stadium, projecting a $2.5 million deficit. People don't realize the cost of education has gone up dramatically."

Most people believe that whatever Michigan does, it does correctly. So when Schultz announced the Michigan deficit, no one ever suspected it was the ego of Michigan's now-retired athletic director, and not the rising cost of education, that caused it.

Winners of both the 1989 Rose Bowl and The Final Four, Michigan's twenty-one men's and women's varsity intercollegiate athletic teams usually are Big Ten powerhouses. One hundred and twenty salaried people coach and administer to 600 varsity athletes, 324 of whom attend Michigan on athletic scholarships.

The annual budget of Michigan's athletic department is $20 million, exactly double the budgets of most other big-time universities. Michigan's athletic department also presides over assets worth $225 million, consisting of a brand new $9 million natatorium, the Track and Tennis Building, the Football Services Building, Michigan Stadium, Chrysler Arena (basketball), the hockey rink, an indoor football practice field, golf course, and 125 acres of playing fields.

Football, by far, is Michigan's biggest revenue-producing sport, contributing $12.8 million (sixty-four percent) to the athletic department's annual gross. Basketball is second with $2.4 million, and the remaining $4.8 million comes from hockey, investment income, royalties, fundraising, and various on-campus sports camps. Michigan's biggest expense is payroll, which amounts to $4.2 million per year, up ninety-eight percent since 1978. The increase in salaries has far outpaced inflation because Michigan has hired more and more people each year. Today, Michigan has ten paid assistant football coaches and three paid assistant basketball coaches when, compared to a dozen years ago, Bo Schembechler had three assistants, and Michigan's basketball coach had only a student team manager by his side.

The university spends close to $2.5 million per year on recruiting, an average of $38,460 for every high school recruit who decides to attend Michigan, which is three times more than what it spends on the recruit once he is a student.

Recruiting that one superstar is worth the effort and expense, though, because he can produce a huge windfall for the university. Boston College earned an extra $10 million from Doug Flutie, and Georgetown University benefited by $30 million when Patrick Ewing played for the Hoyas.

Like most other big-time colleges, the Michigan athletic officials complain about the rising cost of education (grants-in-aid), and never about the bigger increases in salaries, recruiting, and equipment and facilities expenses which they are responsible for.[14]

For twenty years, Don Canham served as Michigan's athletic director, a man of boundless self-esteem. Canham fancied himself a modern corporate manager, not an ex-coach. He was forever preaching, "No longer can an athletic director just hire coaches and arrange schedules. He now has a multimillion dollar business he must run like a chief executive officer."

In fact, Canham believed so much in his multimillion dollar

business analogy that he persuaded the powers-to-be at Michigan to form a separate corporation for the athletic department which, similar to Vince Dooley's situation at Georgia, removed him from the scrutiny and authority of the university. Canham organized the corporation so that he became its chief executive officer reporting to a handpicked board of directors. Notably, the president of Michigan was not among them.

In 1989, one year after Canham had retired, Michigan reported the deficit that sent shock waves throughout the NCAA.

When asked to confirm this figure, Bob DeCarolis, Michigan's assistant athletic director for business, said, "That number is highly misleading. If it weren't for Don Canham leaving us holding the bag, we'd be in real good shape."[15]

DeCarolis explained that several years ago, Don Canham became obsessed with building a natatorium which, according to DeCarolis, "no one at Michigan wanted." Rather than wait to finance the new swimming pool facility through a debt-free fundraising process, which is Michigan's usual way to pay for such undertakings, Canham took out a $9 million mortgage entirely on his own. "If it weren't for Canham's half-assed swimming pool, we'd be okay," DeCarolis said. "It's the annual mortgage payment of $875,000, plus the natatorium's annual maintenance expense of $500,000, that caused the deficit."

A month after Michigan's new swimming complex was named the Donald B. Canham Natatorium, its namesake retired.

According to a 1989 survey, fourteen of the top forty-seven big-time schools operated at a deficit, a finding that provoked widespread sympathy within the NCAA community.[15] No one stopped to consider whether the deficits were legitimate, or whether they were caused by athletic directors who, like Don Canham, were looking for immortality.

But rather than reduce recruiting expenses, discontinue separate athletic dormitories, limit scholarships and the number of coaches, all steps that might jeopardize their chances for winning, most athletic directors continue to spend at the same high levels, hoping that an invitation to a post-season tournament or bowl game will bail them out.

Unlike real businesses, however, which must make a profit to survive, athletic directors have the safety net of the university, the endowment fund, or some rich booster. Athletic directors operate under either a false sense of security or a false sense of alarm because they know that, ultimately, coaches and athletic directors get fired for failing to win, not for deficits.

Whenever an athletic director becomes dependent on post-season tournaments to solve his financial problems, he becomes entrapped in a cycle that often leads to even bigger financial problems. They think once they win a bowl game or a basketball tournament, and the payoff is deposited in the bank, this is the way it will always be.

But to get invited to the NCAA's Men's Basketball Championship, "the tournament with the $400,000 free throw," for example, requires a winning record. Winning requires the best players and coaches. The best players and coaches require the best facilities, scholarships and salaries. The best facilities, scholarships and salaries require the best (most) money.

Winning in the era of the new Final Four now takes on a new meaning as it tempts all Division I basketball teams to engage in a winning frenzy to qualify for an invitation. No football bowl game, however prestigious, has ever distributed $76 million to sixty-four teams as the NCAA's Men's Basketball Championship does. No college event has ever been such an overwhelming temptation for corruption.

The NCAA's greatest success, The Final Four, points out the NCAA's greatest flaw: the conflict between its mandate to promote college athletics and its mandate to enforce the virtues of college athletics. Promotion, which pays the bills, has all but vanquished enforcement which maintains integrity.

Despite their receiving more than $143 million from CBS each year, almost triple the amount received three years ago, a survey of seven members of the twelve-person NCAA Executive Committee [17] revealed they thought the CBS windfall should be used to make the NCAA more comfortable, not more effective or more vigilant. "I think we ought to increase the travel expenses for championships," suggested Al Witte, current president of the NCAA.

Every NCAA Executive Committee surveyed did not endorse the notion of enlarging the NCAA staff of fifteen enforcement investigators who currently oversee 250,000 intercollegiate athletes.

Judith Sweet, NCAA secretary-treasurer, said, "With respect to enforcement, we want fair competition throughout the NCAA system. We feel we have that now. There's always room for improvement, of course, and I am more than glad to improve what is already in place, but I don't think more money is necessarily the answer." [18]

According to Dr. Edward Bozik, a member of the NCAA Executive Committee and athletic director of the University of Pittsburgh, "Asking if the NCAA should increase its enforcement resources now that we have all this money implies that college athletics is going to hell in a handbasket, and that it requires a gestapo unit to enforce the rules. That is not true. It's only what the media likes to portray. When a student makes a 3.99 gpa, that is not news. But when an athlete gets arrested, that's front-page event. The vast majority of all that goes on in college athletics today is pretty decent. It's the fault of the media that college athletics have a bad name. I don't believe we need a large enforcement staff. We just increased it anyway." [19]

Bozik was referring to the field investigative staff's increasing from ten to fifteen in 1988.

James Delany, The Big Ten commissioner, said, "We don't need any more enforcers or investigators. We know who the offenders are."

Robert J. Minnix is one of five NCAA directors of enforcement. A lawyer, Minnix joined the NCAA in 1975 at an annual salary of $22,000 per year. In 1989, after fourteen years of service, Minnix was promoted to director, at an annual salary of $35,000 per year. [20] Quite often, Minnix and his associates contend with high-powered law firms specializing in NCAA law that are hired by universities under NCAA investigation for fees of $300,000 and more.

When asked about increasing the resources of the enforcement department, Minnix did not directly contradict any of the NCAA officials. But he did say, "We're only fifteen people. All we do is push paper, and try our best to monitor what goes on out there."

Nor did any NCAA Executive Committee member surveyed feel that the association's budget should be increased to meet the mounting challenges of drug abuse. In 1988-89, the NCAA spent $1.7 million on drug testing and education, just .03 percent of the NCAA's annual revenue. [21]

"One million, seven hundred thousand is a lot of money to spend

on anything. More than we spend on public relations or rent,''[22] said
Louis J. Spry, the NCAA's controller and associate executive director.

The NCAA did manage to buy Dick Schultz a Lear jet, though.

"We bought the plane, second-hand," said NCAA controller
Louis Spry, "I won't tell you what it cost, but it's worth more today
than when we bought it in 1988. Dick felt he needed it because he
travels to schools often in out-of-the-way locales. He claims the
plane saves him enough time that he can spend an extra month in the
office.''[23]

However, Al Witte, NCAA president, thought the plane was a
gift, not a multimillion dollar purchase. "Dick said the Greyhound
Corporation donated the plane to the NCAA, and all we need to do is
pay for the fuel and its maintenance.''[24] Several other NCAA
executive committee members thought the plane was leased.

Buried in the NCAA's 1987-88 annual report was this note: "The
Association purchased an aircraft for a net cost of $1,670,000 with a
note in the amount of $1,750,000 from the United Missouri Bank of
Kansas City." In addition to the purchase price of the plane, the
NCAA also spends $273,074 per year maintaining the plane, includ-
ing the salaries of two pilots.

But the oft-forgotten element in NCAA activities, the athletes,
would like to see a change in their status result from the new CBS
money. As noted earlier, almost fifty percent of big-time college
football and basketball players are black and the majority of these
black athletes are from homes whose median income is less than
$20,000.[25] There is little money for the family, much less for the
incidental expenses incurred while a college student. Summer and
part-time jobs are difficult or impossible to hold because of the time
demands imposed by most big-time football and basketball programs.

Consider Ronnie Harmon, a black football player from Queens,
New York, whose two older brothers played in the NFL.

After starring for Bayside High School, Harmon followed the
example of his brother, Kevin, and enrolled at the University of
Iowa, a Big Ten school of 29,000 students.

As a streetwise kid from New York, it did not take long for
Harmon to learn that his coach, Hayden Fry, earned close to
$345,678 per year in salary, television and radio show fees, shoe

endorsements, low-interest mortgages, annuities, country club memberships and a car.

Harmon knew that six times each fall, the Iowa football stadium was packed with 67,000 fans who had come to watch him and his teammates play. Harmon also knew there were several million other fans watching him on television, which advertisers paid big sums to reach. All told, Harmon and his 124 teammates generated about $7.8 million net per year for the University of Iowa.

Hayden Fry, Iowa's fiery coach who criticized his boss, President Rawlings, when the latter advocated freshman ineligibility, was forever referring to the job each member of the team had to perform. Ronnie Harmon put in over thirty-three hours a week at his job, playing, practicing and studying football, nearly three times the hours he spent in class. Measuring his job output in dollars and cents, Harmon generated $125,000 per year for Iowa. In return, he received a full athletic grant-in-aid worth $13,546 per year which covered his room, board, tuition, books and miscellaneous student fees.

Harmon also thought about security. If Coach Fry, for whatever reason, were to lose his job, he would be protected by a severance agreement worth half a million dollars. Harmon knew that if he lost his job because of injury, he'd leave Iowa with nothing.

Knowing that Iowa made nearly $450,000 profit on him over the course of his four-year career, Harmon had a difficult time accepting the fact he only had $25 per week for expenses, including clothes, dates, laundry and trips home to New York.

What happened, of course, was that Ronnie Harmon, and the many players like him, got money, somehow.

The summer before his junior year, Harmon signed a secret contract with an agent named Norby Walters. In return, Walters over the next two years loaned Harmon $57,000 against his future earnings as a pro.

Walters had been a booking agent for Dionne Warwick, Miles Davis and other black entertainers of similar marquee appeal for ten years before Lloyd Bloom, who looks like a scowling Li'l Abner, convinced him there was more money to be made in sports. In July 1984, Walters and Bloom formed a partnership called World Sports & Entertainment, Inc., and set out to sign black college athletes, the poorer the better.

But when they first started out, Walters and Bloom frequently encountered prospects who, as early as their sophomore years, had already signed agent contracts in violation of NCAA regulations. In return, these agents would advance cash to their clients in the form of loans against their future pro earnings. Leigh Steinberg, a California agent, estimates that twenty-five to fifty percent of all college athletes headed for the pros violate the NCAA regulation pertaining to agents.[26]

Walters and Bloom quickly adapted to the realities of doing business in college athletics, and perfected their own recruiting techniques. Besides being fluent in street jive, Walters would drop $50 bills, one by one, at the feet of a college athlete as an inducement to sign. If that failed, Walters would fly a prospect to Los Angeles or New York to mingle and socialize with his entertainment clients. In a short time, Norby Walters and Lloyd Bloom had signed an impressive roster of clients.

As successful as Walters and Bloom were, they had problems with a few greedy clients. About a dozen athletes who had been on WS&E's payroll as sophomores and juniors, switched to other agents in their senior years and then balked at repaying Walters and Bloom the money the two had advanced them.

Enraged, Walters and Bloom tried to dissuade the defectors with threats. The two agents said that their silent partner, Michael Franzene, an alleged member of a notorious crime family, would break the legs of any clients who either reneged on his contract or failed to repay his loans. When these threats did not persuade six of WS&E's former clients to return, Walters sued them for breach of contract.

Then, in March 1987, Kathe Clements, an associate of agent Steve Zucker, a competitor to Walters and Bloom, was slashed and beaten in her Skokie, Illinois, office by a man wearing a ski mask. Zucker had just signed three of Walters' former clients.

Shortly thereafter, a group of prominent universities, Michigan, Michigan State, Notre Dame, Purdue and Iowa among them, brought federal racketeering and fraud charges against Walters, Bloom and eight of their own athletes.

The suit contended that Walters and Bloom defrauded the universities when they signed the eight athletes to secret agent contracts, thereby rendering the athletes ineligible since they were no longer amateurs in the eyes of the NCAA. The suit also contended that the eight athletes defrauded the universities by continuing to accept scholarship benefits when they knew their agent relationships violated their amateur status and made them ineligible.

The defense retaliated by attempting to demonstrate it was Walters and Bloom who were wronged by the greed and deceitfulness of the universities and their intercollegiate athletic system. The defense showed that the universities had been treating the athletes as full-fledged professionals all along, admitting them to play football, but not to educate them.

The defense attorneys called Ronnie Harmon to the stand. Harmon told the courtroom he took Watercolor Painting, Billiards, Slo-pitch Softball, Recreational Leisure, and Ancient Athletics. Harmon also revealed that he failed to graduate from Iowa because the school allowed him to "cherrypick" the easier courses without concern for the standard requirement that each course should lead toward a specific and recognized degree.

Defense attorney Dan Webb then called Fred Mims, Iowa's assistant athletic director for academic services, to the stand and asked, "Since Ronnie Harmon violated the NCAA regulation requiring athletes to be in good academic standing and to be making satisfactory progress towards a degree, and since he also violated the Big Ten's requirement that all fourth-year athletes have at least a 1.85 grade point average, how could the University of Iowa allow Harmon to play football his senior year?"

Mims could not answer the question.

Walters was found guilty and sentenced to five years in prison and Bloom to three years. Later, the United States Court of Appeals for the Seventh Circuit reversed both convictions, citing an error by the judge. Ronnie Harmon now plays for the San Diego Chargers in the NFL, as do many former WS&E clients. Nothing happened to Iowa or any other universities involved in the case.

Over a three-year period, Walters and Bloom, with the aid of cash and the threat of mafia violence, signed almost sixty players from the thirty top schools in the country. In all that time, not one coach, athletic director, university administrator or NCAA official ever noticed or became suspicious of a flamboyant man handing out over $800,000 to sixty high-visibility and underprivileged athletes who immediately converted the cash into BMW's, gold jewelry and a life of ostentatious luxury in small towns like Ames, Iowa; Ann Arbor, Michigan; South Bend, Indiana; and Columbus, Ohio.

"You think we were the first?" Walters asked, after his conviction. "There are 20,000 agents who, for fifteen years now, have been illegally chasing kids bound for the NFL and the NBA. Nobody noticed this before?"[27]

Many people believe the way to solve situations like Ronnie Harmon's is to pay college athletes for their services. Red Smith wrote, "There is something scandalous about a college collecting hundreds of thousands of dollars in gate receipts and paying off the help with a bowl of rice."[28]

Coaches like Bobby Knight of Indiana, Dean Smith of North Carolina, and Mike Krzyzewski of Duke all want athletes to receive more money. They argue the athletes have never been amateurs anyway since they already receive compensation in the form of scholarships.

But others, most notably Ira Michael Heyman, the chancellor of the University of California-Berkeley, say that to pay a college athlete "would be the last and most dangerous concession to those people in intercollegiate athletics today who are not coaches and educators, but rather are promoters and producers of mass entertainment. Professional athletes get paid, student-athletes do not. Collegiate athletes play for institutions of higher learning, not the San Francisco Giants."[29]

As it stands now, while the NCAA prohibits athletes from receiving even "laundry" money, the association feels perfectly free to dole out $100 million payouts to million-dollar coaches based on how well the impoverished athletes play.

Faced with these contradictions, it is understandable why thirty-one percent of a sample of present and former professional football players admitted accepting illicit payments when they played in college. Fifty-three percent saw nothing wrong with the practice.[30]

College athletes have even more restrictive per diem allowances. According to David Berkoff, Harvard swimmer and a member of the NCAA's Student-Athlete Advisory Committee, "We receive $5 per day meal allowance. It's ridiculous. We have to eat pizza or [at] McDonald's which is terrible for your training."[31]

But the average per diem for both the NCAA staff and volunteer officials is $650.[32] When traveling on official NCAA business, personnel, staff and members may chose their own hotel accommodations and decide whether to fly first-class. Judging from the size of their per diems, not many choose coach.

Unlike the numerous NCAA rules and restrictions limiting an athlete's finances, there are no such restraints to what college coaches can earn.

To the resentment of most university communities, coaches on any big-time campus regularly make three to four times more than the university president does.

Lefty Driesell hired noted lawyer E. Bennett Williams to negotiate his ten-year $3 million pact with the University of Maryland which included a local television show, and endorsements for insurance, shoes and a local haberdashery.

Kentucky hired former New York Knicks coach Rick Pitino at $1 million per year as part of its widely-publicized effort to de-emphasize and reform Kentucky basketball. Three months before, Eddie Sutton, Pitino's predecessor, was forced to resign. Sutton left Kentucky under a cloud, but $650,000 richer because of his severance agreement.

When David Stern, commissioner of the NBA, learned that Pitino left the NBA for $1 million, he said, "I think that the University of Kentucky and the NBA are in the same business of making money from basketball. But I think we're a lot more honest with our approach.[33]

According to the American Association of University Professors, the average salary of a professor at a four-year institution is $50,420. According to Joe Vicinsin, executive director of the National Association of Basketball Coaches, the top seventy-five NCAA Division I basketball coaches average $195,467 in total income, which he felt was justified. Vicinsin said, "In 1988-1989, one out of every six Division I basketball coaches lost his [job], a turnover rate no doubt increased by the pressure to get into the NCAA's Men's Basketball Championship. Coaches don't get tenure or the security of a regular faculty member so they deserve to make more."[34]

As Tom Penders of the University of Texas once said, "Pressure is making $50,000 and having your athletic director expect you to compete against Michigan."

Besides Pitino's $1 million deal, other coaches have Wall Street incomes, too.

Before Pitino, Notre Dame football coach Lou Holtz was believed to be the top earner among college coaches. Besides his salary, and money from his television show, Holtz has income from speaking engagements. Holtz booked thirty-two appearances at $18,000 apiece in 1989 for a total of $576,000.

Georgetown coach John Thompson earns $317,000 in salary, compared to Georgetown's president, Rev. Leo O'Donovan, S.J., who earns $180,000. In addition Thompson has an endorsement contract with Nike worth $200,000 per year, which is nine times greater than what Nike normally pays a college coach.

Nike's contract with Thompson explains why, in December 1989, the Georgetown players suddenly appeared on a nationally televised game wearing uniforms with only the Nike logo emblazoned on their chest. Anyone watching the game could have easily concluded that Alonzo Mourning and his teammates played for Nike, not Georgetown. Whatever extra money the shoe manufacturer paid for such valuable television exposure went to Thompson, not Georgetown or the players.[35] All told, Thompson earns nearly $700,000 per year, a suitable income for a man who proclaimed to the NCAA's 1988 convention, "I'm a capitalist, and I'm in this for the money. Who in this room isn't?"

In March of 1989, a week before the NCAA's Men's Basketball Championship began, Bill Frieder, the University of Michigan's basketball coach, announced he was resigning after the tournament to accept a position at Arizona State with a guaranteed annual income of $750,000.

Bo Schembechler, Frieder's boss and Michigan's athletic director and football coach, fired him on the spot, stating contemptuously, "Only a Michigan man is going to coach the Wolverines in The Final Four." Nine months later, Schembechler left Michigan to become the president of the Detroit Tigers.

Pat Dye became Auburn's football coach in 1981, and negotiated an imaginative incentive. If he stayed at Auburn for more than thirteen years, which meant if he won enough games to last that long, Auburn would pay off his $400,000 home mortgage. Having recruited Bo Jackson, and beaten Alabama, Dye has nothing to worry about.

Some big-time coaches can earn upwards of $250,000 annually

from weekly television and radio shows, whose biggest sponsors are local beer distributors.

Severance or termination packages have taken on a special meaning in the past several years, particularly when they have been invoked by coaches who have lost their jobs because they have violated NCAA regulations. When the Texas A&M football program narrowly missed the NCAA's death penalty, Jackie Sherrill, the coach, was disgraced and lost his job. The university gave Sherrill $542,000 in cash, in addition to paying off his $140,000 home mortgage. The payments went directly to Sherrill's corporation, J.S.J.S. Inc. of Pennsylvania.

Jim Valvano, North Carolina State's basketball coach, resigned after ABC News alleged a point-shaving scheme took place while he was coaching. He left North Carolina with a settlement worth over $500,000, and was then hired by ABC Sports for $900,000 over three years.

Two years after Len Bias died, Lefty Driesell left Maryland to become James Madison's basketball coach at a salary which was $30,000 less than what he was earning at Maryland. Driesell's termination agreement with Maryland required the university to pay him the $30,000 difference for the next eight years.

Other perquisites for coaches include the use of a car, expense accounts, country club memberships, multimillion dollar life insurance policies and retirement annuities, and local retailers supplying them with free clothes or other goods and services.

Many athletic directors believe football coaches are worth every penny they get. Bobby Bowden, Florida State University's football coach, makes $350,000 per year, a sum Hootie Ingram, former athletic director at FSU, vigorously defended. "Bobby Bowden was the reason the financial picture was as good as it was, and he was justly rewarded for that."[36]

CHAPTER 9

Recruiting

For the people of Texas, football teaches the most important lesson of life, how to be a real Texas man. But to the alumni of Southern Methodist University, football is even more important. It validates their business and amatory triumphs when SMU wins, and it stirs up life-long insecurities when it loses, especially to Texas and Texas A&M.

Founded in 1915, SMU's 5,500 undergraduates are virtually all white, Protestant, inclined to party, and personify the school's nickname, "Rolexville,"

SMU's Georgian campus, a studied replication of an Ivy League school, is located in a hilltop enclave populated by families whose surnames appear on many campus buildings.

Although owned by the United Methodist Church, nearly two dozen millionaires used to run the university like they still run Dallas. No meetings, no memos. Just make the decision, and get on with it.

From 1964 to 1975, SMU's once-great football team had deteriorated badly, causing alumni fears to bubble over. In January 1976, in an attempt to restore SMU football to its former glory, a special committee of alumni, all members of SMU's Board of Governors, bypassed the school's president, James Zumberge, and hired Ron

Meyer, the head football coach of the University of Nevada, Las Vegas.

The board of governors appointed Ron Meyer because he had just finished turning the woeful UNLV football team into a contender in much the same way many of these men had made their first million, through intuition, shrewdness and the courage to go against the grain and take radical action.

After seeing what he had to work with on the first day of spring practice in 1976, Meyer simply remarked, "If they can't play, I can't coach." It was a terse way of announcing a new era of SMU recruiting which would be every bit as ambitious and as pragmatic as the alumni were.

That first year, Meyer and his assistants crisscrossed Texas, exhorting seventeen-year-old all-stars to believe their futures lay in the resurrection of SMU football. Meyer was good, but not as good as Texas, Texas A&M, and Houston.

The next year, 1977, knowing he had to be more convincing, Meyer persuaded selected SMU alumni to establish a pay-for-play fund that would bankroll the school's future football stars. A committee consisting of Meyer and several alumni would decide how much, if anything, to pay each player. Thereafter, the task of actually distributing the cash fell to an assistant coach.

One of Meyer's typical donors was Sherwood Blount, a twenty-nine-year-old alumnus who had played linebacker for SMU in the late Sixties. Another donor was Bobby Folsom, former mayor of Dallas. Both men, real estate millionaires, were thrilled to tithe the SMU football team.

As Meyer's recruiting fund grew, so did SMU's recruiting success. By 1978, the Mustangs were attracting first-rate Texas high school stars and they beat Rice, Baylor and Texas Christian University that year. As a result, attendance shot up to 52,000 per game, an increase of nearly a 100 percent, and SMU's endowment funds did just about as well. Shortly thereafter, SMU abandoned its campus football facility, Ownby Stadium, in favor of Texas Stadium, the home of the Dallas Cowboys.

In 1979, the Meyer fund bankrolled even more outstanding talent, including running back Eric Dickerson, the future NFL great. Meyer had secured the inside track with Dickerson by courting

Dickerson's mother, grandmother and aunt. But on the eve of National Letter of Intent signing day, the day Dickerson was to formally commit to SMU, Texas A&M provided him with a brand new Pontiac TransAm. That same day, another school's recruiter arrived at Eric's home carrying a suitcase that contained $50,000 in cash. Dickerson kept the TransAm but rejected the last-minute offers in favor of SMU's, which had suddenly gotten richer.[1]

Another member of SMU's 1979 recruiting class was Houston's Craig James, now a standout for the New England Patriots, who teamed up with Dickerson to form The Pony Express, an SMU legend that rivals Doak Walker.

A year later, 1980, SMU beat Texas 20-6, and SMU football's rise from the ashes was confirmed. In fact, from that day until 1985, Southern Methodist won the coveted Southwest Conference title three times and ranked in the Top Ten for four years running.

Impressed with SMU's resurgence, UCLA recruited James Zumberge to be its president in May 1980. His replacement was L. Donald Shields, president of Cal State-Fullerton, who looked like a door-to-door Fuller brush salesman.

In the fall of 1980, aroused by rumors, President Shields investigated allegations that Sherwood Blount, one of Meyer's original payroll masters, was paying football players to come to SMU. When his investigation confirmed the allegations, Shields reported his findings in writing to Robert Stewart III, chairman of SMU's Board of Governors, and to Edward Cox, chairman of Cox Gas & Oil and of SMU's Board of Trustees. Both men simply ignored the report.

Eight months later, in February 1981, Bob Hitch, a Mississippian, was named SMU athletic director.

Several months later, responding to the same rumors that caused Shields to act the preceding fall, the NCAA announced it was beginning a full-scale investigation to determine if SMU was indeed hiring its football team. But after investigating eighty-one allegations of recruiting improprieties, including charges that SMU alumni had paid two SMU sorority members $400 to provide a weekend of sex for high school prospects, the NCAA investigators could only substantiate a few minor charges. An assistant coach, for example, played racquetball with a recruiting prospect, an event that constituted an illegal workout. The NCAA penalized the Mustangs with two years' probation, including a one-year ban on bowl games and television appearances.

In 1981, SMU compiled a 10-1 record and the AP ranked the Mustangs fifth in the nation.

On January 15, 1982, after six wildly successful years at SMU, Ron Meyer was named head coach of the New England Patriots. President Shields and athletic director Bob Hitch hired Bobby Collins from Southern Mississippi University to replace Meyer.

In 1982, the first year Collins coached Meyer's recruits, the Mustangs went 11-0-1, and beat Pitt, quarterbacked by Dan Marino, 7-3, in the Cotton Bowl.

After the 1982 season, the alumni, led by Sherwood Blount, virtually took over SMU's recruiting. It seems that Coach Collins, accustomed to Southern Mississippi's recruiting ways, was still getting used to the Meyer system.

By February 1983, the alumni had managed to recruit four *Parade* magazine All-Americans. It was the most talented SMU class of recruits ever, better even than Dickerson's and James's class.

In March 1983, the NCAA sent SMU its sixth letter in eighteen years announcing yet another investigation of recruiting violations. Someone had told the NCAA that Ronald Morris, one of the *Parade* All-Americans, was offered a ''signing'' bonus of $4,000 and a monthly salary of $400 by two Dallas alumni.

On May 15, 1983, Bill Clements, who had just been defeated after serving one term as governor of Texas, replaced Bobby Stewart as chairman of SMU's Board of Governors. Clements, a crony of George Bush, had been an Under Secretary of Defense in the Nixon and Ford administrations.

A year later, *The Dallas Times Herald* revealed that eighteen SMU football players had purchased Datsun 280ZX's and Datsun 300ZX's from Dallas auto dealer W. O. Bankston, an SMU alumnus and friend of Sherwood Blount.

In 1984, the Mustangs had a 9-2 season, and beat Notre Dame in Hawaii's Aloha bowl.

In February 1985, Sherwood Blount admitted to the NCAA that he had offered a Pennsylvania prospect, Sean Stopperich, a $5,000 signing bonus, a new Datsun 300ZX, $300 per month salary, a rent-free apartment for the Stopperich family, and help in getting Mr. Stopperich, who was unemployed at the time, a job in Dallas.

Several months later, SMU president Donald Shields banned Sherwood Blount and eight other alumni from having any contact or involvement with the school's football program.

On April 26, 1985, the NCAA's Committee on Infractions met in Kansas City to hear the results of the NCAA twenty-five-month investigation of SMU.

President Donald Shields presented SMU's case. Shields blamed most of the infractions on alumni-booster Sherwood Blount who acted solely on his own accord. Shields swore that no one from the university was aware, much less approved, of Sherwood Blount's actions.

Bill Clements, chairman of SMU's Board of Governors, also appeared before the NCAA's Committee on Infractions and personally guaranteed there would be no more SMU recruiting violations.

The NCAA Committee on Infractions found SMU guilty of some fifty recruiting violations associated with the recruitment of Sean Stopperich. The NCAA withheld the actual penalty pending an appeal to the NCAA Council, the overseer of the Committee on Infractions.

Later that summer, Bill Clements announced he would seek a second term as Texas governor in the election of November 1986. He agreed to remain chairman of SMU's Board of Governors, however.

SMU's president, Donald Shields, presented the school's appeal to the NCAA council. Two days later, the NCAA announced SMU's penalties, which consisted of losing forty-five football scholarships over two years, a one-year television ban, a two-year bowl ban, and the demotion of the staff recruiting coordinator. Both Shields and Clements, in ensuing media interviews, insisted the violations were committed only by an enthusiastic but errant member of the Mustang Club, whom they had already banned from SMU's recruiting process. "We are tired of this monkey business," Clements proclaimed.[2]

Three months later, Bill Clements defeated the incumbent Texas governor, Mark White. During his four-year administration, White had alienated more than a few voters by championing the "no pass, no play" law which requires Texas high school students to pass all their courses before they can participate in sports.

Within days of the election, David Stanley, a former SMU

lineman, appeared on Channel 8, a Dallas ABC television affiliate. Stanley admitted he received a $25,000 signing bonus and $750 per month thereafter as an inducement to attend SMU. Channel 8 then segued to a segment taped earlier that day where sportscasters met with SMU athletic director Bob Hitch, football coach Bobby Collins and assistant athletic director Henry Lee Parker on the school's campus. When asked to identify an envelope addressed to Stanley that had allegedly been used to convey a cash payment, all three SMU athletic officials denied it was their handwriting. Channel 8 then showed a handwriting expert testifying that the handwriting on the "cash envelope" was Harry Lee Parker's.

The program, toward the end, showed Stanley taking a lie detector test, which he passed.

A week later, L. Donald Shields, SMU's president, resigned.

Hitch, Parker and Collins resigned shortly thereafter. The three men walked away with $863,013 in severance money.[3]

On February 25, 1987, at a jam-packed press conference held in SMU's student center, a pallid and sweating David Berst, head of NCAA's enforcement department, revealed the association's findings of its two-and-a-half-year investigation. All told, from September 1985 to December 1986, thirteen SMU football players had received $61,000 in payments ranging from $50 to $750 per month. The room gasped. Up until then, people suspected that only David Stanley and maybe one or two other players were on salary.

In view of these repeated and egregious offenses, Berst announced, the NCAA Committee on Infractions invoked the death penalty, a new and much harsher punishment for repeat offenders. SMU was prohibited from participating in intercollegiate football for the 1987 season, and limited to seven away games for the 1988 season.

Members of the press were disappointed that the names of the paid players, and the names of those paying them, were not divulged. This compromise was struck, Berst explained, so that all the facts, however anonymous, could come to light.

In the question and answer period that followed, Channel 8's John Sparks, the man who first broke the SMU scandal, asked the school's interim president, William Stallcup, "Did the university's investigation determine that Texas governor Bill Clements participated in the decision to pay these football players?"

Stallcup replied, "There is no evidence that Governor Clements was involved."[4]

As a curious adjunct to the death penalty, the NCAA ruled that SMU players could transfer immediately to other schools. By 8:00 A.M. the next day, 180 college football coaches had flown through the night and were now clustered in the gym like vultures, recruiting SMU football players. Forty of SMU's fifty-six scholarship football players found homes at such schools as Houston, Texas, Texas Southern, UCLA, Michigan State, Auburn, Oklahoma, Georgia, Penn State, Illinois and Hawaii. Many coaches, it is believed, violated NCAA recruiting regulations that day.

On March 4, 1987, at a press conference in Austin, Governor Bill Clements revealed he had authorized the continued payments of SMU football players' salaries. He went on to admit that as many as twenty-six players, not thirteen, were involved in the scheme, and that at least eight members of SMU's Board of Governors understood what was going on, and that the remaining board members accepted in good faith what he had done.

Clements rationalized his actions by saying, "We made a considered judgment decision over several months that the commitments had been made, and in the interest of the institution, the boys, their families and to comply with the NCAA that the program [paying players] would be phased out."[5]

When he learned of Clements's comments, David Berst said, "To imply the NCAA condoned winding down the payments is absurd. Mr. Clements intentionally misled us. If he's typical of the people who are in charge, then there really isn't any hope for integrity in college athletics."[6]

When Mark White, who was defeated by Clements in November, heard of Clements's confession, White said, "Had these things come to light just a few months back, Clements would never have beaten me."

On March 20, 1987, SMU's twenty-one-member Board of Governors was abolished.

The Special Bishops Committee of the South Central Jurisdiction of the United Methodist Church on June 19, 1987, censured the following men for participating in and then covering up the scheme to pay its football players: Texas Governor Bill Clements, former chairman of SMU's Board of Governors; Robert H. Stewart, III,

CEO of First International Bancshares and former chairman of SMU's Board of Governors; Edward Cox, chairman of Cox Gas & Oil and former chairman of SMU's Board of Trustees; William Hutchinson, chairman of Texas Gas and Oil Corp. and former chairman of SMU's Board of Governors; Paul Corley, former oil company executive and member of SMU's Board of Governors; Bobby Folsom, former mayor of Dallas and member of SMU's Board of Governors; L. Donald Shields, former SMU president; William Stallcup, interim SMU president; Leon Bennett, SMU's vice president for Legal Affairs; and Robert Thomas, SMU's attorney for the NCAA investigation.

On May 17, 1989, Bill Clements signed a Texas law that makes it a felony to bribe high school athletes to attend college. The crime carries a jail sentence of two to five years, and a fine of $5,000.

The same year SMU received the death penalty, five of its eight Southwest Conference rivals were placed on probation by the NCAA for recruiting violations. Texas Tech received a three-year probation from the NCAA for sequestering a prospect in a motel four days before National Letter of Intent signing day, and providing him with prostitutes. In 1988, Texas A&M terminated its football coach Jackie Sherrill because a former player, George Smith, told *The Dallas Morning News* that Sherrill had paid him to lie to NCAA enforcement representatives who were investigating the Aggies for recruiting violations.

But the SMU death penalty did little to dissuade other colleges from violating recruiting regulations.

In February 1990, the NCAA sent the University of Illinois a letter of inquiry, its third in six years, containing these allegations committed by its basketball team, a team that reached The Final Four in 1989.

1. During East St Louis high school star LaPhonso Ellis's official paid visit in September 1987, Illinois assistant coach Jimmy Collins offered him $5,000 to sign with the school, and an additional $5,000 for each year he played for the Illini— $20,000 over four years.

2. During that same visit, Collins gave Ellis's student host $140 to spend on the recruit. (Regulations permit $40.)

3. On more than one occasion, Collins promised Ellis a car if he enrolled at the university. Collins also offered to provide financial assistance toward the purchase of a new home for Ellis's mother.

4. In the spring of 1987, during his junior year of high school, Ellis asked Collins for $200 to $300 so he could attend a school prom. Ellis later received it from a third party at the prom.

5. In the fall of 1987, a recruit received a pair of Converse basketball shoes and an Adidas sweatshirt from Collins.

6. During a visit to Champlain in January 1989, Collins offered Chicago prospect Deon Thomas $80,000 and a new Chevy Blazer if he signed with Illinois.

7. In January 1989, Collins made an off-campus recruiting contact with Thomas, while Thomas was eating breakfast at Aunt Sonya's Restaurant in Champaign. (NCAA regulations permitted only on-campus, in-person recruiting contacts during January 1989. The NCAA apparently found that Aunt Sonya's was off-campus.)

8. In late November or early December 1988, Collins offered financial assistance to Thomas's grandmother, with whom he lived, if she wanted to move to a more comfortable and secure building. When Thomas told Collins that his grandmother did not want to move, Collins then offered to have her current residence refurbished and made more secure.

9. Members of the university's coaching staff visited Thomas more than once during the week of April 3, 1989. (NCAA regulations permit coaches to visit prospects only once during any given week.)

10. During the 1985-86 academic year, Collins made a recruiting contact with a high school junior. (NCAA regulations restrict recruiting contacts to prospects who have completed their junior year.)

11. Collins conduct was unethical, and he demonstrated "a knowing and willful effort to violate NCAA legislation."[7]

All the while Illinois assistant coach Jimmy Collins was allegedly offering mega-bribes to high school basketball stars, Stanley Ikenberry, president of the Illinois University system, served as chairman of the American Council on Education, a group of university leaders pressing for college athletics reform. He also was appointed to the NCAA's Presidents Commission.

And if that were not embarrassing enough, on the same day the NCAA enforcement department announced the Illini violations, Dick Schultz, the association's executive director, introduced Illinois University's athletic director John Mackovic at a special NCAA seminar for a group of the nation's top sportswriters and sportscasters. Mackovic and other big-time athletic officials spoke about recent successes in cleaning up college athletics at Illinois and elsewhere.

The envy of any college football recruiter is Notre Dame University, the once small Indiana college that Knute Rockne and The Four Horsemen transformed into the nation's ideal of what a Catholic college should be.

Notre Dame's football prowess dates back to 1887, but certainly no day contributed more to its legend than November 10, 1928, when Notre Dame faced Army. The gnarly, broken-nosed Rockne, the Daniel Webster of lockerroom oratory, pleaded with his hopelessly outmatched team to beat Army: "Let's win this one for The Gipper." George Gipp, a Notre Dame football player who died eight years before, was, according to Notre Dame legend, the greatest college football player who ever lived. Rockne was so demonically convincing that Notre Dame did in fact beat Army that day, 12-6, a victory that helped elect Ronald Reagan to the presidency fifty-two years later.

One of the men responsible for Notre Dame's excellence was Rockne's boss, Father Matthew Walsh, president of Notre Dame from 1922 to 1928. Father Walsh was courageous and crafty enough to keep Rockne's considerable ego and ambitions in check so that the players he recruited were capable of receiving Notre Dame degrees as well as All-America honors. While keeping Rockne in line, Walsh also brooked no interference from other university contingents, most notably alumni and trustees. Walsh's tough stance precluded a demi-god coach and/or a football-loving alumni from ever undermining his objective of producing winning football teams without sacrificing academics and without cheating.

Establishing this militaristic chain of command was Walsh's legacy to his successors, the most famous of whom was Father Theodore Hesburgh, who ruled the school for thirty-five years beginning in 1952.

An uncommonly handsome and congenial man, Father Hesburgh thrived in the limelight of the football team. Within a remarkably short period of time, Father Hesburgh became the nation's celebrity priest, known to Presidents from Eisenhower to Nixon as "my good friend, Father Ted."

Father Hesburgh enhanced Notre Dame's already accomplished public relations skills, and the Indiana school with the golden dome became a national treasure like baseball, *Time* magazine, hot dogs and Father Flanagan's Boys Town. Over the course of Father Hesburgh's administration, seven Notre Dame football players won the Heisman Trophy, and Father Hesburgh himself received 116 honorary degrees, enough to make the *Guinness Book of World Records.*

But Father Hesburgh was not just a dilettante glad-hander who sat back and basked in the glory that his charm induced. Hesburgh is a man of conviction who once was fired by Richard Nixon from the Civil Rights Commission because he refused to agree with the President on a key issue.

Like his predecessor, Father Walsh, Father Hesburgh did not take kindly to anyone who would undermine his authority. "When I was president, I was president," Father Hesburgh said. "I used the power I was given. But everytime we hired a new coach, I had the final word on whether we hired him or not. During that five-minute interview, I would say, 'Do you know our rules? Are you prepared to adhere to them meticulously? You have five years on this job, at the very least. During this time, you can lose every game we play, and you'll still be the coach. You maintain the integrity of the school, and I'll keep people off your back. But you break one rule, and I'll have you out of here by nightfall.' "[8]

Father Hesburgh, now retired, was speaking from his office on the thirteenth floor of Hesburgh Library, the tallest building on campus. The library's entire south exterior wall side is occupied by the astonishing "Touchdown Jesus" mural, a giant mosaic of Jesus

Christ, struck in a Rockne-like pose, exhorting the Irish on to yet another victory.

Father Hesburgh continued, "In the eighteen years Digger Phelps has been the basketball coach here, every player, 100 percent, has graduated. And with respect to our football players, many of whom are blacks who were insufficiently educated in high school, we still graduate ninety-four percent of them."[9] By comparison, most of Notre Dame's opponents graduate less than twenty-three percent percent of their players.

"Most of our football and basketball players today are predominantly black who come from urban high schools of dubious quality," Hesbugh said. "These athletes are obviously academically disadvantaged, a condition that can be exacerbated by their concentration on athletics while in college. But we attempt to make sure they receive the appropriate attention through a program known as the Preparation for Life. We've had a good success rate with minorities, and that's why we are good recruiters."[10]

But as rival coaches are quick to point out, another reason Notre Dame has become such a good recruiter rests on the fact the Fighting Irish appear on television more frequently than Johnny Carson. All twelve of Notre Dame's regular-season games are televised, ten of them nationally. "My god, who couldn't recruit like Notre Dame if you had their television contract?" asked Vince Dooley, Georgia's athletic director.[11]

Notre Dame's dependence on television perhaps explains why it unexpectedly broke ranks with a consortium of other big-time schools in 1990 to strike its own, more lucrative deal with NBC directly.

"It was nothing but greed," Vince Dooley said. "And it's ironic that Notre Dame would be the ones to break away like that since, as recently as three years ago when the Southeastern Conference wanted to go out on its own, they were the ones always telling the rest of us to stick together."

Each year, of the 150,000 high school seniors who play basketball, only 680, or one out of every 221 high school senior basketball players, receive scholarships to play big-time college basketball. In football, of the 265,000 seniors playing high school football, only 2,253, one out of every 118 high school senior football players, receive scholarships.[12]

These odds explain why recruiting violations represent sixty to seventy percent of all NCAA infractions.

What follows are samples of recruiting regulations, rewritten so a lay person might understand them, that demonstrate the folly of the NCAA's attempt to do the impossible: legislate morality through a bewildering, petty and ever-changing set of rules.

Virtually any athlete, no matter how young, may be recruited.

When Indiana whiz, Damon Bailey, was in the eighth grade, Indiana coach Bobby Knight said Bailey was a better point guard than any playing for Indiana at the time. Almost two years later, as a fourteen-year-old high school sophomore, Bailey signed a National Letter of Intent to attend Indiana in the fall of 1990. Bailey finished his high school basketball with a career total of 3,134 points, an Indiana state record, and led his team to the Indiana high school state championship.

Only those coaches listed on an institution's official NCAA coaching roster may recruit. No alumnus or booster may be involved in any aspect of recruiting, including telephoning and corresponding with prospects.

Obviously, this rule was passed in 1987 after the SMU incident. Each year, approximately 1,133 Division I-A football coaches recruit 2,253 high school seniors, and approximately 1,465 Division I basketball coaches recruit 680 high school seniors. The odds inevitably lead to abuses and ego-inflated prospects.

A coach may not bribe a prospect, or his family, to attend an NCAA school. Forms of bribes include, but are not restricted to, cash, clothing, merchandise or equipment; co-signing loans; providing loans to a prospect's relatives or friends; free or reduced-cost services and rentals; and employing a prospect's relatives.

Dale Brown, basketball coach of LSU, does not hire a prospect's relatives, but he does hire their high school coaches. From 1974 to 1988, Dale Brown hired four high school coaches, all of whom brought their high school stars with them to Baton Rouge.[13]

Georgia Tech basketball coach Bobby Cremins gave a full scholarship to Giuseppe Liantonio, a student manager for New York

City's Archbishop Malloy High School basketball team, the school that the highly acclaimed Kenny Anderson attended. In exchange for the scholarship, Liantonio gave Cremins regular reports on Anderson.[14]

A college head coach may contact a prospect in person only after he has completed his junior year in high school, but phone calls and letters are permitted at anytime.

Kenny Anderson, who led Georgia Tech to the 1990 Final Four, said he selected Georgia Tech because: "They were the only school on their p's and q's. I got letters every day, left and right. Last week there were twenty letters just from Tech. From everybody. The whole Georgia Tech was sending letters, assistant coaches, the president, vice president, everybody. That showed me some kind of character."[15]

A football coach may contact a prospect as many times as he wants to, provided it's at the prospect's high school. He also may contact a prospect three times away from his high school. But a basketball coach is restricted to six visits per year, three at a prospect's high school and three at a site other than the prospect's high school.

This rule has changed five times in the last seven years, making it difficult for any college recruiter to know what's right and wrong. A high school coach, working with an outdated NCAA manual, has an almost impossible time of it.

A head coach is not permitted, for example, to take a prospect out for dinner one evening, and then see him for breakfast the next morning.

The average big-time school spends between $400,000 and $1 million on recruiting. Coaches' travel expenses make up fifty percent of the budget, which is why many big-time athletic departments own or lease planes especially for recruiting.

"Contacts" are defined as any face-to-face meeting between a coach and a prospect or his parents during which any party says more than hello. If the face-to-face meeting is accidental, and if nothing more than a flicker of mutual recognition is conveyed, and if it takes place in a site other than the prospect's home, high school, competition or practice site, it is regarded as a permissible "bump." A pre-arranged, face-to-face meeting constitutes a contact, regardless of what is said.

The NCAA Manual devotes an unseemly amount of space to articulating the differences between a simple exchange of greetings and a solicitous conversation. It devotes even more space to articulating how many and where these conversations may take place.

The contact, of course, is when the forty-five-year-old coach, fighting hard to keep his job, unleashes all of his persuasiveness on the seventeen-year-old superstar. Former Maryland coach Lefty Driesell once told a prospect bound for North Carolina State: "If you go to State, son, you're gonna get your name in *The Raleigh Observer*. But if you come to Maryland, you're gonna get your name in *The Washington Post*. And the President reads *The Washington Post*."[16]

The school year is divided up into periods during which only certain recruiting activities are permitted to take place. Here is the 1990–91 recruiting calendar for basketball, which is completely different from the football recruiting calendar.

June 1–July 4, 1990	Quiet Period
July 5–July 31	Evaluation Period
August 1–September 10	Quiet Period
September 11–October 10	Contact Period
October 11–November 12 (8 A.M.)	Quiet Period
November 12 (8 A.M.)–November 30	Quiet Period
December 1–December 11	Evaluation Period
December 12–January 19, 1991	Quiet Period
January 20–January 30	Evaluation Period
January 31–February 17	Quiet Period
February 18–February 28	Evaluation Period
March 1–March 3	Quiet Period
March 4–March 22	Contact Period
March 23–March 27	Quiet Period
March 28–April 2 (noon)	Dead Period
April 2 (noon)–April 3 (8 A.M.)	Quiet Period
April 3 (8 A.M.)–April 8 (8 A.M.)	Contact Period
April 8 (8 A.M.–April 10 (8 A.M.)	Dead Period
April 10 (8 A.M.)–April 19	Contact Period
April 20–July 4	Quiet Period

In its rather impractical attempt to define and legislate virtually every type of recruiting contact possible, this calendar of permissible activities provokes as much confusion as a Byzantine liturgy.

During an evaluation period, a coach may assess a prospect's academic and/or athletic ability. No in-person, off-campus recruiting contacts may be made with a prospect during evaluation periods.

Georgia Tech's Bobby Cremins saw Kenny Anderson play forty times before he ever spoke to him. Cremins started evaluating Anderson when Anderson was in the ninth grade.

Video and film expense constitutes twenty percent of a typical recruiting budget, reflecting the predominant practice of evaluating the skill of prospects through videos.

During a dead period, a coach is not permitted to make in-person, on- or off-campus recruiting or evaluation contacts. Expense-paid "trips" by prospects to college campuses are prohibited, as well. Also, a coach may not speak to or attend a banquet where prospects might be in the audience. He may, however, telephone and write a prospect during a dead period

In the forty-eight-hour dead period preceding the day he was to decide what school he was going to attend, Alonzo Mourning, the nation's number-one basketball prospect in 1988, spent ten of the forty-eight hours talking to anxious coaches from Georgetown, Maryland, Georgia Tech, Syracuse and North Carolina on the telephone.

Telephone recruiting expenses have increased considerably for most schools. Clemson, for example, will incur $85,000 in telephone expense in 1990. A portable phone is not a luxury when it comes to recruiting.

During a quiet period, a coach can make in-person recruiting contacts only on his campus. No in-person, off-campus recruiting contacts or evaluations can take place during quiet periods.

These restrictive periods, the forty weeks where coaches are prohibited from making "in-person, off-campus recruiting contacts," have given rise to middlemen who have vested interests in a college basketball program and who serve as a coach's surrogate.

As unlikely as this might seem, athletic shoe manufacturers have become middlemen in college basketball recruiting, exerting influence far beyond what the general public might logically imagine possible. Between network and cable television, over 300 college games are televised each season, and Nike, for example, believes that television viewers notice, and are swayed by, the brands of athletic shoes worn by the college basketball players appearing on the screen. Because of this exposure, Sonny Vaccaro, Nike's head of basketball promotions, pays college coaches to turn their teams into running and jumping billboards for his company.

Through the efforts of Vaccaro, an ex-gambler from Las Vegas, Nike leads in this athletic shoes advertising battle. Armed with a $4 million-per-year promotional budget, Vaccaro has hired more than sixty big-time college basketball coaches, including John Thompson at $200,000 per year, Jim Valvano at $160,000 per year, Bobby Cremins of Georgia Tech at $125,000, Jerry Tarkanian of UNLV at $100,000, and even ESPN's Dick Vitale.

Vaccaro said, "My dream was that Nike would own basketball at every level. I think I accomplished my goal without abusing the kids."[17]

It just so happens that the period between July 10 and July 31 is an ideal time for college coaches to evaluate prospects. Knowing this, Vaccaro created the Nike Academic Betterment and Career Development Camp (Nike/ABCD) in 1983.

Held at Princeton University each summer, the Nike/ABCD camp offers unparalleled basketball competition for the nation's 120 best college basketball prospects who, while attending the camp, wear only Nike products. On any given day that the Nike camp is in session, at least ten big-time college basketball coaches, television sportscasters, major sportswriters and NBA scouts are sitting in the stands of Princeton's Jadwin Gym, scrutinizing future All-Americans.

Vaccaro staffs the Nike Camp coaching jobs with high school basketball coaches who invariably have the nation's stars playing for them. While the camp is in session, these select high school coaches establish and nurture future employment contacts with the leaders of big-time college basketball.

Vaccaro, representing Nike, also sponsors AAU summer leagues, and All-Star basketball tournaments such as the Dapper Dan of Pittsburgh, and the Las Vegas Invitational. Vaccaro sponsors this extensive network of grass-roots basketball so that he may funnel the very best high school talent to those schools that "play" the Nike brand.

Spurned coaches are still shaking their heads over what Vaccaro did for his best friend, John Thompson of Georgetown. In 1987, during two different "dead" periods, Vaccaro went to Chesapeake, Virginia, a remote town 150 miles southeast of Richmond, to visit Alonzo Mourning, the nation's top high school basketball star that year. Vaccaro claims he was just passing through, and decided to stop by and confirm a summer league sponsorship deal with Bill Lassiter, Mourning's high school coach, who was also a coach at the Nike/ABCD camp the previous summer. A day after Vaccaro's second visit, Mourning announced his decision to play for Nike's $200,000-per-year friend, John Thompson of Georgetown. Thompson did nothing to quell the complaints when he said, "I certainly hope my friendship with Sonny helped me get Alonzo."[18]

Finally, Vaccaro gives some college basketball programs an almost unlimited supply of free Nike shoes. The investigation that led to the eventual demise of Jim Valvano at North Carolina State revealed that his players regularly sold extra pairs of Nikes to supplement their incomes.

A prospect may receive one official paid visit per college, and five official paid trips, overall. Helicopters and limousines may not be used during official paid visits, nor can the prospect receive any frequent flyer bonus miles that may result from his trip. Football programs may host no more than eighty-five official paid visits, and basketball programs may host no more than eighteen official paid visits.

Official paid visits, or "tripping," is when most prospects finally make their final decisions. Many times decisions are based on the most capricious things, such as what kind of ice cream the cafeteria serves.

A school may not arrange for excessive entertainment during official paid visits.

The University of Georgia once spent $2,500 to stock a field with quail so the prospects could go shooting.

Georgia Tech took Alonzo Mourning to an Anita Baker concert where he met Baker backstage. Mourning then went to an Atlanta night club where the Atlanta Hawks's Dominique Wilkins and Spud

Webb just happened to be. The three players got along famously.[19] Five of the last six ACC Rookies of the Year have come from Georgia Tech.

The official paid visit may not exceed forty-eight hours, which begins when the prospect arrives on campus. A prospect may receive round-trip transportation, coach or tourist, between his home and the campus. If a university uses its own plane to transport a prospect to and from the campus on his trip, neither his friends nor his family may accompany him on the plane. Once on campus, his parents may receive food and lodging from the college. Lodging for the prospect must be consistent with normal student life. A student host may acquaint the prospect with the campus, and may spend $20 per day doing so. But none of this money can be used to purchase college souvenirs for the prospect. A school may not provide a prospect or his student host with an automobile during an official paid visit.

Again, high school star Alonzo Mourning stayed in Atlanta's luxurious Peachtree Plaza Hotel which, according to the NCAA's Dan Dutchery, "probably was a violation."[20]

A prospect confirms his decision to attend a particular school, and the school confirms its decision to award the prospect a scholarship, by signing a National Letter of Intent. Basketball intent letters may be signed twice a year, in November and in the early spring. Football intent letters are signed in February. A big-time head football coach may not be present if a prospect signs a National Letter of Intent at an off-campus site.

In theory, the letter of intent is voluntary. But in actual practice, few big-time schools grant scholarships just on a prospect's verbal commitment. A letter of intent is a contract, vigorously enforced, that decidedly favors the school, not the prospect.

The letter-of-intent commitment can pose problems, especially when a prospect is recruited by a coach who leaves the school, or when a school is put on NCAA probation, in the interim between when the letter is signed and when the prospect starts school. Since championships are won or lost on signing day, few colleges are willing to let prospects back out of their commitments. Even if the school does release an athlete, he loses a year of eligibility. When the school refuses, the athlete loses two years of eligibility. Those who advocate paying college athletes, cite intent letters as evidence that college athletes are professionals merely masquerading as amateurs.

Certain sections of Georgia, Texas and Oklahoma, follow the activities of signing day closer than they do the Dow Jones averages. Some people think National Letter of Intent Signing Day should be televised.

Perhaps the most notorious case of a prospect successfully getting out of his commitment involved Sean Higgins, a California basketball wonder. In the fall of 1986, Higgins signed up to attend UCLA. Several weeks later, he had second thoughts. He claimed he really wanted to attend the University of Michigan to be closer to his father who lived outside of Detroit but that he signed with UCLA because his stepfather threatened him with a baseball bat. Eventually the Pac-10 conference released Higgins from his UCLA commitment, and in 1989, Sean Higgins helped Michigan win The Final Four.

Recruiting and evaluation contact restrictions do not apply to a coach who is the parent or the legal guardian of a prospect.

A few years back, University of Nevada-Las Vegas's basketball recruiting coordinator, Mark Warkentien, became the legal guardian of Lloyd ''Sweet Pea'' Daniels, a player touted as the next Magic Johnson. Although Daniels never played for UNLV, the NCAA launched an inquiry to determine if Daniels's relationship with Warkentien was born out of parental concern or out of mischief. Specifically, the NCAA wanted to know if the items Warkentien gave Daniels—cash, a car, an $1,800 motorcycle—were merely the gifts a guardian bestows on a ward, or the inducements of an illegal recruiting scheme.

NCAA probes are a way of life for UNLV basketball coach Jerry Tarkanian. Ever since he began coaching at Riverside City College in 1961, Tarkanian has maintained a fatal attraction for superb athletes who are also academic and social cast-offs. Daniels, for example, read on a third-grade level and was a drug addict.

Tarkanian once said, ''The way I look at it, if you bring a kid in that can't read and write, somebody nobody will touch, and you keep him here for four or five years, teach him to follow the rules, make him responsible for what he does, at the end if he can read and write a little, you've done him a favor. Even if he doesn't have a piece of paper, you've given him a chance to straighten out. I don't see anything wrong with that."[21]

Tarkanian's philosophy finally paid off when his inner-city Running Rebels annihilated the Duke suburbanites in the 1990 NCAA Men's Basketball Championships. In addition to earning a bonus of $140,000, winning The Final Four in full view of many of the NCAA officials who had been badgering him for fifteen years was a special kind of vindication for Jerry Tarkanian. But the NCAA had the last word.

In 1977, after uncovering major recruiting violations, the NCAA insisted that University of Nevada-Las Vegas suspend Tarkanian for two years. Tarkanian responded by bringing suit against both UNLV and the NCAA, asserting that both parties had denied him due process when they considered terminating him without so much as a hearing.

The NCAA appealed a series of Nevada court decisions favoring Tarkanian to the United States Supreme Court, which found in favor of the NCAA by the slim margin of 5-4. In writing the majority's decision, Justice John Paul Stevens claimed that the NCAA, because it is a private organization, is not bound by the constitutional requirement of due process that public agencies must observe.

Far beyond whatever personal difficulties it may cause Tarkanian, the real significance of the Supreme Court's decision was the determination that the NCAA, as a private organization, may treat its members in any manner it wants to. The ruling permits the NCAA much more leeway in enforcing its rules.

Schools are allowed to send prospects: "one annual athletics press guide (with only one color of printing inside the covers) per sport, or one annual recruiting brochure (with only one color of printing inside the covers) per sport; one student-athlete handbook (with only one color of printing inside the covers); one wallet-size playing schedule per sport; general correspondence and greeting cards; newspaper clippings, which may not be assembled in any form of scrapbook; weight-lifting program information, provided the prospect has signed a National Letter of Intent."[22]

Before this rule was adopted, some prospects' post offices could not handle the avalanche of posters and four-color brochures.

A school may not advertise for prospects.

This rule does not apply to the school that leads the unsuspecting prospect into its 100,000-seat stadium where his name is emblazoned in twenty-foot letters on the electronic scoreboard, blinking in rhythm to the fight song. Even if it is the end of January and the stadium is empty, it can have quite an effect on a seventeen-year-old.

There are only two instances when a school can provide transportation to a prospect: when he is on an official paid visit, and when the prospect is on an unofficial visit and he wishes to view a practice or competition site or some other institutional facility, provided they are within a thirty-mile radius of the campus and the prospect is accompanied by an institutional staff member. However, the prospect may not receive transportation to attend a home game during an unofficial visit.

The NCAA obsesses over giving prospects rides, and it becomes particularly alarmed if the ride takes the prospect thirty miles from the center of the campus.

Maryland University's Bob Wade eventually lost his job because *The Washington Post* discovered that an assistant Maryland coach drove Rudy Archer, a former Maryland player, to his junior college classes. It prompted Maryland University's chairman of the Board of Trustees at the time, Peter O'Malley, to say, "I've issued instructions to all my coaches that they can give players rides to classes any time."[23]

Florida coach Galen Hall was censured by the NCAA because he had instructed a graduate assistant to drive a Florida football player to court to answer charges of nonpayment of child support.

A tiny southwestern college was severely reprimanded because prospects on their official paid visits were allowed to attend an Alabama-Louisiana State football game that was forty miles away.

Like an idiot savant, the NCAA regards all infractions, serious and inconsequential, on an equal footing. Mega-bribes are brandished and accepted at some NCAA member-schools because the NCAA is too busy bringing to justice coaches who play racquetball with prospects at other schools.

Moreover, when it comes time to enforce these regulations, the NCAA is strapped with administrative law, a system of legal reckoning which is totally inappropriate for the rough-and-tumble world of big-time collegiate football and basketball. The NCAA, for example, cannot subpoena witnesses, seize evidence, pay informants, impose contempt sanctions, or even tape record testimony.

Every Wednesday morning, Steve Morgan and David Berst, the NCAA's Associate Executive Director for Enforcement and Assistant Executive Director for Enforcement, respectively, discuss that week's infraction tips from media reports, anonymous tipsters, competitors and institutions themselves. In those cases where Berst and Morgan believe that an intentional violation has occurred, they notify the suspected institution by letter that an NCAA enforcement representative will soon conduct a preliminary or fact-gathering inquiry to determine whether an official inquiry should be launched.

In conducting these preliminary investigations, by necessity the NCAA must rely greatly on the suspected institution's cooperation. According to Robert Minnix, an NCAA Director of Enforcement, "We can't bully our way in. We can't establish martial law. Violations are first handled by the university, then the conference, and only then does the NCAA get involved." [24]

Berst and Morgan review the findings of the preliminary inquiry to decide the seriousness of the violations, if any. When they suspect a major violation might have occurred, they send an official letter of inquiry to the institution's chief executive officer conveying specific allegations.

At this juncture, the institution usually launches its own internal investigation. In the meanwhile, the NCAA enforcement staff defers to the institution in recognition of "home rule," which allows an institution to control its own destiny, even in matters dealing with its own corruption. This conflict is camouflaged by the fable that both the NCAA enforcement staff and the institution are "like partners engaged in a dispassionate search for the truth." [25]

Both the institution and the NCAA enforcement staff then appear before the Committee on Infractions, the NCAA's version of federal court. As noted earlier, a $28,000-per-year enforcement representative is usually matched against either the president of a university or a high-priced attorney specializing in compliance law. Frequently, the NCAA representative acquiesces to his more experienced antagonist.

After hearing the suspected institution and the NCAA enforcement department, the six-man Committee on Infractions renders a decision. In doing so, the committee is inordinately swayed by demonstrations of "self-disclosure" and cooperation from the suspected institution.

Leniency, of course, takes the form of a lesser penalty, and is also manifested in the NCAA's eagerness to drop many of the more flagrant charges. That's why the allegations contained in a preliminary letter of inquiry, as opposed to those listed in the final resolution of a case, invariably reflect what really went on at the institution. It also explains why the final resolution contains many more trivial infractions than major violations.

If the committee hands down a sanction, the institution may appeal to a subcommittee of the NCAA Council, the association's version of the Supreme Court. Inevitably, the appeal committee agrees with the Committee on Infraction, but out of deference to the appealing institution it dilutes the charges and the penalties even more. Exacerbating the already-endangered effectiveness of the NCAA's enforcement capability is the fact that the department consists of only eighteen enforcement representatives who must monitor 750 NCAA member-schools and 250,000 athletes.

Of course, it is awkward for the association's enforcement department to investigate the very people who pay its salaries. The same people who run the NCAA serve as plaintiff, defendant, defense attorney, prosecutor and judge. A school suspected of a violation is judged by a jury of its peers, the Committee on Infractions, which is comprised of six people with the same interests and outlooks who might be friends, opponents, or past or future employers of the accused.

When this conflict of interest was presented to David Berst for comment, he replied, "I don't accept that view. We [the NCAA] stack up quite well against any other volunteer organizations that impose penalties on their members."[26]

David Berst's sole experience prior to joining the NCAA enforcement department in 1971 consisted of being the baseball coach of MacMurray College in Jacksonville, Illinois. The diffident, bespectacled David Berst, 44, started as a field investigator and became the head of the department in 1977.

Berst does not feel impaired by his lack of legal training. He maintained, "You don't need to know Greek and Latin phrases to understand what is right and wrong."[27]

Berst is also satisfied with his department's budget of $1.8 million per year even though he and his associates have crushing work loads. "I'm always for improving the enforcement department," Berst said, "but I don't know if more money would necessarily do that. What is needed more than more money is an enhanced commitment on the part of NCAA member-schools to run their athletic programs honestly."[28]

The average salary of an enforcement representative is $28,000, which, together with the work load (thirty to forty cases apiece), and the heavy travel schedule ($30,000 annual travel expenses per investigator), explains why the average enforcement representative stays on the job less than two years. Several years ago, when Marist College was being investigated, seven different enforcement representatives were assigned to the case.

All these hindrances may explain what many consider is the NCAA's greatest enforcement blunder.

In 1985, the *Lexington Herald-Leader* wrote a series of Pulitzer Prize-winning articles that revealed how Kentucky alumni routinely gave $100 handshakes and other monetary signs of affection to Kentucky basketball players. Both the university and the NCAA followed up with investigations that lasted nearly three years. Incredibly, neither investigation could confirm a Pulitzer Prize-winning charge.

Michael Garnes, a former NCAA enforcement representative who helped conduct the Kentucky investigation, claimed that the NCAA's investigation of Kentucky lacked real commitment. Garnes said, "I was pulled off the Kentucky investigation to work on a small black college by my boss, Chuck Smrt. He told me money was the reason. Yet I spent just as much of the NCAA's money investigating that small black college as I did investigating Kentucky. I had a big argument with Smrt. I told him it didn't look right. Told him it looked like selective enforcement. Smrt got real nervous. He said, 'You're stepping on toes.' "[29]

Those "toes," according to Creed Black, then chairman and publisher of the *Lexington Herald-Leader*, belonged to Kentucky's president, Otis Singletary, and the NCAA's executive director at the time, Walter Byers. "There was no question Singletary stonewalled the investigation, and that Byers eased off," Black said. At the time, Otis Singletary, who had been Kentucky's president for eighteen years, was a founding member of the President's Commission, the organization the NCAA formed to reform college athletics in 1984.

In March 1988, the NCAA's Committee on Infractions reprimanded Kentucky for conducting a half-hearted investigation of the *Herald-Leader*'s charges, but it imposed no penalties.

One month later, another Kentucky basketball scandal hit the newspapers. This time, an assistant coach, Dwayne Casey, allegedly sent $1,000 to Claud Mills, the father of a Kentucky basketball player. Casey sent the money via Emery Delivery Service. Apparently the envelope broke open while being processed, and a number of Emery employees observed its contents, twenty $50 bills and a videotape. A short time later, the incident was reported to a local newspaper, complete with who the sender and the recipient were.

After its second investigation, this one lasting a year, the NCAA found Casey guilty of sending the money to Claud Mills. The NCAA also discovered that another Kentucky player, Eric Manuel, had cheated while taking an ACT test. (Under the NCAA's Proposition 48, an athlete must score a 15 or better on the test before he can receive an athletic scholarship.) Manuel, a native of Macon, Georgia, first took the test in his home state and scored a 3. When Manuel took the test again, in Lexington, Kentucky, he scored 18. Two hundred and eleven of his answers matched a student's who sat beside him during the test.

The NCAA fell short of delivering the death penalty, imposing instead a two-year ban on post-season play, a one-year ban on television and certain restrictions on the number of scholarships Kentucky could grant.

Many thought the penalty was too lenient, considering Kentucky's thirty-five-year history of infractions which began in the early Fifties when five of its players, including the famous Alex Groza, were convicted of point-shaving. In fact, members of the Committee on Infractions admitted they had considered handing down the death penalty but were persuaded otherwise because of the cooperation of Kentucky's new president, David Roselle. Two months after the NCAA announced the penalties, Roselle, who had been in office for less than two years, resigned from Kentucky and became the president of the University of Delaware.

To correct the situation, Kentucky hired a new athletic director, C. M. Newton from Vanderbilt, who in turn replaced Eddie Sutton, Kentucky's basketball coach, with Rick Pitino, coach of the New York Knicks, at a salary of $5.7 million over seven years. Pitino, however, did not come to Lexington with a clean bill of NCAA health. In 1981, the NCAA recommended to the University of Hawaii that it fire Pitino, then an assistant coach, because he had been found guilty of eight recruiting violations, including arranging free air travel for a player, using season tickets as currency to purchase a new car, and distributing free meal tickets to players.

Eric Manuel, the Kentucky basketball star who allegedly cheated on the SAT's, surely could not have concocted that elaborate scheme by himself. Manuel was banned for life from the NCAA while Chris Mills, the alleged recipient of the $1,000 bribe, transferred to Arizona. As Chris Mills's father, Claude, said, "What happened was bad for Kentucky, but it wasn't a big deal for Chris, personally."

When UNLV's Jerry Tarkanian heard that Kentucky did not get the death penalty, he said, "The NCAA is so mad at Kentucky that they'll probably slap another two years' probation on Cleveland State."[30] Tarkanian was referring to the NCAA's proclivity for seldom matching the punishment with the crime.

Tarkanian's point is perhaps even better illustrated by the sanctions the NCAA imposed on Southeastern Louisiana University.

Southeastern Louisiana is not a big-time basketball powerhouse. It is a small school, with a student body of 9,500, located in the Steel Magnolia-like town of Hammond, Louisiana, forty miles from Baton Rouge. The Lions have never been to The Final Four. They have lost sixty percent of their games in the last ten years. And their 1988-89 season was unusually bad, three wins and twenty-four losses. And if that weren't enough, Southeastern was forced to suspend the 1989-90 basketball season because its football team had run up a $476,000 deficit the previous year.

But somehow the school ran afoul of the NCAA and in October 1989, Southeastern was cited for these infractions.

1. In June 1986, Southeastern's basketball coach Newton Chelette agreed to help three of his players rent an apartment

together. "The coach visited the manager of the apartment complex and wrote, 'I will be responsible for $150 deposit,' on the top of a security deposit receipt and then signed his name below the statement."[31] No money changed hands between the coach and the apartment complex manager, and within a few days, the players came up with the $150 deposit on their own.

2. At that time, however, Coach Chellette did loan the boys $200 for the first month's rent which they repaid a month later.

3. A few days later, Coach Chelette contacted Mary Barger, owner and manager of the local McDonald's, and arranged for a job for one of his players. The player worked from mid-June until early August at the rate of $3.35 per hour, the normal rate for all employees. Barger also paid the player a supplemental wage of $1.65 per hour. In addition, on at least two occasions, Chelette drove the player to work.

4. On November 7, Southeastern's assistant basketball coaches Leo McClure and Ronnie Devall watched four prospects who were on their official paid visits that weekend shoot baskets. Then, McClure asked one of the prospects to perform a particular "move" while being guarded by another prospect.

5. The same day, McClure permitted the four prospects to attend the Alabama-LSU football game in Baton Rouge, which is forty miles from Hammond. By doing this, McClure violated the NCAA rule that states prospects on official paid visits may not be entertained outside of a thirty-mile radius from the campus. McClure also gave the prospects cash to spend at the game. Only student hosts may give prospects cash for incidental entertainment on official paid visits.

6. McClure also offered a pair of sneakers to a prospect if he would sign a letter of intent for Southeastern the following week.

7. During that same fateful weekend, another coaching staff member indicated to a prospect from Alabama that since a number of Southeastern students come from Alabama, the prospect would probably be able to hitch a free ride home if he came to Southeastern.[32]

For these infractions, the NCAA imposed a five-year probation on Southeastern, and coaches Chelette, McClure and Devall lost their jobs.

It's the disparities between Southeastern's five-year probation and Kentucky's two-year probation that make critics suspect the NCAA enforces justice selectively. With Southeastern, the NCAA's punishment was swift and it certainly did
not match the crime. But with Kentucky, the punishment was
anything but swift, and anything but commensurate with Kentucky's violations.

Of the twenty-two schools currently serving NCAA probation sentences, eight are small-time schools like Southeastern
Louisiana. Critics think more big-time schools with death
penalties should be on the list.

People ask why, when a school is found guilty of major
violations, its NCAA representatives do not resign from key
NCAA committee positions. Kentucky president Otis Singletary, for example, should have resigned from the Presidents
Commission several years ago.

One intelligent innovation the NCAA has implemented in
the last several years is the formation of a separate department
that helps NCAA member-schools understand and comply with
the rules before they are tempted to break them. Compliance
has already reduced the number of infractions committed by
small-time schools, which usually commit violations out of
ignorance, not gain. But the NCAA's new compliance department has yet to deter the big-time schools' violations.

Consciously or otherwise, the public expects the NCAA to
enforce the rules of college sports like the commissioner of the
NBA or major league baseball does. But the NCAA is unable
to do so because it functions more as a chamber of commerce
than an arbiter.

David Berst inadvertently pointed out the NCAA's greatest
handicap. The NCAA is a volunteer organization with no real
enforcement powers. Under the circumstances, it is amazing
the NCAA can do what it does.

CHAPTER 10

Reform

On January 8, 1989, Richard D. Schultz announced to the 83rd Annual NCAA Convention that the NCAA's virtue had reached new heights. "The state of college sports," said Schultz, "is as good as it's been in a long, long time. Ninety-nine percent of everything is positive."[1]

But while Schultz proclaimed the innocence of college sports, the nation's front pages told a different story.

Almost every day another newspaper or television station chronicled how players or coaches at Oklahoma, Kansas, SMU, Texas Tech, Houston, North Carolina State, Clemson, South Carolina, Texas A&M, Oklahoma State, Illinois, Colorado, Minnesota, Kentucky, Iowa, Michigan State, Ohio State, Florida, and many other institutions committed academic fraud, recruiting violations, bribery, embezzlement, drug dealing, rape, and attempted murder.

Finally, even the NCAA could no longer deny these contradictions, and Schultz conveyed a different message to the 1990 NCAA Convention: "There is a very strong and urgent feeling that we need reform."[2]

Responding to this need, the 1990 NCAA Convention delegates adopted several reform measures, including shortening spring football practice, reducing the length of the basketball season, banning repeat steroid offenders for life, and publishing the graduation rates of athletes.

After the convention, *The NCAA News*, in a front-page, five-column story, exclaimed: "If the NCAA's first official event of the new decade accurately set the tone for the 1990s, college athletics may have taken the first steps on its most dynamic adventure in history."[3]

But Arthur Ashe disagreed.

Ashe said, "To me, most of the NCAA [1990 Convention] actions show it would rather tinker with the real problems than tackle them."[4]

As Ashe intimates, *The NCAA News* failed to remind its readers the 1990 Convention reform measures were nothing more than either watered-down compromises or ideas forced on the NCAA by Congress. The original thought on spring football, for example, was to eliminate it completely. And, had it not been for Senator Bill Bradley's Student-Athlete Right to Know Bill, graduation rates would still be one of the NCAA's best-kept secrets.

For reform to take place, several pivotal attitude changes must occur.

First, the NCAA must stop heralding compromises that perpetuate the status quo as true reform measures. This, of course, will be a challenge since the association, through *The NCAA News*, is at its best when launching public relations campaigns that convince its membership all is well in college athletics.

Second, both the public and Congress have to realize that the NCAA under Dick Schultz is no different from what the association was under Walter Byers. Schultz is "more accessible and open" than his predecessor, and certainly the NCAA is considerably richer thanks to Schultz's television negotiating skills. But it hasn't gotten ethically better. The NCAA has not developed a moral sense that now makes it want to fight the corruption of college sports. Despite the rhetoric, the NCAA's new-found wealth makes the association more eager than ever to protect the present state of college athletics. The NCAA's current talk of reform is window-dressing, aimed at appeasing the media and Congress. It is also part of its anti-reform defenses.

Throughout its history, the NCAA has always mounted clever and effective shields against reform.

The NCAA first denies anything is amiss with an argument not dissimilar from Nixon's Watergate defense. An NCAA official says something like, "Yes, college athletics has a few problems, but none are graver or more widespread than those besetting society in general. The media, however, in their attempt to sell more newspapers and boost ratings, irresponsibly blow these isolated instances out of proportion."

Schultz exhibited this form of denial in his 1989 NCAA Convention speech.

Then, only if and when the contrary evidence becomes overwhelming and the NCAA can no longer deny the problem, the association appears to cooperate by offering its own reform legislation that it announces with headlines such as "the first steps on its [the NCAA's] most dynamic adventure in history."

The reformers, lulled by the NCAA's cooperation, agree to the compromises before realizing they are just cosmetic changes that merely continue the association's dubious practices. Embarrassed, the reformers say nothing for fear their naivete might be exposed. A good example of this occurred when the NCAA diluted Proposition 48 with the partial qualifier amendment.

The NCAA old-guard can also abandon artful compromise and resort to hand-to-hand combat if its authority is seriously threatened. This is how and why the Presidents Commission was created.

In 1984, the Bok Committee, the same group that proposed Proposition 48 the year before, presented the Board of Presidents proposal to the NCAA Convention. In effect, this proposed board would have wrested control of the NCAA away from the athletic directors by vesting sweeping NCAA legislative powers to college chief executive officers. Walter Byers, a vigorous ally of the athletic directors, termed the proposal and the Bok Committee, "power-hungry." To this day, Ted Tow, a Byers crony and publisher of *The NCAA News*, refers to the proposal as "the Board of Omnipotent Presidents."

In explaining why the presidents required such control, Bok claimed, "The NCAA was dominated by athletic directors who were dedicated to only one purpose, bigger and better athletics."[5]

But once in the trenches of the 1984 NCAA convention floor battle, the college presidents proved to be no match for their athletic directors. Even though the Bok Committee's Proposition 48 had been seriously compromised by the partial qualifier loophole at the previous NCAA convention, the victory had been so skillfully executed by the athletic directors that few college presidents realized their proposal had lost. As a consequence, the Bok Committee came to the 1984 NCAA convention underestimating just how zealously the athletic directors would try to defeat the Board of Presidents proposal. Bok said, "We did a lot of telephoning before the '84 Convention. We had the votes. Even the *Chronicle of Higher Education* said so."[6]

The athletic directors fought off the Board of Presidents proposal with an alternative of their own, entitled the Presidents Commission. By design, this title lulled the public and the press into thinking both measures were comparable. But the athletic directors were not inclined to relinquish their NCAA power to anyone, least of all to college presidents. Therefore, they constructed the Presidents Commission to be an advisory and ceremonial group with no authority except for the anemic prerogative to convene special NCAA conventions.

The athletic directors, who comprised the convention majority, prevailed and the Presidents Commission proposal was adopted.

In explaining the defeat, Bok said, "When it came time to vote, many athletic directors went against the instructions of their presidents who did not attend the convention."[7]

As a matter of course, the majority of college presidents do not attend NCAA conventions, preferring instead to delegate this responsibility to their athletic directors and faculty athletics representatives. In theory, the delegates vote according to their presidents' instructions. But in reality, once on the floor of a convention, delegates vote their own minds.

This time the defeat registered with Bok and his associates. Appropriately stung, all the Bok Committee presidents retreated from the NCAA rather than serve on the Presidents Commission, and most soon lost interest in their institution's athletic programs.

Edward T. (Tad) Foote, University of Miami president and a member of the Bok Committee, for example, no longer attends NCAA conventions because "I now have better things to do with my time."[8] Since 1984, Sam Jankovich, Miami's athletic director, has beaten Foote many other times as well. When Miami, for example, had to replace football coach Jimmy Johnson who went to the Dallas Cowboys in March, 1989, Jankovich did not allow Foote to interview, much less approve of, Johnson's replacement, Dennis Erickson.

The presidents who did become members of the Presidents Commission were either too naïve or too political to admit that it had no real authority, although it did enjoy a brief flurry of reform activity during its first year of operation.

In June 1985, the commission called its first special convention, a move that temporarily perplexed the NCAA's athletic directors. They did not know what to expect. In the resulting confusion, the Presidents Commission managed to get a significant piece of reform legislation passed, the so-called death penalty.

Puffed up by the victory, the commission then thought it was well on its way to taking over the NCAA.

"This was not a convention," said Hoke Smith, president of Maryland's Towson State. "It was an invasion."[9]

The Presidents Commission called another special convention in June 1987, to reduce the ever-increasing costs of big-time college athletics.

If 1985 was the NCAA convention of triumph for the commission, then the 1987 NCAA convention was its humiliation. The Presidents Commission's chair, Maryland's John Slaughter, preoccupied with the Len Bias scandal, was politically devoured by the athletic directors. All eight commission reform measures were defeated by embarrassing margins.

Robert Atwell, president of the ACE, said, "It was the end of the so-called reform of college athletics."[10]

To add insult to injury, the NCAA old-guard used the Presidents Commission's special reform convention to overturn a recent, cost-saving measure that reduced the number of allowable basketball scholarships from fifteen to thirteen. In speaking in favor of more scholarships, Jim Valvano, North Carolina State's athletic director and basketball coach at the time, said, "When you are down to thirteen, the desire to run off, so to speak, and do some things that we certainly don't want associated with our profession is apparent. It might lead to abuses."[11] Two and a half years later, Valvano was fired for wholesale recruiting violations and academic abuses.

From June 1987 to January 1990, the Presidents Commission accomplished nothing more than to stage the National Forum, a series of debates on what the proper role of college athletics should be. The value and quality of these debates are illustrated by what Dr. Frank Horton, then president of the University of Oklahoma, had to say. Advocating big-time football programs, Horton con veyed his belief that Sooner football, besides offering great entertain-ment for the citizens of Oklahoma, also enriched them culturally.

Horton said, "When people are drawn to the University of Oklahoma to watch our football, many tour our museums and our libraries as well."[12] A year later, Horton resigned when five mem-bers of the Oklahoma football team were arrested for rape, at-tempted murder and cocaine trafficking.

When it comes to the NCAA conventions, which is the only time change in the NCAA can be effected, the athletic directors and faculty athletic representatives outnumber and outmaneuver the reform-minded presidents mercilessly. Any reform that passes does so because the NCAA old-guard allows it, and not because the Presidents Commission achieves it. Occasionally, for appearances' sake, the athletic directors allow the commission to enjoy a tempor-ary victory, as was the case with the death penalty's passing. Although a solid piece of legislation, its effectiveness has been reduced considerably because it has only been invoked once in five years.

Even though the NCAA manual makes it look remarkably easy, it is difficult for a college president to operate as the final word over a successful big-time college football or basketball program, espe-cially when a winning coach or athletic director has direct ties to trustees and governors. Virtually every unpopular step the president might take can be contradicted. There are few presidents who have the courage and the independent income to defy trustees and gover-nors. Paul Hardin did it at SMU in the early Seventies and lost his job, as did David Roselle at Kentucky in the mid-Eighties.

For lasting, positive change of college athletics to take place, the powers to be—the general public, the NCAA, the American Coun-cil on Education and the federal government—must agree on a few basic tenets.

• We must distinguish between true reform and the counterfeit compromise, and insist on the former.

• True reform must come from within the NCAA. As well-intentioned as they are, outside reform groups, like the Carnegie Commission Report, the American Council on Education or the newly created Knight Commission do nothing but capture fleeting publicity. Nothing ever comes of it.

• Only the top sixty-five big-time football and basketball programs are plagued by serious moral and ethical problems. The rest of college athletics, as Schultz misleadingly claims, is relatively free from scandal.

Of the top sixty-five big-time schools, only Duke and Stanford achieve the balance between excellent athletics and excellent academics. Admittedly, both schools have national reputations that attract the very best student-athletes with little to no recruiting. Stanford and Duke never compromise their educational principles, unlike other schools, like Georgetown and Notre Dame. When coaches make $700,000 per year, as Lou Holtz and John Thompson do, it is a clear indication that athletics take priority over academics. When athletes do not have the same academic qualifications as the rest of a school's student body, like Georgetown's basketball team and Notre Dame's football team, then again athletics have superseded academics.

To reform big-time college football and basketball is to reform the NCAA. And today's circumstances are remarkably similar to those that existed at the turn of the century when the NCAA was founded.

• Big-time college football and basketball can never be abolished or deemphasized. They mirror our national character traits, our aggressiveness, competitiveness and acquisitiveness too well. Only the University of Chicago could afford to drop football. Oklahoma or UNLV can't and shouldn't.

• There will always be abuses in big-time college football and basketball. It's how some people react to competition. But the inevitability of these abuses does not mean they should be tolerated.

• The top sixty-five big-time football and basketball programs have been professional enterprises for over 100 years now, ever since the first paid coach was hired. Athletic scholarships and National Letters of Intent only confirm and strengthen this professionalism. Amateurism does not exist at Oklahoma or Georgetown or Texas A&M or Georgia Tech as it does at Denison University or Harvard.

In the next ten years, the top sixty-five big-time college football
and basketball programs will earn over $1.5 billion from television
rights fees, mostly through the NCAA's ability to stage captivating
Final Four basketball tournaments. One hundred and sixty million
dollars per year, split among sixty-five NCAA institutions, is the
most convincing refutation of amateurism, or proof of professionalism, there could be.

• The NCAA has to concede that after eighty-five years of trying to
make it work, the principle of "home rule"—self-regulation or
institutional control—has failed in the top sixty-five big-time college football and basketball programs. The NCAA must judiciously
bow to the majority of schools and stop deferring to the individual
school. Any program that relies on self-regulation is doomed. It will
capture headlines, and it may satisfy critics initially, but eventually
it will fail. Dick Schultz's test experiment, the certification program, is a good example of a self-regulated program that will fail.
Despite *The NCAA News* rhetoric, certification is nothing more than
a trumped-up version of what NCAA presidents have been doing for
years, namely, attesting annually that their institutions comply with
association regulations when many of them don't.

• The reform of intercollegiate athletics should be approached in a
balanced manner. It does not compare to Savonarola's bonfires of
the vanities. To violate an NCAA regulation, even when a coach
offers a recruit a $100,000 bribe, is not a felony. It isn't even a
misdemeanor, except in Texas.

On the other hand, a cheating university represents an especially
virulent form of corruption because it violates a public trust, the
university's mission to demonstrate value and principle to all of
society, college and non-college person alike.

• The corruption of college athletics is a systemic problem.
Coaches do not cause it by themselves. In fact, to place the blame
on errant coaches is to ignore the fact most universities employ
every conceivable inducement, including outrageous incomes, to
encourage coaches and athletic directors to win at any cost. If they
truly wanted them to stop, universities would never hire aggressive,
obsessive coaches in the first place. Every university knows what it
has in its coaching staff.

Either through commission or omission, coaches have many
accomplices: fans, students, faculty, president, trustees, alumni,

boosters, governor, athletes and their parents. For this reason, it is impossible for an assistant basketball coach to offer $100,000 bribes without his coach, his athletic director, his president, his trustees and his governor knowing about it.

• The academic emphasis for athletes must shift from merely gaining admission and maintaining playing eligibility to obtaining a degree in five years or less. The SAT should be eliminated as a criterion for judging an athlete's classroom abilities. The test was first arbitrarily suggested by the Sapelo Island group which, although well-intentioned, was not qualified to devise academic standards. Moreover, there is little doubt SAT's discriminate against the culturally deprived and the exceedingly creative.

• With respect to how to help black athletes—through waivers, set-asides and exceptions as John Thompson and Harry Edwards argue, or through equal but fair treatment as Arthur Ashe argues— both views are correct, up to a point. SAT's, for example, should be discontinued as a concession to the Thompson-Edwards school of thought. But a certain minimum high school grade point average in college prep courses should be required in recognition of the college-isn't-for-everyone philosophy that Ashe and Bobby Knight advocate.

• The financial responsibility for an athletic program, both its surpluses and deficits, must shift from the athletic department to college presidents. Allowing athletic departments to be financially independent gives them license to overemphasize athletics: "We can't reduce the basketball season by three games because of the revenue-loss."

• In the hierarchy of major college football and basketball programs, no one should be allowed to claim, "I don't make that decision. The chancellor (assistant coach, coach, athletic director, president, trustees, governor) does." No one can avoid the responsibility of managing big-time college football and basketball. Irrespective of job security and political realities, the person most responsible for athletics is the college president.

• Like it or not, college coaches are not members of a faculty. They are far more important. They are surrogate parents, and should be respected and judged accordingly.

• The legislative process of the NCAA must change. As it stands now, the athletic directors outnumber and outwit anyone who opposes them at annual conventions. The theory that college presidents control an NCAA convention by instructing their athletic directors how to vote, is exactly that, a theory. Once involved in a convention floor battle, an athletic director votes the way he wants to, irrespective of traceable, recorded votes.

• Big-time college football and basketball players should be held to the same academic standards as the rest of a university's student body.

But when it comes to conduct, big-time athletes are not representative of the student body. They are celebrities, entertainment stars, public figures bound by a different standard of behavior. Big-time college football and basketball players affect the image of a university and all of higher education. University of Minnesota president Ken Keller was right in refusing to reinstate three basketball players to the team after they were accused and then acquitted of rape. "To play basketball for the University of Minnesota requires a code of conduct higher than merely being acquitted for rape charges," he said.

Statistics prove college football and basketball players are not average. There are 1.3 million undergraduates in the top sixty-five big-time schools. Less than thirty men play in The Final Four finals before thirty million people. Less than 200 athletes go on to pros each year and earn $1 million in the NBA and $500,000 in the NFL. College football and basketball players are drawn from the regular student body at Princeton and Franklin Pierce, but not at Illinois, Michigan, or LSU.

• Athletes should be given a much bigger voice in determining their own NCAA fate.

• This is an ideal time to finance a reform. Whatever incremental expenses that a reform might require can easily come from CBS. In 1991, the annual CBS payments to the NCAA go from $57 million per year to $143 million, a jump of 250 percent.

• Because the Supreme Court has categorized the NCAA as a private organization, the NCAA should now require agreement to its rules and regulations as a condition of membership. If a school or an athlete has a problem with drug testing, then the school or the athlete should not belong to the NCAA.

• The NCAA has to upgrade its staff. It needs people of larger vision and greater experience in key positions like enforcement, finance, and sports medicine.

• *The NCAA News* should have a competitor, a publication that can present the other side of the issues.

• Any reform of intercollegiate athletics must address the victimization of black football and basketball players. The black athlete, because of his athletic superiority, provides this country with unparalled thrills and entertainment. He also provides the university, the conference and the NCAA with unprecedented gate and television receipts. In return, the black athlete receives little else but broken promises: no degree and no pro career.

We must also remember what Professor R. Tait McKenzie of the University of Pennsylvania told the first NCAA Convention:

> Intercollegiate athletics should strive for what the ancient Greeks termed "aidos." It's the quality that instills in an athlete the thrill and joy of athletic combat, but restrains him from using his strength like a brute. Aidos is the quality that enables an athlete to earn honor and respect, in victory or in defeat. It enables a team to risk defeat rather than to win under dubious circumstances. It is a spirit of modesty and dignity that obeys the law, even if the decisions seem unjust, instead of piercing the air with protestations.[13]

Because games and athletics mirror human behavior, they serve as glimpses into the best and the worst in man. But college sports offer a far more important opportunity. College athletics reflect the personality and character of institutions of higher education, institutions that are supposed to symbolize truth and enlightenment. Although regrettable, it is one thing for hooliganism to tarnish the World Cup. But it is quite another thing for scandal to taint the University of Oklahoma. The former reflects badly on any country's lowest class of people. The latter reflects badly on what should be America's best class.

CHAPTER 11

Epilogue

The reform of college sports will never occur until the NCAA corrects an organizational flaw that has thwarted the association since 1955. Many will consider the suggestions for reform in this epilogue to be unrealistic. However, major changes—not simply cosmetic ones—are called for.

The NCAA must install a system of checks and balances that separates the association's basic functions. No longer, for example, can the same people who created The Final Four and who negotiated the $1 billion deal with CBS be responsible for the tournament's drug testing and rules enforcement. As presently constructed, the NCAA possesses too many conflicts of interest.

The NCAA's system of checks and balances should consist of four autonomous and equal branches: legislative, judicial, compliance, and operations/promotions.

1. LEGISLATIVE

The NCAA Legislative branch will consist solely of college presidents or chief executive officers. They, and they alone, will be empowered to propose, approve, modify or rescind all NCAA rules and regulations.

The NCAA will create a new division, called the Professional Division, consisting of the top sixty-five big-time football and basketball powers. All other existing divisions, and their assigned institutions, will remain the same.

The NCAA Legislative branch will be organized by division. Presidents of the Professional Division schools will make the rules for that division, just as presidents for Division III schools will legislate for their group of institutions.

The NCAA Legislative branch—each division's presidents—will meet three times a year to consider legislation. These meetings will replace the NCAA annual convention.

A two-thirds majority will be required to approve or amend legislation within each division's presidential deliberations.

The NCAA presidents will have complete financial authority over all other association branches, including negotiating each division's television contracts.

The NCAA presidents will have ultimate responsibility over the NCAA compliance and operations-promotions branches. They will not have responsibility over the NCAA judicial branches.

The NCAA presidents may organize into committees, hold hearings, and solicit the testimony of expert witnesses, e.g., athletes, coaches and athletic directors.

The NCAA president will be assisted by a full-time, paid staff which currently is the association's ten-person legislative services department.

The NCAA's legislative services department will sever its reporting relationship with the association's executive director, and report to the NCAA presidents. The NCAA presidents' staff will move from Overland Park, Kansas, to some other city.

The incremental expenses associated with transforming the NCAA's legislative services department into the NCAA presidents' staff is estimated to be $1 million per year.[1]

2. JUDICIAL

The present NCAA Committee on Infractions, consisting of volunteers employed by NCAA member-schools, will be disbanded and replaced by a seven-member panel—the NCAA Judicial Commission—consisting of paid, jurisprudence professionals. The NCAA Judicial Commission shall have the sole power to adjudicate all charges brought before it by the NCAA Compliance Commission.

The NCAA Judicial Commission will be completely autonomous, answerable to no one.

The NCAA presidents will appoint members to the NCAA Judicial Commission members for five-year, non-succeeding terms. The Professional Division presidents will appoint four members, and the remaining three members will be appointed by the presidents of the three other divisions. NCAA Judicial Commission members will be paid $3,000 per day.

The NCAA Judicial Commission will serve all four NCAA divisions.

A full-time staff of one professional and one administrative assistant will assist the NCAA Judicial Commission. The staff will be headquartered in the same building as the NCAA presidents' staff. Estimated annual incremental cost to maintain the NCAA Judicial Commission and its staff will be $826,500.[2]

3. COMPLIANCE

The NCAA's current enforcement and compliance departments, consisting of twenty-eight people, will be spun off and established as an autonomous entity, to be known as the NCAA Compliance Commission.

The NCAA Compliance Commission will be responsible for enforcing regulations and conducting drug tests.

The NCAA Compliance Commission will be divided into subgroups, corresponding to the NCAA's four divisions. The newly transformed twenty-eight-member staff, because of its experience, will oversee the Professional Division. Twenty additional compliance-enforcement attorneys will oversee the three remaining divisions. These new attorneys will start at $40,000 per year. Veteran NCAA compliance-enforcement professionals will receive raises to a minimum salary of $45,000, depending on experience and time in grade. Twenty drug testers will be hired on a per diem basis.

The NCAA Compliance Commission will be headquartered in the same city with the NCAA Boards of Presidents staff and the NCAA Judicial Commission.

The estimated annual incremental cost for The NCAA Compliance Commission is $2.8 million.[3]

4. THE NCAA OPERATIONS-PROMOTION COMMISSION

The remaining functions of the current NCAA organization—promoting and staging championships, publishing, maintaining statistics—will fall under the renamed NCAA Operations-Promotions Commission.

The NCAA's athletic directors and faculty athletic representatives, as presently constituted, will now serve on this commission and convene at least once a year to discuss operational matters pertaining to their responsibilities.

Since many of the services previously performed at NCAA headquarters in Overland Park, Kansas, will now be performed by other branches in other locations, there will be an estimated annual savings of $750,000 per year.

All told, splitting the existing NCAA organization into four branches will cost an additional $3.9 million per year.[4]

Once this new structure is established, then the NCAA presidents should effect these rule-changes.

1. COMPLIANCE

The NCAA presidents will grant the NCAA Compliance Commission subpoena powers. Failure to comply can result in penalties as severe as those meted out for actual violations. The NCAA Compliance Commission will now audit and verify the academic progress of all athletes.

2. FINANCES

All athletic corporations and separate financial entities relating to the athletic departments will be dissolved. The athletic departments will be treated as a university cost center.

All funds generated by the athletic department in both regular season and post-season play will be turned over immediately to the university's general fund. All funds generated by the NCAA

Operations-Promotions Commission will be turned over to the NCAA presidents for distribution. Aside from adhering to a pre-approved budget, the athletic department is not to have any financial responsibility for its operations.

The athletic directors for all Professional Division institutions shall report directly to the university's president.

The football season will be reduced to ten games, and begin on the second weekend in September. Football practice will begin on August 15 of each year. With the exception of the Professional Division, spring football practice will be eliminated. Football squads will be reduced to eighty players (the size of NFL squads). No game may begin in the evening merely to accommodate television.

Basketball squads will be reduced to thirteen players, and the regular season will be reduced to twenty-three games, including practice and exhibition games. The regular basketball season will start on January 1 of each year. No game may begin later than 7:30 P.M., local time.

The finals of The Final Four basketball tournament will be held in a centrally-located city each year, and played on Sunday afternoon, at 5:00 P.M., EST. No school may play outside its geographic regions during the first five rounds of the NCAA Men's Basketball Championship.

Athletic scholarships will be replaced by need-based financial grants. If a star football player, for example, demonstrates he needs financial help, then the university's financial aid office, not the athletic department, will provide it.

All Professional Division football and basketball players will receive a monthly salary of $600 per month. The NBA and the NFL will pay for this annual expense, estimated to be $36.3 million per year,[5] Each club will contribute $758,000,[6] annually.

The top 150 Professional Division football players and the top seventy-five Professional Division basketball players will be covered by death and disability insurance during their third year of eligibility. The payoff will be twice the NFL's or NBA's current average salary. The NCAA will pay for this insurance, the cost of which is estimated to be $1.4 million.[7]

When a Professional Division football or basketball player graduates in four years, he will receive a $20,000 bonus. If he graduates in five years, he will receive a $10,000 bonus. The NCAA will fund this $7 million annual expense.[8]

All endorsement contracts from athletic equipment and shoe manufacturers will be prohibited.

Booster clubs will make donations directly to the university's general fund.

Separate dormitories for athletes will be prohibited.

3. ACADEMICS

All universities will adhere to a minimum graduation rate of fifty percent. Failure to do so will result in a school's suspension until this minimum graduate rate level is attained.

All NCAA athletes must take a minimum of twelve college credits each semester, and must declare a major by the beginning of their junior year (fifth semester). They must also achieve a minimum 1.800 cumulative gpa by the end of the second semester. Every year thereafter, athletes must attain a cumulative 2.000 gpa. Failure to do so will result in suspension from athletics until the cumulative gpa minimums are attained. Two consecutive semesters below this gpa minimum will result in the loss of all financial aid and salary.

All college athletes will have three years of eligibility. Freshmen athletes are prohibited from intercollegiate competition and practicing in any form.

4. RECRUITMENT

In the Professional Division, recruitment will be replaced by a draft. Each big-time college football program may draft up to twenty-two athletes annually, and each Professional Division basketball program may draft up to six athletes annually.

To be eligible for the draft, a high school prospect must be nominated by *USA Today*, and have a minimum cumulative gpa of 2.300 in college prep courses.

High school prospects who do not wish to participate in the draft, or fail to qualify for it, are still eligible to be recruited in the traditional manner by schools in the other NCAA divisions.

5. GOVERNANCE

A university's governing board shall attest annually that it did not interfere in the president's management of the athletic department. If the NCAA Judicial Commission determines that a school's trustees have terminated a president unfairly—the president fought for athletic reform, and the trustees resisted it—the school must pay the president $750,000 over and above the normal severance agreement.

The NCAA Professional Division presidents will eliminate all rules pertaining to recruitment and amateurism. No added inducements other than those already specified will be permitted.

Student athletes will have voting privileges with the NCAA Promotion and Operation Commission.

Athletic directors, coaches and athletes will have ample opportunity to influence the legislative process.

A Professional Division football and basketball player is subject to immediate suspension if he provokes adverse publicity. The NCAA Judicial Commission will make this determination on an ad hoc basis.

Professional Division football and basketball coaches will be paid $175,000 per year, and be eligible for periodic raises. They are not to engage in any other activity—television shows, summer camps, endorsement relationships, etc.—for supplemental personal income. If Professional Division football and basketball coaches are fired, they will receive a sum equivalent to five times their annual salary. If a coach is dismissed because of moral turpitude or an NCAA infraction, he will forfeit his severance pay.

6. DRUGS

Every NCAA member-school must initiate year-round, unannounced drug testing for all athletes. The tests will be for street drugs as well as steroids.

A positive drug test result carries an immediate and lifelong ban from NCAA athletics. The athlete will also forfeit all aid and salary.

7. ALCOHOL

All NCAA athletes must refrain from alcohol during their practice and playing seasons. Alcohol will be placed on the list of banned substances, and a positive drug test will result in an immediate and lifelong ban from the NCAA.

Alcoholic beverage advertising, including beer and wine, will be banned from all NCAA activities.

Notes

Chapter One—Hank Gathers

1. "Hank Gathers, The Death of a Dream," *Los Angeles Times*, April 1, 1990.
2. Interview with Rich Yankowitz, basketball coach, Murrel¹ Dobbins Vocational High School, April 27, 1990.
3. *Los Angeles Times*, April 1, 1990.
4. Interview with Rich Yankowitz, April 27, 1990.
5. *Los Angeles Times*, March 9, 1990.
6. Ibid., April 1, 1990.
7. Interview with Barry Zepel, Assistant Director of Athletics, Loyola Marymount University.
8. Ibid.
9. *The Philadelphia Inquirer*, March 9, 1990.
10. Interview with Frank Uryasz, Director of Sports Science, NCAA, April 26, 1990.
11. Ibid.
12. M.Koss, "National Institute of Health Survey of Sexual Crimes Nation's Top 100 Universities, 1988," NIH, 1988.
13. G. Ezkenazi, "The Male Athlete and Sexual Assault," *The New York Times*, June 3, 1990.
14. Interview with Al Witte, President, NCAA, May 12, 1989.
15. *The Washington Post*, August 31, 1985.
16. Interview with Al Witte, May 12, 1989.
17. *The New York Times*, December 13, 1989.
18. *The New York Times*, January 10, 1989.
19. Interview with Charles Driesell, Assistant Director of Athletics, University of Maryland, September 9, 1987.

20. Interview with Dr. John B. Slaughter, Chancellor, University of Maryland, September 9, 1987.
21. Ibid.

Chapter 2—Drugs

1. Interview with Betsey Richardson, former Vice President, Reebok International, March 19, 1990.
2. Interview with Lee Fentress, Managing Director, Advantage International, March 19, 1990.
3. Interview with Charles Driesell, Assistant Director of Athletics, University of Maryland, September 9, 1987.
4. Interview with Colonel Thomas Fields (USMC Retired), President, Maryland Terrapins Club, January 19, 1989.
5. The official report, dated May 5, 1987, of Michael G. Ferriter, Prince George's County Police Department, the investigating homicide detective of the Bias death.
6. Ibid.
7. Ibid.
8. Ibid.
9. Interview with Detective Michael Ferriter, Prince George's County Police Department, retired, December 28, 1988.
10. Interview with Lee Fentress, March 19, 1990.
11. Interview with Arthur Marshall, former State's Attorney, Prince George's County, December 29, 1989.
12. Ibid.
13. Transcript ABC's "Good Morning America," June 20, 1986, p. 4.
14. Interview with James and Lonise Bias and Attorney Wayne Curry, October 7, 1987.
15. *USA Today*, June 23, 1986.
16. Interview with Betsey Richardson, May 9, 1990.
17. Interview with Arthur Marshall, December 29, 1988.
18. Ibid.
19. Interview with Attorney Wayne Curry, October 10, 1988.
20. Interview with James and Lonise Bias and Attorney Wayne Curry, October 7, 1987.
21. Interview with Michael Ferriter, December 28, 1988.

22. Interview with John B. Slaughter, Chancellor, University of Maryland, September 10, 1987.
23. Interview with Margaret Bridwell, M.D., Director, Health Services, University of Maryland, March 19, 1990.
24. Interview with Rep. Tom McMillan, U.S. House of Representatives, 4th District, maryland, January 24, 1989.
25. Interview with former Secretary of State Dean Rusk, now professor of law at the University of Georgia, Athens, Georgia, March 15, 1989.
26. *Los Angeles Times*, July 23, 1987
27. NCAA Manual, 1989-1990, p. 46.
28. Interview with Robert Minnix, NCAA director of enforcement, May 5, 1989.
29. *The New York Times*, November 17, 1989.
30. *The NCAA News*, September, 1987.
31. *The New York Times*, September 18, 1988.
32. Richard Schultz's address to the 1990 NCAA Convention, Dallas, Texas, January 10, 1990.
33. The National Study of the Substance Use and Abuse Habits of College Student-Athletes, conducted by the College of Human Medicine, Michigan State University, October 1989.
34. Ibid., Table 11.
35. Interview with Dr. Robert O. Voy, physician, former head of USOC drug testing program, current member of NCAA Drug Testing Committee, March 19, 1990.
36. S. Huffman, "I Deserve My Turn," *Sports Illustrated,* August 27, 1990, p. 26.
37. Interview with an NFL consulting physician who wishes to remain anonymous.
38. R. Telander, "Tommy Chaikin's Steroid Account," *Sports Illustrated*, October 24, 1988.
39. Interview with Dr. Robert O. Voy, March 19, 1990.
40. Ibid.
41. *The New York Times*, May 15, 1989.
42. Interview with Al Witte, President, NCAA, May 12, 1989.
43. "NCAA Stiffens Drug Penalties and Expands Testing in Football," *The New York Times*, January 10, 1990.
44. Tom Wicker, "Warning About Tests," *The New York Times*, December 1, 1989.

45. Congressional testimony of William Fralic, Atlantic Hawks, before the Biden Committee on Anabolic Steroids, May 12, 1989.
46. Ibid.
47. Congressional Record, June 23, 1988.
48. Interview with Dr. Robert O. Voy, March 19, 1990.

Chapter 3—100 Years Ago

1. R. Whittingham, *Saturday Afternoon*, New York: Workman Press, 1985, p. 46.
2. Interview with David Roberts, former oarsman, Cambridge University crew, March 23, 1989.
3. R. Smith, *Sports and Freedom*, New York: Oxford University Press, 1989, p. 66.
4. G. Santayana, "Philosophy on the Bleachers," *Harvard Monthly,* Cambridge, Mass., 1894, p. 183.
5. Theodore Roosevelt, *The Strenuous Life: Essays and Addresses.* New York: Century, 1902, p. 56.
6. *The Harvard Alumni Magazine*, December 1905.

Chapter 4—Academic Fraud

1. *The Atlanta Constitution*, February 12, 1986.
2. Draft of letter given to the author by Dr. LeRoy Ervin in Atlanta, Georgia, February 24, 1989.
3. Interview with Jan Kemp, Professor, University of Georgia, Athens, February 8, 1989.
4. Testimony at the trial of Kemp vs. University of Georgia, February 12, 1986.
5. Interview with Jan Kemp, February 8, 1989.
6. Interview with Vince Dooley, Director of Athletics, University of Georgia, February 8, 1989.
7. Interview with Dr. Charles Knapp, President, University of Georgia, February 24, 1989.
8. Interview with Dean Rusk, Professor, University of Georgia Law School, February 24, 1989.
9. Interview with Dr. LeRoy Ervin, University of Georgia, Atlanta, February 24, 1989.

10. *The Atlanta Constitution*, February 8, 1986.
11. Interview with Jan Kemp, April 6, 1989.
12. Interview with Jan Kemp, February 8, 1989.
13. Ibid.
14. *The Atlanta Constitution*, February 9, 1986.
15. Interview with Barbara Carson, Professor of English, University of Georgia, February 18, 1989.
16. Ibid.
17. Interview with Dr. LeRoy Ervin, February 24, 1989.
18. *The Atlanta Constitution*, February 6, 1989.
19. Interview with Dean Rusk, February 24, 1989.
20. Interview with Chance Dobbs, football player, University of Georgia, February 8, 1989.
21. *The Atlanta Constitution*, February 12, 1986.
22. Georgia Board of Regents Audit of the Developmental Studies program, University of Georgia, Athens, March, 1986.
23. Interview with Dr. Fred Davison, former President, University of Georgia, Athens, May 12, 1989.
24. *The Atlanta Constitution*, February 9, 1986.
25. Ibid.
26. *The Atlanta Constitution*, February 12, 1986.
27. Ibid.
28. Interview with Dr. LeRoy Ervin, February 24, 1989.
29. Interview with Dr. Fred Davison, May 12, 1989.
30. *The Atlanta Constitution*, February 9, 1986.
31. Interview with Dr. Ted Hummock, former Dean of Studies, University of Georgia, May 12, 1989.
32. Interview with Robert Minnix, NCAA Director of Enforcement, May 4, 1989.
33. Interview with Jan Kemp, February 8, 1989.
34. Interview with Dr. Charles Knapp, February 24, 1989.
35. Ibid.

Chapter 5—The Black Gladiator

1. Interview with David Stern, NBA Commissioner, New York, April 4, 1989.
2. Interview with Dr. Harry Edwards, professor, University of California-Berkeley, April 6, 1989.

3. Interview with Arthur Ashe, Washington, D.C., April 6, 1989.
4. Interview with Dr. Richard Lapchick, Northeastern University, Boston, Mass., April 6, 1989.
5. Interview with Dr. Harry Edwards, Professor, University of California—Berkeley, April 6, 1989.
6. Interview with Jan Kemp, Professor, University of Georgia, February 8, 1989.
7. *The Washington Post*, April 7, 1988.
8. Interview with Arthur Ashe, April 6, 1989.
9. The Government Accounting Office audit of NCAA graduation data, reported by *The New York Times*, September 10, 1989.
10. Interview with Robert Atwell, President, American Council on Education, Washington, D.C., March 22, 1989.
11. Interview with Arthur Ashe, April 6, 1989.
12. Ibid.
13. Interview with Dr. Richard Lapchick, April 12, 1989.
14. Ibid.

Chapter 6—Proposition 48, Freshmen Eligibility, and
Satisfactory Progress

1. *People*, January 12, 1990, p.12.
2. Interview with Dr. Fred Davison, former President, University of Georgia, Athens, May 12, 1989.
3. Interview with Vince Dooley, Director of Athletics, University of Georgia, February 8, 1989.
4. Interview with Father Timothy Healy, S.J., President, Georgetown University, February 23, 1989.
5. Interview with Robert Atwell, President, American Council on Education, November 19, 1989.
6. Interview with Dr. Harry Edwards, University of California—Berkeley, April 6, 1989.
7. The NCAA 1983 Convention Proceedings, p. 45.
8. Ibid., p.67.
9. Interview with Father Timothy Healy, S.J., February 12, 1989.
10. Interview with Dr. John B. Slaughter, Chancellor, University of Maryland, September 9, 1987.
11. *Des Moines Register*, April 12, 1989.

12. Remarks made by Leo Miles, former football coach, Howard University, at Black Athlete Seminar, Washington, D.C., April 6, 1989.
13. Interview with Father Timothy Healy, S.J., February 12, 1989.
14. *The New York Times*, January 12, 1989.
15. Interview with Father Timothy Healy, S.J., February 24, 1989.
16. Extrapolated from NCAA and TV Bureau data.

Chapter 7—Beer

 1. *The New York Times*, December 12, 1987.
 2. Interview with Dr. William A. Anderson, Associate Professor, Office of Medical Education, Michigan State University, East Lansing, Michigan, January 19, 1990.
 3. Interview with Dr. Gordon Gee, President, University of Colorado, March 4, 1990.
 4. Interview with James Delany, Commissioner, The Big Ten, in his Chicago, Illinois home, December 7, 1989.
 5. *Time*, November 30, 1987, p.90.
 6. Statistics and quote from an interview with Dick Bast, senior technical advisor, National Clearinghouse for Drug and Alcohol Abuse, January 19, 1990.
 7. Koop, Dr. C. Everett press conference regarding the Surgeon General's Workshop on Drunk Driving: Proceedings, May 31, 1989, Washington, D.C.
 8. Interview with Dr. Denise Kandel, Professor, School of Public Health, Columbia University, January 9, 1990.
 9. Ibid. Surveys were filled out by 7,611 students in fifty-three public and private schools in the spring 1988.
10. N. Gordon and A. McAlister. "Promoting Adolescent Health," Adolescent Drinking: Issues and Research. New York: Academic Press, 1982, p. 204.
14. Data published by MADD, September, 1989.
15. Interview with Robert King, Executive Director, MADD, December 5, 1989.
16. Statistical Abstract of the United States, 1989, p.173.
17. Interview with Teddie Penziger, January 8, 1990.
18. Interview with Bob Stratton, Marketing Manager, AAA Foundation for Traffic Safety, January 11, 1990.

19. Koop, Dr. C. Everett, press conference remarks, Washington, D.C., May 31, 1989.
20. Interview Robert King, December 5, 1989.
21. Interview with Victoria Davis, American Medical Association, Chicago, Illinois, December 4, 1989.
22. Interview with C. Hikawa, Vice President, Continuity Practices, ABC, January 9, 1990.
23. "Beer. How It Influences The Games We Play and Watch," *Sports Illustrated* August 8, 1988.
24. N.R. Klinefeld, "The King of Beer Raises the Ante," *The New York Times*, December 24, 1989.
25. *USA Today*, December 12, 1989.
26. Television Bureau Research Department.
27. Advertising Age Research Department.
28. Anheuser-Busch 1988 Annual Report
29. C.E. Phelps, "Estimating the Effects of Increased Federal Excise Tax on Alcoholic Beverages," Surgeon General's Workshop on Drunk Driving Proceedings, December, 1988, p.25.
30. Surgeon General's Workshop on Drunk Driving, December 14-18, 1988, background papers, p. 10.
31. Ibid.
32. Beer Marketers Insight, 1989
33. Statistical Abstract of the United States, 1989, pp. 13 and 15. The 1989 population, 16 +, was 191.5 million, whereas it was 157.3 million in 1975, an increase of 21.7 percent.
34. R.G. Smart, "Does Alcohol Advertising Affect Overall Consumption?" *Journal of Studies on Alcohol*, Vol 49, No. 4, 1988, p. 314.
35. "Drugs and the Athlete . . . A Losing Combination." NCAA Publications, Mission, Kansas, p.4.
36. *The Sporting News*, May 5, 1989
37. Interview, with Richard Schultz, Executive Director, NCAA, Mission, Kansas, May 4, 1989.
38. N.R. Klinefield, "The King of Beer Raises the Ante," *The New York Times*, December 24, 1989.
39. Interview with Edward E. Bozik, Athletic Director and Assistant to the President, University of Pittsburgh, December 9, 1989.

40. Interview with David Gavitt, Commissioner, The Big East Conference, December 6, 1989.

41. Press Conference, NCAA Offices, Mission, Kansas, November 21, 1989.

42. Interview with Joe Anastos, Executive Director, SADD, December 4, 1989.

43. Repeated telephone calls to Anheuser-Busch executives Michael J. Roarty and Steven J. Burrows during the week of December 4, 1989 were stonewalled by pleasant but adamant secretaries who kept saying the two executives were "out of town." Finally, Mark Abels of Fleischman-Hillard returned my call, and rejected my request to talk with either executive on the grounds I was not a writer for a recognized, national publication.

44. Interview with Ben Mason, Manager, Alcohol Issues, Coors Brewery, Golden, Colorado. December 6, 1989.

45. Interview with Robert King, December 8, 1989.

46. Interview with Jeff Becker, Vice President, Alcohol Issues, The Beer Institute, December 5, 1989.

47. Interview with James Delany, Commissioner, The Big Ten Conference, December 2, 1989.

48. R. Sandomir, "CBS Postpones Plan to Scramble NFL Games," *The New York Times*, September 2, 1990, Section 8, p. 8.

49. Interview with Emmie Morrissey, Program Coordinator, NCAA Foundation, May 3, 1990.

50. Interview with Frank Uryasz, Director of Sports Science, NCAA, May 4, 1990.

Chapter 8—Greed

1. Interview with Werner Michel, Senior Vice President, Bozell, New York, December 8, 1989.

2. Randall Rothenberg, *The New York Times*, December 1, 1989.

3. Interview with Steven Leff, Media Head, Interpublic, December 2, 1989.

4. Interview with Lisa Donneson, media analyst, County Nat-West, December 7, 1989. Ms. Donneson, who specializes in CBS stock, figured an average spot cost of $105 thousand for

the first twenty five games. Each game has forty-two spots at 105,000 per spot = $110.25 million. Then, the final game has an average cost of $180,000 × 42 = $7,560,000 gross for the game. Overall gross will be $117.8 million. Rights fees will be $143 million, plus $10.4 million in production and talent ($400,000 per game × 26 games) for a total of $153.4 million. Net loss first year is ($153.4 minus $117.8 million) $35.6 million.

5.

	1990:	1992:
Daytona	30	30
Masters	30	30
US Open	18	32
NFL	112	250
NCAA	55	143
Olympics	--	240
baseball	--	275
coll ftbl	21	21
coll bbl	15	15
	$281	$1.038

6. NFL Management Council, 1989.

7. D.A. Klatell and N. Marcus. *Sports For Sale*, New York: Oxford University, 1989, pp. 36-38.

8. Essay by Walter Byers, *The New York Times*, August 5, 1986.

9. Season totals for the number of college and professional basketball games on television were compiled by the A.C. Nielsen Company.

10. Interview with Dave Gavitt, Commissioner, The Big East, Providence, Rhode Island. December 11, 1989.

11. Interview with John Paquette, Director of Sports Information, Seton Hall University, South Orange, New Jersey. February 1, 1990.

12. *The Sporting News*, February 12,1990, p.14.

13. K. Hannon, "That Championship Season," *Main Event*, February, 1989, pp. 45-56.

14. Interview with Bob DeCarolis, Assistant Athletic Director—Business, University of Michigan, December 11, 1989.

15. Ibid.

16. 1988 College Football Association Financial Survey of forty-seven of its members.

17. Interviews with Al Witte, Edward Bozik, Judith Sweet, Jim Delaney, Lou Spry, Francis Bonner, Alvin Van Wie, the week of December 6, 1989.
18. Interview with Judith Sweet, Secretary-Treasurer, NCAA, Athletic Director, University of California—San Diego. December 6, 1989.
19. Interview with Dr. Edward Bozik, Director of Athletics, University of Pittsburgh, December 6, 1990.
20. Interview with Robert J. Minnix, Director of Enforcement, NCAA, Mission, Kansas. May 4, 1989.
21. The NCAA Annual Report, 1988-1989, Fiscal Year ending August 31, 1989.
22. Interview with Louis J. Spry, Controller and Associate Executive Director, NCAA. December 8, 1990.
23. Ibid.
24. Interview with Al Witte, President, NCAA, May 12, 1989.
25. Interview with Bill Shapland, Georgetown's Sports Information Director, January 12, 1990, confirmed this fact.
26. *The Sporting News*, November 16, 1987.
27. Trial testimony of Norby Walters, Chicago, Illinois, March 12, 1989.
28. *New York Herald Tribune*, August 12, 1951.
29. Remarks made to the NCAA Special Convention, Presidents Commission Forum, Dallas, Texas, June 29, 1987.
30. Survey conducted by Allen Sack, Professor of Sociology, University of New Haven, 1989.
31. Interview with David Berkoff, student-athlete, Harvard University, December 7, 1989.
32. NCAA staff travel expenses for the year 1989 were $1,784,790, whereas they were $1,289,112 for NCAA volunteer officials. Between the two groups, there are an estimated 4700 travel days which, when divided into the two budgets, results in a $650 per diem.
33. *The Sporting News*, June 19, 1989.
34. Interview with Joe Vicinsin, Executive Director, NABC, December 8, 1989.
35. Interview with Bill Shapland, January 12, 1990, confirmed this fact.

36. *The New York Times*, June 6, 1989.

Chapter 9—Recruiting

1. C. Dufresne, "Dickerson Says SMU Paid Him," *Los Angeles Times*, May 9, 1987.
2. *Dallas Morning Times*, August 26, 1985.
3. D. Whitford, *A Payroll to Meet*, New York: Macmillan, 1989, p. 181.
4. Ibid., p. 204.
5. *Dallas Morning News*, March 5, 1987.
6. Ibid., March 8, 1987.
7. *Chicago Times*, February 17, 1990.
8. Interview with Father Theodore Hesbugh, retired President, Notre Dame University, March 29, 1989.
9. Ibid.
10. Ibid.
11. Interview with Vince Dooley, Director of Athletics, University of Georgia, February 12, 1989.
12. Ibid.
13. Data according to the NFSHSA: 525,000 high school basketball players, of whom an estimated 150,000 are seniors. There are 4,400 basketball players (293 schools × 15) in big-time NCAA schools, of which 1,365 are freshmen. There are approximately 680 college freshmen who receive scholarships, so we are talking about 680 players out of 150,000 who receive scholarships, or 1 in 221. There are approximately 12,875 football players playing in the NCAA's Div 1-A (103 schools × 125 players each school). Of this group, 35 percent are freshmen (4,506). Of this group, 2,253 are awarded scholarships.
14. *The New York Times*, January 4, 1988.
15. W.C. Rhoden, "The Recruitment of Kenny Anderson," *The New York Times*, November 28, 1988.
16. *The New York Times*, November 28, 1988.
17. *The Washington Post*, June 16, 1976.
18. "Vaccaro Has a Foot in Every Door," *The Sporting News*, February 22, 1988.

19. *The Washington Post*, December 12, 1987.
20. William Brubaker, "The Recruitment of Alonzo Mourning," *The Washington Post*, February 8, 1988.
21. Interview with Daniel Dutchery, Legislative Assistant, NCAA, April 10, 1990.
22. W.C. Rhoden, "Success Muted by Scrutiny," *The New York Times*, November 12, 1989.
23. The NCAA Manual 1989-90, p.83.
24. Interview with Peter O'Malley, Chairman, Board of Trustees, Maryland University System, May 12, 1989.
25. Interview with Robert Minnix, Director of Enforcement, NCAA, May 4, 1989.
26. The Supreme Court majority decision, written by Justice John Paul Stevens, of Tarkanian vs. the NCAA where the Court found in favor of the NCAA.
27. Interview with David Berst, Assistant Executive Director for Enforcement, NCAA, April 11, 1990.
28. Ibid.
29. Ibid.
30. Interview with Michael Garnes, former NCAA field enforcement investigator, May 12, 1989.
31. A. Wulff, "The Blue Devils vs The Devil Blue," *Sports Illustrated*, November 3, 1988.
32. *The NCAA News*, October 2, 1989.
33. *The NCAA News*, October 2, 1989, and interviews with Al LeBlanc, acting athletic director, and Larry Hymel, public information assistant, Southeastern Louisiana University, April 12, 1990.

Chapter 10—Reform

1. 1989 NCAA Convention Proceedings.
2. *The NCAA News*, January 10, 1990.
3. Ibid., January 17, 1990.
4. *The Washington Post*, March 27, 1990.
5. Interview with Dr. Derek Bok, President, Harvard University, May 9, 1990.
6. Ibid.

7. Ibid.
8. Interview with Edward Foote, President, University of Miami, March 13, 1989.
9. *The New York Times*, June 22, 1985.
10. Interview with Robert Atwell, President, American Council on Education, March 23, 1989.
11. The NCAA's Sixth Special Convention Proceedings, June 29-30, 1987, p. 162.
12. The NCAA Convention Proceedings, January, 1987.
13. J. Falla, *NCAA: Voice of College Sports*, 1982, National Collegiate Athletic Association, Mission, Kansas, page 56.

Epilogue

1. Rent—$750,000;   utilities—$175,000;   supplies—$25,000; travel—$50,000.
2. NCAA Judicial Commission Member Fees: seven members × $3,000 @ day × 30 days = $630,000 annually.

Staff salaries $75,000, benefits $16,500 = $91,500 annually. Rent $45,000; utilities $45,000, misc $15,000 = $105,000
Grand total: $826,500 annually.

3. 20 new attorneys hired = $800,000 annually.

Benefits	= 200,000	"
5 more assistants	= 125,000	"
Benefits	= 31,250	"
Total raises/incumbents	= 300,000	"
Rent	= 750,000	"
Utilities	= 125,000	"
Travel	= 450,000	"
Drug testers	= 50,000	
TOTAL	= 2,831,250	

4.
NCAA Presidents	=	$1,000,000
NCAA Judicial	=	826,500
NCAA Compliance	=	2,800,000
NCAA Oper/Prom	=	− 750,000
TOTAL		$3,876,500

5. 65 schools × (80 football players + 13 basketball players = 93 athletes) × 10 months × $600 per month = $36,270,000

6. There are 50 teams in the NBA and the NFL, divided into 36,270,000 = \$725,400 per team.

7. (150 football players + 75 basketball players) × annual premium of \$6,000 = \$1,350,000.

8. There are 6,045 athletes in the top sixty-five big-time colleges (5,200 football players and 845 basketball players). Assuming that 1,200 in any given year are seniors, and assuming a fifty percent graduation rate, then 600 athletes will graduate each year. Of these, estimate that 120 will graduate in four years, the balance in five. 120 × 20,000 = \$2,400,000; and 480 × 10,000 = \$4,800,000, or a total of \$7,000,000.

Bibliography

1. Baker, L. H. *Athletics and Princeton—A History*. New York: Prentice-Hall, 1900.
2. Bureau of the Census. *Statistical Abstract of the United States, 1989*. Washington, D.C.: U.S. Department of Commerce, 1989.
3. Cole, Lewis. *Never Too Young to Die*. New York: Pantheon Books, 1990.
4. Condon, David, Bob Best and Chet Grant. *Notre Dame Football: The Golden Tradition*. South Bend, Ind.; The Icarus Press, 1982.
5. Durso, Joseph, *The Sports Factory*, New York: Quadrangle Books, The New York Times Book Co., 1975.
6. Falla, Jack. *NCAA: The Voice of College Sports*. Mission, Kansas: NCAA Publications, 1981.
7. Feinstein, John. *A Season on the Brink*. New York: Simon and Schuster, 1986.
8. ———*A Season Inside*. New York: Villard Books, 1988.
9. Fisher, James L., Martha W. Tack and Karen J. Wheeler. *The Effective College President*. New York: American Council on Education—Macmillan Publishing Company, 1988.
10. Gardiner, E. Norman. *Athletics of the Ancient World*. London: Oxford University Press, 1930.
11. Golenbock, Peter. *Personal Fouls: The Broken Promises and Shattered Dreams of Big Money Basketball at Jim Valvano's North Carolina State*. New York: Carroll & Graf Publishers, 1989.

12. Hesburgh, Theodore, C.S.C. *The Hesburgh Papers: Higher Values in Higher Education.* Kansas City: Andrews and McMeel, 1979.
13. Juvenal. *The Sixteen Satires.* New York: Penguin Classics, 1987.
14. Klatell, David A. and Norman Marcus. *Sports for Sale.*New York: Oxford Univerity Press, 1988.
15. Lapchick, Richard E. and Robert Malekoff. *On the Mark.* Lexington, Mass.: Lexington Books, 1987.
16. ———, and John Brooks Slaughter, *The Rules of the Game.* New York: MacMillan, 1989.
17. Malloy, John W., Jr and Richard C. Adams. *The Spirit of Sport.* Bristol, Ind.: Wyndham Hall Press, Inc, 1987.
18. McCabe, Peter. *Bad News at Black Rock: The Sell-Out of CBS News.* New York: Arbor House, 1987.
19. McCallum, John D. *College Basketball, USA.* Briarcliff Manor, N.Y.: Stein & Day. 1974.
20. Meserole, Mike. *The 1990 Information Please 1990 Sports Almanac.* Boston: Houghton Mifflin Co., 1989.
21. Michener, James A. *Sports in America.* New York: Fawcett, 1983. 12. National Collegiate Athletic Association. *NCAA Manual 1989-1990.* Mission, Kan.: NCAA Publishing, 1989.
22. Newman, John Henry. *The Idea of a University.* Notre Dame, Ind.: Notre Dame University, 1986.
23. Novak, Michael. *The Joy of Sports: End Zones, Bases, Baskets, Balls and the Consecration of the American Spirit.* New York: Basic Books, 1976.
24. Pindar. *The Odes.* New York: Penguin Classics, 1988.
25. Rader, Benjamin G. *American Sports: From the Age of Folk Games to the Age of Spectators.* New York: Prentice-Hall, 1983.
26. Roosevelt, Theodore. *The Strenuous Life: Essays and Addresses.* New York: Century, 1902.
27. Rosovsky, Henry. *The University: An Owner's Manual.* New York: W.W. Norton and Company, 1990.
28. Simon, R.L. *Sport and Social Values.* Englewood Cliffs, New Jersey: Prentice-Hall, 1985.
29. Smith, Ronald A. *Sports and Freedom.* New York: Oxford University Press, 1988.

233 WIN AT ANY COST

30. Taylor, Lawrence and David Faulkner: *LT: Living on the Edge*. New York: Times Books, 1987.
31. Telander, Rick. *The Hundred Yard Lie*. New York: Simon and Schuster, 1989.
32. Underwood, John D. *Death of an American Game*. Garden City, New York: Doubleday, 1980.
33. Veysey, Lawrence. *The Emergence of the American University*. Chicago: University of Chicago Press, 1965.
34. Weiss, Paul. *Sports: A Philosophic Inquiry*. Carbondale, Ill.: Southern Illinois University Press, 1969.
35. Whitford, David. *A Payroll to Meet*. New York: Macmillan, 1989.
36. Whittingham, Richard. *Saturday Afternoon*. New York: Workman Publishing, 1985.
37. Wolff, Alexander and Armen Keteyian. *Raw Recruits*. New York: Pocket Books, 1990.

Index

Abels, Mark, 140
Advantage International, 33
Ainge, Danny, 34
Allen, Forrest C. "Phog," 74
Allen, Mel, 148
Almand, Hale, 86
Anastos, Joe, 140
Anderson, Kenny, 104, 151, 181, 183
Anderson, William A., 126–27
Anheuser-Busch Brewery, 132–34,
    138–40, 142–43
Archer, Rudy, 189
Arnold, Thomas, 58
Ashe, Arthur, 98–105, 107, 198, 205
Askew, Vincent, 154
Astaphan, Jamie, 51
Atwell, Robert, 100, 114, 115, 201
Auerbach, Red, 32, 34, 36, 40

Bailey, Damon, 180
Bailey, Wilford S., 30
Baker, Anita, 185
Bankston, W.O., 171
Barger, Mary, 195
Bast, Dick, 128
Baxter, Jeff, 34, 35, 38
Becker, Jeff, 136, 141
Bennett, Leon, 175
Bennett, William, 55, 143
Berkoff, David, 164
Berst, David, 173, 174, 190–92, 196
Bias, Eric, 35
Bias, James, 33, 35, 38, 40, 41
Bias, Jay, 35
Bias, Len, 31, 32–41

Bias, Lonise, 34, 35, 38
Bias, Michelle, 35
Biden, Joe, 54
Bird, Larry, 33, 34, 40, 109, 151
Black, Creed, 192
Bloody Monday, 58–59
Bloom, Lloyd, 161–63
Blount, Sherwood, 169–72
Bok, Derek, 30, 114, 200
Bok Committee, 114–15, 119,
    199–200
Bolduc, David, 50
Boston Celtics, 34
Bosworth, Brian, 55
Bowden, Bobby, 167
Bowen, Otis R., 127, 136
Bozik, Edward, 139, 159
Bradley, Bill, 99–100, 198
Braman, Norman, 132
Branstad, Terry, 118
Bridwell, Margaret, 43
Brokaw, Tom, 99
Brown, Dale, 180
Brown, James, 110
Brown, Larry, 154
Bryant, Bear, 90, 97
Burciaga, Juan C., 150
Burrows, Steven J., 140
Busch, August A., Jr., 132
Bush, George, 143
Buss, Jerry, 21
Butkus, Dick, 130
Butler, Nicholas Murray, 75
Byars, Walter, 26, 28–30, 149–51,
    192, 198, 199

Camp, Walter, 65–67, 69–72, 75, 76
Canham, Don, 114, 156–57
Carlos, John, 100
Carnesecca, Lou, 125, 130
Carson, Barbara, 88
Casey, Dwayne, 193
Cassell, Ollan, 44
Cawood, David, 28
CBS Sports, 24, 27–28, 110, 137, 139, 140–47
Chaikin, Tommy, 48
Chamberlain, Wilt, 97
Chelette, Newton, 194–95
Chaflin, John, 59
Clarkson, Walter, 62, 63
Clements, Bill, 171–74
Clements, Kathe, 162
Cleveland, Grover, 68
Cogburn, Michael, 36
Collins, Bobby, 171, 173
Collins, Jimmy, 175–76
Colorado University, 127
Connors, Jimmy, 148
Conway, William, 36
Coors Brewery, 127, 140–41
Copas, Richard, 90
Corley, Paul, 175
Courson, Steve, 54
Covington, Keeta, 35
Cox, Edward, 170, 175
Cremins, Bobby, 180, 183, 184
Crump, Marva, 17
Cunningham, Sam "Bam," 97
Curry, Wayne, 41

Daniels, Lloyd "Sweet Pea," 187
Dartmouth College, 68–69
Daugherty, Brad, 32
Davis, Glenn, 133
Davis, John R., 29
Davis, Victoria, 131
Davison, Fred, 80, 85, 91–94, 114
Dawkins, Johnny, 32
DeCarolis, Bob, 157
DeCicciotto, Phil, 33, 35
Delany, James, 127, 141, 146, 159
Dell, Donald, 101
Dent, Richard, 53
Devall, Ronnie, 195
Dickerson, Eric, 169–70

DiMaggio, Joe, 148
Dobbs, Chance, 90
Dooley, Vince, 82–84, 89–90, 92–95, 97, 113, 114, 157, 179
Doran, Richard, 39
Driesell, Lefty, 31, 37–44, 165, 167, 182
Drug testing procedures, 49–51
Duchaine, Dan, 47
Dugal, Robert, 45
Dutchery, Dan, 186
Dye, Pat, 166

Edwards, Harry, 97, 98, 100–105, 108, 109, 115, 205
Eliot, Charles, 70, 76, 117
Elkins, James, 56
Ellis, LaPhonso, 175–76
Ellis, William Webb, 58
England, football in, 58
Erickson, Dennis, 201
Ervin, Leroy, 78–80, 84–89, 91, 93, 94
Evert, Chris, 148
Ewing, Patrick, 156
Ewings, Landry, 85–86, 106

Fagel, Bruce, 22
Fentress, Lee, 33–35, 38, 39
Ferriter, Michael G., 38, 42
Fields, Tom, 35
Fireman, Paul, 33, 34, 41
Flutie, Doug, 156
Flying wedge, 67
Folsom, Bobby, 169
Foote, Edward "Tad," 114, 200–201
Fralic, Bill, 54
Francis, Charlie, 45
Franzene, Michael, 162
Free, Ken, 122
Friday, William, 114
Frieder, Bill, 166
Fritts, Edward, 136
Fry, Hayden, 118, 160, 161

Galbraith, John Kenneth, 136
Garnes, Michael, 192
Gathers, Charles, 16
Gathers, Derrick, 16–18
Gathers, Eric Wilson (father), 16

Gathers, Hank, 13–24, 27
Gathers, Lucille, 16, 17, 22
Gatlin, Keith, 35
Gavitt, Dave, 139, 152
Gaze, Andrew, 153
Gee, D. Gordon, 127
Georgetown University, 122, 166
Georgia University, 81–83, 91–93, 113
Gerdy, John R., 108
Giamatti, Bart, 132
Gill, Pramjit, 50
Gipp, George, 177
Goode, W. Wilson, 132
Graf, Steffi, 33
Gregg, David, 35–39
Groza, Alex, 193
Gulik, Luther, 73

Hagen, Father Dave, 16–18, 23
Hall, Galen, 189
Hall, G. Stanley, 63
Hamilton, Kenny, 17
Hardin, Paul, 202
Harmon, Kevin, 160
Harmon, Ronnie, 160–64
Harris, Joe Frank, 79
Harvard University, 56–60, 62, 68,
    75–76, 117
Hattori, Vernon, 15, 22, 23
Hayes, Elvin, 98
Healy, Father Timothy, 114, 115, 117,
    121, 122
Hearn, Thomas, 118
Heffelfinger, Pudge, 65
Heinsohn, Tommie, 110
Heisman, John William, 60, 70
Heisman Trophy, 84, 178
Helm, Dewitt, 136
Helmick, Robert, 51
Henderson, Keith, 95
Henry, Hue, 90
Hesburgh, Father Theodore, 114,
    178–179
Heyman, Ira Michael, 164
Higgins, Sean, 187
Hikawa, Christine, 132
Hitch, Bob, 170, 171, 173
Hoffman, Steve, 46
Hogan, James, 69, 70
Holtz, Lou, 46, 166, 203
Horton, Frank, 202

Hummock, Ted, 93
Hurley, Bobby, 151
Hutchinson, William, 175
Hyslop, Daniel, 14

Ikenberry, Stanley, 176–77
Illinois University, 175–77
Ingram, Hootie, 167
Iowa University, 118

Jabbar, Kareem Abdul, 20
Jackson, Bo, 166
Jackson, Derrick Z., 109–10
Jackson, "Jeep," 44
Jackson, Jesse, 40, 116
Jackson, Collie F., III, 123
James, Craig, 170
Jankovich, Sam, 200–201
Jefferson, Ben, 35
Jensen, Kurt Enemar, 49
Jimmy the Greek, 98–99
Johnson, Ben, 47, 149
Johnson, Dennis, 34
Johnson, Jimmy, 200–201
Johnson, Joseph B., 116
Johnson, Magic, 20–21, 151
Jones, Tom, 34
Jordan, Michael, 21

Kansas University, 154
Keller, Ken, 206
Kemp, Jan Hammock, 78–81, 86–88,
    92–95
Kennedy, Chris, 123
Kennedy, Edward, 99
Kentucky University, 192–94, 196
Kimble, Bo, 14, 15, 17, 18, 23
King, Billie Jean, 148
King, Martin Luther, Jr., 100–102
King, Robert, 131, 141
Knapp, Charles, 83, 94–95
Knight, Bobby, 92, 114, 123–24, 164,
    180, 205
Koop, C. Everett, 127, 128, 136, 139
Korbut, Olga, 149
Krzyzewski, Mike, 164

Lapchick, Richard, 98, 106, 109
Lassiter, Bill, 185
Laver, Rod, 148

Leff, Stephen M., 146–47
Lemp, Michael, 121
Levant, Simone, 52
Lewis, Carl, 44, 149
Lewis, Tommy, 18
Liantonio, Giuseppe, 180–81
Liken, Peter, 31
Livingston, Carol, 14
Lodge, Henry Cabot, 67
Long, Terry, 31, 34–39
Los Angeles Lakers, 20–21
Louisiana State University, 26
Loyola Marymount University, 13, 15, 18–24, 27

MacCracken, Henry, 75
MacCracken Group, 75
Mackovic, John, 177
Malcolm X, 100
Malone, Moses, 33
Manley, Dexter, III, 128
Manning, Danny, 154
Mantle, Mickey, 148
Manuel, Eric, 193, 194
Marable, Chris, 16, 18
Marino, Dan, 171
Marshall, Arthur, 39, 41
Martin, David, 137
Maryland University, 31, 42–44
Mason, Ben, 140–41
Massenburg, Tony, 35
Mather, Cotton, 57
Matt, Francis X., 134
McClure, Leo, 195
McEnroe, John, 33, 148
McKay, Jim, 149
McKenzie, R. Tait, 207
McKinney, Jack, 20
McMillan, Tom, 43
Mellman, Michael, 15, 22
Merriwether, Frank, 65
Meyer, Ron, 168–69, 171
Michel, Werner, 144
Michigan University, 155–57
Miles, Leo, 118
Mills, Chris, 194
Mills, Claude, 193, 194
Mills, Terry, 119
Mims, Fred, 163
Minnix, Robert J., 44, 94, 159, 190
Moore, Harold, 74–75

Morgan, Steve, 190
Morris, Ronald, 171
Morrison, Stan, 18
Morrissey, Emmie, 143
Mourning, Alonzo, 166, 183, 185, 186
Mullin, Chris, 125–26, 128, 130, 131

Naismith, James, 73–74
NCAA
    drug testing by, 49–51
    membership in, 25
    objectives of, 26–27
    reforms needed, 202–207
    rules of, 180–90
Neines, Chuck, 114
Nelson, Don, 125–26
Newton, C.M., 194
Nike, Inc., 166, 184–85
Nixon, Richard, 178
Notre Dame University, 150, 177–79

O'Donovan, Reverend Leo, 166
Oklahoma University, 202
O'Malley, Peter, 189
O'Toole, John, 136
Overton, Doug, 17

Packer, Billy, 110
Paley, William, 145
Palmer, Arnold, 148
Paraseghian, Ara, 94
Parker, Henry Lee, 173
Paterno, Joe, 114
Penders, Tom, 165
Perkins, Sam, 33
Perot, H. Ross, 107
Person, Chuck, 32
Phelps, Digger, 179
Philip Morris, Inc., 134
Phillips, Stone, 39
Pierce, Franklin, 56
Pilson, Neal, 142, 144, 146, 147
Pitino, Rick, 165, 194
Powell, William, 91
Proposition 42, 120
Proposition 48, 114–116, 121, 199
Purnell, Oliver, 39

Ramsey, Jack, 20
Rangel, Charles B., 54–55

Rasul, Amjad, 38
Raveling, George, 18
Rawlings, Hunter, 118, 161
Reagan, Ronald, 177
Reebok International, 33, 40
Reid, William, 76, 122
Rice, Grantland, 82
Rice, Homer, 92
Richardson, Betsey, 33, 40
Richmond, Lee, 62
Riggs, Bobby, 148
Roarty, Michael J., 133, 140
Roberts, David, 60
Robinson, Jackie, 103
Robinson, Rumeal, 119
Rockne, Knute, 177
Rodman, Dennis, 109
Rogers, Don, 44
Rogers, Kenny, 81
Roosevelt, Theodore, 25, 61, 68
Rose, Bill, 142
Roselle, David, 193, 202
Ross, Kevin, 111
Rozelle, Pete, 53, 148
Rupp, Adolph, 74
Rusk, Dean, 44, 84, 90, 91
Russell, Bill, 97

Sanity Code, 112
Santayana, George, 61
SAT exams, 116, 118–20, 123
Schaefer, Chip, 14, 15
Schaffer, Benjamin, 14
Schallhorn, Carl, 40
Schembechler, Bo, 30, 156, 166
Schultz, Richard B. "Dick," 28, 29,
    45, 99–100, 137–38, 141, 142,
    146, 155, 160, 177, 197–99, 203,
    204
Scott, Jack, 55
Seton Hall College, 153
Shelton, Bill, 33, 35
Sherrill, Jackie, 167, 175
Shields, L. Donald, 114, 170–73, 175
Shoup, Harold, 138
Sims, Kenny, 88
Singletary, Otis, 192, 196
Slaughter, John, 31, 42, 44, 201
Sloane, William Milligan, 68
Smialek, John E., 38
Smith, Bubba, 131

Smith, Dean, 114, 164
Smith, George, 175
Smith, Hoke, 201
Smith, Red, 164
Smith, Ron, 60, 63
Smith, Tommy, 100
Smrt, Chuck, 192
Smyth, Dennis E., 39
Southeastern Louisiana University,
    194–96
Southern Methodist University,
    168–175
Sparks, John, 173
Spencer, Dave, 17
Spitz, Mark, 149
Sports and Freedom (Smith), 60, 63
Spry, Louis J., 30, 160
Stagg, Amos Alonzo, 65, 70, 72, 74
Stallcup, William, 173–75
Stanley, David, 172–73
Steinberg, Leigh, 162
Stern, David, 32, 33, 36, 96, 165
Steroids, 45–55
Stevens, John Paul, 188
Stewart, Robert, III, 170, 171, 174
Stewart, Ronnie, 88
Stone, Chuck, 116
Stone, Jesse N., Jr., 115
Stopperich, Sean, 171, 172
Stratton, Bob, 131
Sutton, Eddie, 165, 194
Sutton, Mark, 121
Sweet, Judith, 141, 142, 158
Swerdlow, Charles, 15

Tarkanian, Jerry, 184, 187–88, 194
Tartikoff, Brandon, 144
Taylor, Lawrence, 128
Telander, Rick, 48
Thomas, Deon, 176
Thomas, Isiah, 109
Thomas, Robert, 175
Thompson, John, 120–23, 166, 184,
    185, 203, 205
Tisch, Laurence, 144–47
Tow, Ted, 199
Toy, Mary, 16
Tribble, Brian, 36–38
Trotter, Virginia, 79–80, 84–85,
    90–91, 93, 94
Turner, Frederick Jackson, 67

Turner, Ted, 145
Tyson, Mike, 19

Ueberroth, Peter, 144, 145
Universities. *See* specific name e.g.
    Maryland University
Uryasz, Frank, 24, 28, 30, 143

Vaccaro, Sonny, 184–185
Valvano, Jim, 167, 184, 185, 201
Veal, Herman, 43
Vicinsin, Joe, 165
Vitale, Dick, 184
Von der Ahe, Christophe, 132
Voy, Robert O., 45, 50, 51, 55

Wade, Bob, 89
Wagner, Robert, 39
Walker, Doak, 170
Walker, Herschel, 83–85, 87, 95, 98
Walker, Kenny, 32
Walker, Veronica, 88
Walsh, Father Matthew, 177–78
Walters, Norby, 161–64
Ward, Horace T., 78
Warkentien, Mark, 187

Washburn, Chris, 32
Webb, Dan, 163
Webb, Spud, 186
Webb, William, 65
Westhead, Paul, 13–15, 18–24
White, Andrew D., 64
White, Mark, 172, 174
Wicker, Tom, 53
Wilkins, Dominique, 185
Williams, E. Bennett, 42, 165
Witte, Al, 29, 30, 51, 141, 158, 160
Wood, William, 59–60
Woods, Marilyn, 35
Worley, Tim, 95
Wyman, Tom, 145, 146

Yale University, 56–60, 65, 67, 69,
    117
Yankowitz, Rich, 16, 17, 21–22
Yost, Fielding H., 71
Young, Charles, 118

Zepel, Barry, 23
Ziegler, John, 46
Zucker, Steve, 162
Zuffellato, Raphael, 50
Zumberge, James, 168, 170